WAR ON THE WESTERN FRONT

OSPREY
PUBLISHING

WAR ON THE WESTERN FRONT

Editor

DR GARY SHEFFIELD

First published in Great Britain in 2007 by Osprey Publishing,
Midland House, West Way, Botley, Oxford OX2 0PH, United Kingdom.
443 Park Avenue South, New York, NY 10016, USA.
Email: info@ospreypublishing.com

Previously published as Elite 78: *World War I Trench Warfare (1) 1914–16* by Dr Stephen Bull; Elite 84: *World War I Trench Warfare (2) 1916–18* by Dr Stephen Bull; Warrior 12: *German Stormtrooper 1914–18* by Ian Drury; Warrior 16: *British Tommy 1914–18* by Martin Pegler; and Warrior 79: *US Doughboy 1916–19* by Thomas A. Hoff.

A CIP catalogue record for this book is available from the British Library

ISBN: 978 1 84603 210 3

Adam Hook has asserted his right under the Copyright, Designs and Patents Act, 1988, to be identified as the illustrator of Warrior 79: *US Doughboy 1916–19*.
Gary Sheffield has asserted his right under the Copyright, Designs and Patents Act, 1988, to be identified as the author of the foreword to this book.

Index by Alison Worthington
Typeset in Adobe Garamond and Helvetica Neue
Originated by PDQ Digital Media Solutions
Printed in China through World Print Ltd.

07 08 09 10 11   10 9 8 7 6 5 4 3 2 1

For a catalogue of all books published by Osprey please contact:

NORTH AMERICA
Osprey Direct c/o Random House Distribution Center
400 Hahn Road, Westminster, MD 21157, USA
E-mail: info@ospreydirect.com

ALL OTHER REGIONS
Osprey Direct UK, P.O. Box 140, Wellingborough, Northants, NN8 2FA, UK
E-mail: info@ospreydirect.co.uk

www.ospreypublishing.com

Front cover: *Gassed*, painting by John Sargent, 1856–1925 (The Art Archive / Imperial War Museum)
Back cover: Red poppy (Peter Garbet/iStockphoto)
Endpapers: Third battle of Ypres (IWM, C02265)
Note on British Tommy chapter: First-hand accounts are from the author's interviews with World War I veterans. These interviews are on tape and are held in the Imperial War Museum archives.
Note on measurements: Both the Imperial and metric systems were in use during the World War I era. No attempt has been made to standardize to one system in this book, though approximate conversions have been provided where necessary.

Imperial War Museum Collections
Many of the photos in this book come from the Imperial War Museum's huge collections which cover all aspects of conflict involving Britain and the Commonwealth since the start of the 20th century. These rich resources are available online to search, browse and buy at www.iwmcollections.org.uk. In addition to Collections Online, you can visit the Visitor Rooms where you can explore over 8 million photographs, thousands of hours of moving images, the largest sound archive of its kind in the world, thousands of diaries and letters written by people in wartime, and a huge reference library. To make an appointment, call (020) 7416 5320, or e-mail mail@iwm.org.uk. Imperial War Museum www.iwm.org.uk

CONTENTS

FOREWORD

Dr Gary Sheffield

World War I was fought in many parts of the globe. The Middle East, East and West Africa, Turkey, Italy, Poland, Russia, the Balkans, even the Falkland Islands and the South Pacific: all of these regions saw combat. But it was the Western Front, a narrow band of territory stretching from the Belgian coast to the Swiss frontier, where the war was decided. Here, from August 1914 to November 1918, was the primary focus of two of the major belligerents, France and Britain, and it was where a third, Germany, in March 1918 chose to make an all-out, make or break effort to win the war. That is not to underplay the importance of other theatres of war, especially the Eastern Front, but although Germany won a decisive victory over Russia in 1917–18, catastrophic defeat in the West rendered these successes in the East worthless. In November 1918 Germany, militarily vanquished by the Western Allies, collapsed into defeat and revolution. There could be no starker illustration of the primacy of the Western Front during World War I.

The campaigns on the Western Front fall into several easily identifiable phases. The first began with Germany's execution of the Schlieffen Plan in August 1914. Mobile operations had by mid-September evolved into semi-open warfare as rudimentary trenches began to appear. The failure of the Germans to break through the Allied lines at Ypres in early November marked the effective end of the first phase of fighting on the Western Front. Periods of temporary stalemate had occurred in earlier conflicts such as the American Civil War (1861–65) and the Russo–Japanese War (1904–05). At the end of 1914, there was every reason to believe that the deadlock would soon be broken. World War I repeated the pattern of previous wars, in that trench warfare did prove to be a hiatus before the resumption of mobility; but it was a phase that lasted longer than anyone could have imagined at the end of 1914.

The reason for the stalemate lay in the temporary dominance of the defensive over the offensive. Quick-firing artillery and machine guns, barbed wire and trenches dominated the battlefield. The sheer numbers of troops crammed into a relatively small area without flanks to turn made fluid warfare much more difficult to achieve than on the plains of eastern Europe. Unlike Napoleon and Wellington a century before, or Rommel and Patton a generation later, generals of 1914–18 could not exercise voice control over their corps and divisions. Armies were now too big and dispersed for such personal control, and radio communications too primitive. And unlike their counterparts at Waterloo and D-Day, they lacked an effective instrument of exploitation. Horsed cavalry, although by no means as useless on the Western Front as many have asserted, could no longer carry out its traditional role of exploiting battlefield success, and its eventual natural successor, the tank, was only invented in the middle of the war and was too rudimentary to do much more than demonstrate the potential of armoured forces. To this lethal cocktail we must add industrialized societies, fuelled by nationalism, organized for total war and producing armies of unprecedented size with war-making *materiel* to support them. The challenges facing the armies on the Western Front were unprecedented.

The year 1915 saw the first, fumbling attempts to break the deadlock, but, in spite of new tactics and weapons, it was marked by battles of attrition on the Western Front. In 1916, this pattern was repeated at Verdun and on the Somme, but warfare was beginning to take on a decidedly modern form. The combination of aircraft and artillery working in close cooperation, and infantry tactics based around the light machine gun, together with the debut of the tank, pointed the way to developments that characterize warfare to the present day. The year 1917 is remembered as one of attritional slaughter, but while the casualties were undoubtedly heavy, tactics were becoming increasingly sophisticated. By the end of the year, as the battle of Cambrai (November–December 1917) demonstrated, it was increasingly difficult for defenders to prevent a skilled and determined attacker from breaking through. This conclusion is reinforced by the initial success of the Germans in March 1918, and the Allies' victorious 'Hundred Days' campaign (August–November). In the end, however, tactical brilliance was not enough. The Germans failed at the operational and strategic levels; the Allies did not make the same mistake.

Ultimately, the war was decided not by generals but by the front line soldiers. For four long years they endured terrible conditions – the sheer resilience of their morale is remarkable. In recent years, historians have increasingly come to reject the idea that they were mere passive victims of the enemy or their own commanders. This book puts the ordinary soldier centre stage by bringing together a number of fascinating studies of Tommy, Fritz, the *poilu* and the doughboy. All contributors have taken their own approach to the subject, and there has been no attempt to impose uniformity of opinion. The resulting book is a treasure-trove of detailed information about uniforms and weapons, tactics and training, placed into context by an authoritative account of the evolution of warfare on the Western Front. Novices to the subject and experts alike will find this an invaluable guide to the Western Front and the soldiers who fought there.

Opposite:
Bombers of 1st Battalion, Scots Guards, in 'Big Willie' trench at Loos, October 1915. (IWM, Q17390)

A silhouetted file of men of the 8th Battalion, East Yorkshire Regiment, going up to the line near Frezenberg. (IWM, Q2978)

PART I

WARRIORS ON THE WESTERN FRONT

GERMAN STORMTROOPER

Ian Drury

At 6.20am on 20 November 1917 a thousand guns opened fire on the German trenches defending the town of Cambrai. Under cover of this ferocious bombardment, 378 tanks lumbered across No Man's Land, spearheading a surprise attack that smashed through the German lines. After three years of trench warfare, the British Army had at last developed the means to crack open the Western Front. The 'green fields beyond' were finally in sight.

For the first time in the war, church bells were rung in England to celebrate a major victory. However, ten days later the Germans counter-attacked. They swiftly recaptured part of the newly created salient, and in some places penetrated beyond the original British front line. Yet the Germans had no tanks. Their attack was led by units of elite infantry: *Stosstruppen* or 'stormtroops'. Fighting in small groups, amply equipped with light machine guns, mortars, grenade-launchers and hand grenades, they advanced at an equally astonishing rate. By midday on 30 November the leading stormtroops had gained 5 miles.

Units of *Stosstruppen* had fought in France before, but never in such numbers. Many more would have been available for the counter-stroke at Cambrai, but most stormtroop formations were still in Italy, where they had played a key role in the battle of Caporetto, nearly knocking Italy out of the war, and compelling Britain and France to send sorely needed divisions to shore-up the Italian Front. However, the victory at Cambrai counted for more to the German military leadership. It proved that the German Army had the capability to rupture the Western Front, to penetrate the defences not only of the gravely weakened Italians, but also of the British Army itself. And unless Germany could achieve victory in the West by the following summer, it was doomed to certain defeat, since the United States' entry into the war had given the Allies overwhelming industrial and numerical superiority.

On 3 December 1917 the Bolshevik leaders were compelled to accept an armistice, taking Russia out of the war. German infantry divisions were already piling into trains to begin the long journey home, and by the spring of 1918 the German forces on the Western Front had gained 400,000 fresh troops – the last reinforcements they would ever receive.

The German soldiers returning from the East had fought a very different war from their comrades in the West, and they had a great deal to learn before they could participate in the great offensive of 1918. The German infantry on the Western Front had been transformed: gone were the uniformly armed and equipped rifle companies of 1914. The 19th-century style skirmish lines employed that fateful autumn had become a distant memory. Infantry companies no longer fought as monolithic blocs, but were divided into platoons that were themselves split into sub-units, each with a discrete tactical role. By late 1916 the organization of German infantry battalions on the Western Front had begun to foreshadow that of World War II.

In their search for tactical progress on the Western Front, the *Stosstruppen* were at the forefront of modern infantry tactics. Those employed at Cambrai and throughout 1918 involved individual squads of soldiers using a combination of weapons. The magazine-loading rifle – the sole weapon of the infantry in 1914 – had become just one element in an array of mutually complementary weapons. While British and French tactics had advanced too, in some respects they had not travelled as far or as fast: by 1918 the German stormtroop battalions were using the same sort of 'gun group' and 'rifle group' minor tactics that 2 Para used at Goose Green in 1982: indeed, the infantry battle on the desolate ridgeline above Darwin would probably have seemed remarkably familiar to a World War I stormtrooper (although the lack of artillery would have astonished him). Trenches were suppressed by machine gun fire, then assaulted with grenades (in 1918 the stormtroops used cut-down Russian field guns and rifle grenades); particularly difficult bunkers were tackled with heavy weapons.

Like the Parachute Regiment, the stormtroopers had a strong *esprit de corps*. Fit and aggressive shock troops, they earned their distinctions – and extra rations – by proven bravery on the battlefield. Their training emphasized individual initiative. Non-commissioned officers were no longer there just to enforce the officers' authority, but to provide tactical leadership throughout the platoon.

The British learned through bitter experience how successful the Germans' defensive tactics had become, and in 1918 they began to reorganize along the same lines. But stormtroops and their

Opposite:
A classic study of a stormtrooper. He wears the M1907 engineers' tunic, and M1917 field-grey trousers. Around his neck is slung a M1917 bandolier for rifle ammunition clips, leaving his belt free to hook on four M1916 stick grenades. (Friedrich Herrmann Memorial Collection)

A stormtroop company poses for a group photograph during 1918. It is at less than half its established strength in riflemen, but it includes two MG08s and one MG08/15. (IWM, Q55371)

This group of nine soldiers has formed an assault party in order to raid an enemy trench in 1916. All wear the standard infantry uniform with M1907 or simplified M1907 field tunics, M1907 trousers and marching boots. (Friedrich Herrmann Memorial Collection)

methods were never fully understood. The effects of their actions were painfully clear, but even when it came to writing the official history, the best explanation the British official historian could offer was that the Germans had copied the idea from a French pamphlet (Vol II of *The Official History of Operations in France and Belgium 1917* credits Captain André Laffargue, whose pamphlet 'The Attack in Trench Warfare' was commercially published in 1916).

In the forefront of tactical development throughout the conflict, stormtroopers were still associated with victory even after Germany plunged to defeat. In the chaos that followed that defeat, many paramilitary groups modelled themselves in the stormtroops' image. One even hijacked the name. When the then-obscure German Workers' Party organized a gang of toughs to deal with its opponents on the street, it called them the *Sturmabteilung* (SA) ('assault detachment') in conscious imitation. The SA was to become the strong arm of the Nazi party until Adolf Hitler achieved supreme power.

CREATING AN ELITE

The first official German stormtroop unit was authorized on 2 March 1915. *Oberste Heeresleitung* (OHL), the High Command of the field army, ordered the VIII Corps to form a detachment for the testing of experimental weapons and the development of appropriate tactics that could break the deadlock on the Western Front. It was considered a natural job for the pioneers – the only element of the pre-war army experienced with hand grenades and trained for siege warfare.

For several decades the German Army had been preparing to invade its neighbours. Not entirely ignorant of German intentions, the French, Belgian and Russian governments had fortified their frontiers, guarding vital road and rail junctions with modern castles of concrete and steel.

CHRONOLOGY

1 August 1914 — Germany declares war on Russia.

3 August 1914 — Germany invades Belgium, France and Luxemburg.

5–10 September 1914 German invasion of France defeated at the battle of the Marne.

9–14 September 1914 German counter-attacks defeat and destroy the Russian armies that have invaded East Prussia.

Oct–Nov 1914 — German attacks at Ypres fail to break the British Expeditionary Force and the front line on the Western Front is established from the Channel to Switzerland. It will barely move for the next three years.

18 January 1915 — The first flame-thrower unit is created by the German Army, commanded by Captain Hermann Reddemann, former chief of the Leipzig fire brigade.

2 March 1915 — The German Army High Command authorizes the creation of the first official stormtroop unit, a company commanded by Major Kaslow of the 18th Pioneer Battalion.

23 May 1915 — Italy declares war on the Central Powers.

August 1915 — Major Kaslow is replaced by Captain Rohr of the Guards Rifles and the unit is renamed Sturmabteilung Rohr.

21 February 1916 — German offensive begins at Verdun. Sturmabteilung Rohr is transferred there.

1 April 1916 — Sturmabteilung Rohr expanded to battalion strength.

May 1916 — German High Command orders all armies on the Western Front to send two officers and four NCOs to Sturmbataillon Rohr to be trained in the new weapons and tactics.

4 June 1916 — Brusilov offensive begins: the Russians inflict a major defeat on Austria-Hungary, forcing the Germans to divert troops, including new stormtroop formations, to the Eastern Front.

1 July 1916 — The battle of the Somme begins. Although the first day is a disaster for the British, by August the Germans have lost more men in this battle than in six months of fighting around Verdun.

15 September 1916 — Tanks are used for the first time in a British operation on the Somme.

23 October 1916 — All German armies in the West ordered to form a stormtroop battalion, although many have created unofficial stormtroop units already.

December 1916 — German Army introduces the MG08/15 machine-gun as a GPMG, but captured Lewis guns remain in widespread use until the end of the war.

31 January 1917 — Germany announces unrestricted submarine warfare.

23 February 1917 — German armies in the West begin to withdraw to the Hindenburg Line.

12 March 1917 — First Russian Revolution. Tsar Nicholas abdicates on 15 March.

30 November 1917 — *Stosstruppen* spearhead the German counter-attack at Cambrai, penetrating up to 5 miles on the first day.

3 December 1917 — Bolsheviks agree armistice, taking Russia out of the war, and releasing 400,000 German troops for operations in the West.

21 March 1918 — Ludendorff offensives begin with an attack on the British Fifth Army that achieves a complete breakthrough, rupturing the Western Front for the first time since 1914.

15 July 1918 — Ludendorff begins the last of his offensives that ultimately fail to break the Allied armies. German casualties in these operations total 963,000.

8–12 August 1918 — At the battle of Amiens, the British break clean through the German front line, overrunning corps HQs with armoured cars.

October 1918 — The influenza pandemic strikes Germany. Killing over 400,000 people, it quickly spreads to the army.

9 November 1918 — Kaiser Wilhelm abdicates.

11 November 1918 — Armistice signed.

A machine gun post in a front line trench during the retreat to the Siegfried Line, February 1917. As German infantry companies received more light machine guns, platoons began to subdivide into 'gun groups' and 'rifle groups', capable of independent fire and movement. (IWM, Q44170)

While the German Army had acquired the heavy artillery and specialist engineer units to storm such strongpoints, it had not anticipated the stalemate that was to follow its failure to defeat the French Army in 1914.

Machine guns were at the heart of the problem. Even more effective than pre-war studies had suggested, they showed a remarkable ability to survive artillery bombardment in sufficient numbers to mow down attacking infantry. All armies had experienced this, but the armaments company Krupp, in Germany, was first to offer a technical solution. If heavy artillery could not succeed, why not try the opposite tack? Krupp designed the *Sturmkanone* – a 3.7cm light cannon that could be easily manoeuvred in the front line – and to test it the first *Sturmabteilung* was created. Commanded by a pioneer officer, Major Kaslow of the 18th Pioneer Battalion, the detachment became known as Sturmabteilung Kaslow. Other equipment they evaluated included steel helmets and body armour. After three months' training the unit was sent into action, parcelled out in detachments to various front line battalions. The Krupp guns proved cumbersome and vulnerable, and the unit suffered over 30 per cent losses in a series of minor attacks.

Kaslow was replaced in August 1915 by Captain Willy Ernst Rohr, a 37-year-old career soldier from the prestigious Garde-Schützen (Guard Rifles) Battalion. Under his dynamic leadership, the assault detachment evolved new tactics to break into an enemy trench system. The *Sturmkanone* were replaced by cut-down field guns captured from the Russians, and the soldiers adapted their uniforms and personal equipment to suit their new methods. Combat operations in the Vosges that autumn suggested Rohr's ideas were sound, and in early February 1916 Sturmabteilung Rohr was transferred to Verdun. It was expanded to battalion strength on 1 April, and in May the High Command ordered all armies on the Western Front to send two officers and four NCOs to Rohr's command to learn the new techniques. Sturmbataillon Rohr was to be an instructional unit with a high turnover in personnel, not an elite formation that simply creamed off the most capable soldiers from line regiments.

FORMATION OF *STOSSTRUPPEN*

On 23 October 1916 General Ludendorff ordered all German armies in the West to form a battalion of stormtroops. Impressed by an honour guard from Sturmbataillon Rohr he had inspected at the Crown Prince's headquarters, Ludendorff soon became aware that the German armies in France and Belgium had changed considerably in the two years he had been away in Russia. By the beginning of December 1916, the First, Second and Fifth German armies each had an assault battalion, and the other 14 German armies established one during the course of the month. However, many of these new *Sturmbataillone* were created by amalgamating existing stormtroop units that had sprung up among the divisions. While Rohr's battalion was created by the High Command (and soon won powerful friends, including the Crown Prince, von Falkenhayn and ultimately Ludendorff), it had no monopoly of new tactical ideas. Since mid-1915 some German regiments had been creating small units of shock troops from within their own ranks. These select troops operated in sections, platoons and even whole companies, and enjoyed a variety of titles. Many favoured *Sturmtrupp* (assault troop), but others included *Jagdkommando* (hunting commando) and *Patrouillentrupp* (raid troop). When the first flame-thrower units were assembled in early 1915, under Captain Reddemann, he called his men *Stosstruppen* (stormtroops). This caught the soldiers' imagination and, regardless of their unit's actual title, the men of these first assault detachments began to refer to themselves as *Stosstruppen*.

OHL did not intend the stormtroops to be a permanent feature of the German order of battle but a model for the rest of the army. Once this had been achieved, the stormtroop formations were

Stormtroopers are inspected outside their rest billets before going into the line. Note the sandbags bulging with stick grenades, and the puttees and boots that have replaced the pre-war jackboots. (IWM, Q85934)

to disappear. Consequently, the stormtroop battalions were never incorporated into the peacetime army structure and were never assigned home barracks or recruiting areas in Germany. They were not associated with historical regiments from the 18th century in the way regular regiments embraced their military heritage; nor did they receive colours.

By November 1916 more than 30 German divisions included some sort of assault detachment. Several independent corps, Landwehr divisions and even the Naval Division had also established a stormtrooper unit on their own initiative. This remarkable process of parallel development stemmed from the training methods and doctrine of the pre-war German Army. In all other major armies training methods were determined by the High Command, but the 22 corps districts of the Imperial German Army were fiercely independent. While the renowned General Staff planned German strategy, peacetime troop movements were left entirely to the corps commanders, who reported directly to the Kaiser. This tradition of tactical independence paid handsome dividends after 1914. The general staffs of other armies worked equally hard to solve the tactical problems of the Western Front, but many handicapped themselves by trying to micro-manage the front line battle. German regimental officers, accustomed to less interference in their tactics, had more freedom to experiment. As a result, by the summer of 1915 stormtroop units were springing up throughout the German armies in the West. Sturmbataillon Rohr would be the most famous, and was instrumental in winning official approval for stormtroops, but the simultaneous appearance of assault detachments in so many divisions demonstrates just how successfully the German military system encouraged individual initiative.

This stormtrooper, shown in a posed study, is demonstrating the use of the M1917 stick grenade. Note at his feet six grenade heads wired around a completed grenade to form a 'concentrated charge'. (Friedrich Herrmann Memorial Collection)

UNIFORMS

German infantrymen began World War I in one of the more practical uniforms worn by the rival armies. Although the style of the German field service dress harked back to the glory days of 1870, the 1910-pattern *feldgrau* uniform was eminently suitable for the opening campaigns of 1914. However, once the German Army went on the defensive in the West, the soldiers' appearance began to change. One of the first casualties was the *Pickelhaube* itself. Its spike served no practical purpose but was the first part of a German soldier to become visible if he peered over the parapet, and front line soldiers soon dispensed with it. The M1915 *Pickelhaube* featured a detachable spike, and the drab cloth cover worn over it lost the red regimental number on the front. The construction of the M1915-pattern *Pickelhaube* reveals a second influence on the German soldiers' appearance, and one that would prove almost as significant as the demands of trench warfare: the effect of the Allied blockade. The *Pickelhaube* was supposed to be made from boiled leather, but felt, thin metal and even compressed cardboard were tried as substitutes.

The stormtroop detachments in 1915 wore standard service uniforms. During that year, the appearance of the front line troops differed only in minor detail from that of 1914. In a change agreed before the war, *steingrau* (stone-grey) trousers were introduced to replace the *feldgrau* ones because the latter seem to have faded too quickly. The M1907–10 tunic was superseded by a more utilitarian version – the distinctive cuffs were replaced by plain turnbacks, and the false skirt pocket flaps disappeared. Soldiers were supposed to blacken their leather equipment, including their boots, belts and cartridge pouches, but this was not always possible in the front line, as captured equipment shows.

WARTIME EQUIPMENT

From 1915 soldiers were issued with a new piece of defensive equipment – one that was to prove indispensable when the German scientists introduced their so-called 'higher form of killing'. The M1915 respirator had a rubberized fabric face piece and a detachable filter (soldiers carried a spare). The increase in the use of poison gas by both sides compelled soldiers to carry respirators and to rig up gas alarms in their front line positions. It also added a unique element of horror to the battlefield. However, for all the suffering it caused, this ghastly application of industrial technology failed to break the deadlock.

German stormtroops, 1917. The centre and left figures are part of a *Flammenwerfer* team, 3rd Guard Pioneer Battalion. This team's weapon is the *Kleif* M1916, which was capable of about 20 metres' (66 feet) range. The centre figure directs the projector pipe, while the figure on the left carries the fuel tank. The figure on the right is the platoon leader. At his belt he carries three 1916 stick grenades. He is hurling a 'concentrated' charge consisting of six grenade heads wired around a complete stick grenade. (Adam Hook © Osprey Publishing Ltd)

On 21 September 1915 the German Army introduced a completely new infantry uniform. The *Bluse* (blouse) was supposed to replace both earlier tunics, although the 1907/10 and 1914 patterns remained in use until the end of the war. Cut slightly looser, it had two large slanted pockets at the front, and looked rather more like a modern combat jacket than the 19th-century style of the earlier tunics. The front buttons – metal, painted grey – were concealed behind a flap, and the shoulder straps were detachable. Manufactured in a dark field grey, it had a fall-down collar faced with green. As before, the jackets of Jäger and Schützen regiments were dyed a much greener shade of *feldgrau*.

The M1895 knapsack, with its distinctive cow hide back, was too cumbersome for trench warfare. While it remained on issue until 1918 and was worn in action on the Russian Front, by late 1915 German infantry in France and Belgium had begun to use an 'assault pack'. They wrapped their greatcoat in a tent cloth and rolled it around a mess tin, creating a smaller, handier pack, more suited to their needs. Their old knapsacks would be used when marching behind the lines, but were often put into battalion stores while the infantry were in the front line.

The first article of uniform that distinguished a stormtrooper from a regular infantryman appeared in early 1916. In time, it would become the trademark of the German soldier in both World Wars. Its very shape has such an emotional charge that the US Army agonized throughout the 1970s before introducing its similarly shaped Kevlar helmet – soon dubbed the 'Fritz'. The M1916 *Stahlhelm* was part of a range of body armour tested by the German Army from 1915. Dubbed by the British the 'coal scuttle' helmet, it was made from silicon-nickel steel and weighed 1.2kg (2$\frac{1}{2}$lb). Extending over the ears and back of the neck, it offered better protection than either the French M1915 mild-steel 'Adrian' helmet or the revived medieval design favoured by the British. It was padded inside and adjusted by leather straps to fit each individual. Thick lugs projected from either side to support an additional steel plate across the front of the helmet. The *Stahlhelm* was issued to sentries and snipers, but was rarely seen by ordinary riflemen.

From its inception, Sturmabteilung Rohr was used to test body armour that might be effective in No Man's Land. The early stormtroops experimented with shields rather like those used today for riot control; but in those pre-Kevlar days, the German shields were made from solid steel and proved too heavy to use during an attack. The protection they offered could not compensate for the loss of mobility. Steel breastplates were similarly restrictive, and tended to be worn by look-outs or other exposed personnel in static positions.

The German Army's pre-war interest in siege warfare paid an unexpected bonus in the autumn of 1914: the arsenals of its border fortresses were packed with hand grenades, originally intended for use by the garrisons. These were shipped to the front line, where they gave the Germans a useful advantage during the first months of trench warfare. Since only the pioneers had been trained in their use, individual pioneers were posted to infantry battalions as supervisors. During 1915 two new types of grenade entered production and soon became standard weapons: the *Eierhandgranate* (egg grenade) and the *Stielhandgranate* (stick grenade).

By February 1916, when the German Army launched its great offensive at Verdun, stormtroop detachments had begun to assume a rather different appearance from soldiers in regular infantry battalions. Stormtroops were among the first to receive the new steel helmet; most of the Fifth German Army's infantry were still wearing the *Pickelhaube* with the spike removed. The stormtroops spearheading the attack were well equipped with stick grenades, each carrying a dozen

or more in a sandbag slung across his chest. Captain Rohr's men had also substituted ankle boots and puttees for their 1866-pattern leather jackboots – another practice that was to spread throughout the assault units over the following two years. The stormtroopers had also started sewing leather patches on their elbows and knees – shielding their most vulnerable joints from the wear and tear of crawling. The first wave over the top at Verdun was primarily armed with hand grenades, so the men carried their rifles slung and did not wear the issue belt and shoulder harness that supported the ammunition pouches. Extra clips of 7.92mm cartridges were carried in cloth bandoliers, each holding 70 rounds.

By the end of 1916 official stormtroop battalions were established throughout the Western armies. Soldiers were selected from regular battalions, posted to a stormtroop formation for a period and then returned to their original unit. A typical infantry battalion of mid-1917 would have included a number of officers and junior NCOs who had served in a stormtroop formation. Exact figures are impossible to obtain, since a high proportion of the Imperial Army's records was destroyed by RAF Bomber Command in 1945.

Men who had served with the stormtroops may well have returned with different uniforms as well as different tactical ideas. In Ludwig Renn's autobiographical novel, *Krieg* (*War*), a newly arrived officer says to an NCO, 'You are wearing puttees and leather knee-pieces. Is that allowed

Six members of an assault detachment pose proudly with a group of dejected French prisoners they have just captured. Some troopers have field-made cloth helmet covers; M1907 infantry field tunics are worn with M1917 trousers, M1866 marching boots or puttees with M1912 ankle boots. They carry locally made grenade sacks, and the corporal (left) has a field torch suspended from a front button. (Friedrich Herrmann Memorial Collection)

in the regiment, sergeant-major?' Learning that the man has just returned from a storm battalion, the captain is delighted, and plans a whole platoon of assault troops. But Renn implies that some line officers were not best pleased with NCOs returning to the battalion with personalized uniforms – and a new sense of their own importance. Renn's real name was Arnold von Golssenau, and he was a career officer who may have encountered such an attitude among his colleagues.

WEAPONS SHORT MAGAZINE

RIFLES AND CARBINES

In 1914 German infantry regiments were uniformly armed with the 1898-pattern Mauser rifle. Chambered for the 8x57mm rimless cartridge, it held five rounds in an internal box magazine that was loaded through the action by brass stripper clips. The side of the stock was cut away on the right, allowing the soldier to slide the cartridges in with the flat of his thumb, rather than push them down with the tip. This had a practical advantage over the British Short Magazine Lee-Enfield (SMLE) in which you had to press home the rounds with the end of your thumb, sometimes splintering the nail in your haste to get the rifle back into action (see p.105). On the other hand, because it was cocked on opening, the Mauser bolt was less tolerant of poor quality ammunition and dirt around the breach. One could not retain his sight picture while working the Mauser's action, and the magazine only held half as many rounds as an SMLE. The Germans attempted to increase the Mauser's firepower by issuing a 25-round magazine, but it only appeared in limited numbers and was rather awkward to handle. With its backsight down, the M1898 was sighted to 200 metres (219 yards), and it could be elevated by 50-metre (55-yard) increments to a maximum of 2,000 metres (1.2 miles). Weighing 4kg (9lb) unloaded, and 1,250mm (4ft) long, the M1898 was a robust and accurate weapon, ideally suited to the open warfare of 1914, but not for the trench fighting that followed.

Sturmbataillon Rohr tested several types of body armour in 1915, rejecting all but the steel helmet as too cumbersome to fight in. This elaborate breastplate was subsequently issued to some snipers and sentries. (Friedrich Herrmann Memorial Collection)

The German Army issued carbines to all other arms: cavalry, artillery, pioneers, independent machine gun companies and motor transport units. The only infantry units to use them at the beginning of the war were the Jäger and Schützen battalions. The standard carbine was the M1898AZ (*Karabiner 98 mit Aufplanz- und Zusammensetzvorrichtung*), which was 1,090mm (3^1/$_2$ft) long and had a 590mm barrel instead of the 600mm of the M1898. Two much shorter carbines had been tested before the war, but were rejected because the muzzle-flash and recoil from a 435mm barrel proved unacceptable.

Sturmbataillon Rohr adopted the K.98 carbine during 1915, and it slowly became the standard armament of stormtroop formations throughout the German armies in the West. It was significantly shorter, and thus handier in the confines of the trenches; but at prevailing combat ranges it was no less accurate or hard-hitting. When it came to re-arm in the 1930s, the German Army adopted a new Mauser with similar dimensions to the K.98 for all infantry units.

A German machine gun platoon on the march during the second battle of the Somme, 1918. They are equipped with captured British Lewis guns, which were used extensively by German machine gun units after 1916. (IWM, Q55482)

AUTOMATIC WEAPONS

The stormtroop battalions also received the world's first effective sub-machine gun, the MP18. Designed by Hugo Schmiesser, the MP18 introduced most of the features that were to make the sub-machine gun the key close-quarter weapon of World War II. Chambered for 9mm Parabellum, the MP18 fired from the open bolt: pulling the trigger sent the bolt forward, where it stripped the uppermost round from the magazine, chambered it and fired it. If the trigger was held back, the bolt continued to cycle, driven directly back by the propellant gas and flung forward again by the return spring. It was mechanically simple and highly effective. Over 30,000 were supplied to the German Army during 1918, but most of them arrived after the great March offensive. General Ludendorff looked to the MP18 to increase the defensive power of the German infantry as the Allies began their assault on the Hindenburg Line.

Some soldiers in the stormtroop battalions had had experience with rapid-fire weapons, if not automatics. NCOs in charge of machine gun or mortar teams were often equipped with pistols capable of doubling as a carbine. Both the P08 Luger and the 'Broomhandle' Mauser were capable of receiving a shoulder stock which gave them an effective range of over 91 metres (100 yards). More practically, it gave the NCOs a handy self-defence weapon that was much better than a rifle when enemy bombing parties were closing in. For close-quarter fighting in the enemy trenches, an Artillery Model Luger with a 32-round 'snail' magazine made much more sense than a bolt-action rifle with a five-round magazine. As Erwin Rommel observed in *Attacks*, 'In a man-to-man fight, the winner is he who has one more round in his magazine.'

HAND GRENADES

The pioneers' hand grenades of 1914 were soon replaced by far more effective weapons. The M1915 *Stielhandgranate* is the most famous, and it became almost the primary weapon of the assault battalions. When stormtroop detachments led the attack at Verdun in February 1916, many of them went into action with their rifles slung, leaving their hands free to lob stick grenades into surviving French positions. The stick grenade consisted of a hollow cylinder about 100mm (4in) long and 75mm (3in) in diameter containing an explosive mixture of potassium perchlorate, barium nitrate, black powder and powdered aluminium. The cylinder had a metal clip on the side,

Germans practise throwing hand grenades. (Ian Drury)

enabling it to be attached to a belt. It also had a hollow wooden throwing handle 225mm (9in) long. A cord projected from the bulbous end; pulling it ignited a friction tube that detonated the main charge 5½ seconds later. Some were issued with 7-second fuses, others with 3-second fuses; the type of fuse was stamped on the handle. There was also a percussion-fused version, detonated by a spring-powered striker when it hit the ground.

In 1916 German infantry began to receive a new grenade, the *Eierhandgranate* or 'egg grenade'. Weighing 310g (11oz) it was made of cast iron, painted black and was the size and shape of a hen's egg. A friction lighter ignited a 5-second fuse, although an 8-second fuse was available if it was fired from a grenade-launcher. This tiny grenade could be thrown as far as 50 metres (55 yards) by an experienced grenadier, but its explosive effect was fairly limited. The egg grenade was first encountered by the British on the Somme: stormtroops counter-attacked north of Thiepval in July 1916, hurling the new grenades into captured trenches and re-taking most of the original German front line.

Both main types of German grenade relied primarily on blast rather than fragmentation, and they were far more effective in the confines of a trench than in the open field. Stormtroopers assaulting particularly well-defended positions tended to tape batches of stick grenades together and then post these deadly packages over the enemy parapet or into the slits of concrete bunkers.

MACHINE GUNS

The German Army did not take to machine guns with the same readiness as the British and French armies: only in 1913 were they issued to line infantry regiments. However, wartime experience soon vindicated the machine gun lobby of the pre-war army, and the number of machine gun companies rose rapidly. In 1914 each infantry regiment included a six-gun machine gun company. During 1915 regiments received supplementary machine gun sections of 30–40 men and three or four machine guns, and by the end of the year many regiments had two full strength machine gun companies. In the winter of 1915/16 specialist machine gun units, known as machine gun marksmen (*Maschinengewehr Scharfschützen Trupps*) were created. Trained specifically for offensive use of machine guns, their personnel underwent a four- or five-week instruction course and were formed into independent companies of six guns. They were first seen at the front line at Verdun.

By mid-1916 the ad hoc development of machine gun units had left some regiments with as many as 25 machine guns, and others with their regulation six. In August a new standard organization was adopted: all machine gun companies were to consist of six weapons and all infantry regiments were to have three such companies, one attached to each infantry battalion. The machine gun marksmen companies were grouped into machine gun detachments (*Maschinen-Gewehr Scharfschützen-Abteilungen*), each of three companies. One such detachment was normally attached to each division engaged in active operations at the front. When the divisional *Sturmbataillone* were formed in December 1916, each battalion had either one or two machine gun companies.

The number of German machine gun units continued to increase during 1917, although the number of machine gun companies per regiment remained the same. Machine gun companies were expanded to eight, ten and finally 12 weapons per company, and the number of independent companies was increased too. A stormtroop battalion could have anything from 12 to 24 machine guns, while independent *Sturmkompagnien* had their own machine gun platoon of two weapons.

Machine gun companies were equipped with the MG08, a modified Maxim gun design. The gun itself weighed 25kg (55lb); on its stout metal sledge and with its water-jacket filled, it weighed 63.6kg (140lb) and was not the most mobile of infantry weapons. Although the MG08 was to exact a fearful toll on Allied infantrymen, it was primarily a defensive weapon. It did not break down to manageable loads and it was a struggle to move it across the heavily cratered battlefields of the Western Front. Nevertheless, when the German Fifth Army made its supreme effort at Verdun, in June 1916, attacking regiments put their machine gun companies in the front line. The Bavarian Life Guard, supported by Sturmbataillon Rohr, seized the village of Fleury and brought up 24 MG08s to fight its way through the ruins.

LIGHT MACHINE GUNS

The German Army recognized the need for a lighter machine gun in 1915, and work began on a modification of the MG08 design. In the meantime, since most of Germany's enemies were already using light machine guns, the German Army formed special battalions to use captured enemy weapons. The first *Musketen-Bataillone* were created in August 1915 and

German stormtroops, autumn 1918. The figure in the right foreground is a section leader from a *Sturmbataillon* formed by a Munich regiment. He advances with the 9mm MP18 sub-machine gun. On the left is a light machine gunner carrying the MG08/15 with its distinctive 100-round drum. In the background is a corporal from a Breslau regiment, preparing to throw an *Eier* or 'egg' bomb. (Adam Hook © Osprey Publishing Ltd)

committed to the Champagne battle in September. These units were armed with Madsen light machine guns, captured from the Russians. The Danish-designed Madsen was a true light machine gun: air-cooled, bipod-mounted and weighing just under 10kg (22lb), it was fed by a 20-round box magazine. The Russian Army had bought the Madsen for its cavalry before the war and it took little effort to re-chamber the weapons. Each *Musketen-Bataillone* consisted of three companies, each with four officers, 160 of other ranks and 30 machine guns. A four-man squad operated each weapon, and the soldiers also carried K.98s, like the regimental machine gun companies.

The *Musketen-Bataillone* were used during the battle of the Somme as part of the German second line. When a breakthrough occurred, they were rushed to plug the gap, machine gunning the leading Allied units and inviting the inevitable attention of British artillery. They suffered heavy casualties, and lost all their Madsens by the end of the campaign.

The British Army was already using the Lewis gun (see p.107): a heavier weapon, weighing closer to 15kg (33lb), but far easier to manoeuvre than an MG08. With a 47-round drum magazine, it could not deliver the sort of sustained fire of a belt-fed weapon, but it gave an infantry platoon the means to suppress an enemy position without relying on heavy weapons further back. By the end of the Somme battle, enough Lewis guns had fallen into German hands for the *Musketen-Bataillone* to re-equip with them. Also re-chambered for German ammunition, the Lewis guns remained in use until the *Musketen-Bataillone* were converted to *Maschinen-Gewehr Scharfschützen Bataillone*, in April 1918. By then, all German infantry regiments contained so many light machine guns that there was no purpose in having a handful of battalions armed exclusively with them. However, the stormtroop battalions seem to have liked the Lewis gun so much that many retained them in preference to the later light machine guns produced by the Germans. Lewis guns remained in front line service until the end of the war, with captured weapons repaired and converted in a factory in Brussels.

In December 1916 the German Army introduced its 'official' light machine gun, the MG08/15 – basically an MG08 mounted on a bipod and fitted with a wooden rifle butt and pistol grip. It was still water-cooled, but the casing was narrower. Weighing 19.5kg (43lb) it was only 'light' in the imagination of its designers. On the other hand, it was arguably the world's first general purpose machine gun (GPMG): light enough to be manhandled over the battlefield, but heavy enough to deliver sustained fire. Fed by 100- or 250-round belts, the MG08/15 could provide a much greater volume of fire than the Lewis or Chauchat light machine guns being used by the Allies and, despite its weight, it anticipated the tactical role of the MG34 in World War II.

The MG08/15 was first encountered on the Western Front in the spring of 1917, when German infantry companies each received three. This increased to six over the course of the year, although units on the Eastern Front were a lower priority, and most made do with a pair of MG08/15s until the Russian campaign was over. The MG08/15s were initially organized as discrete units, effectively forming a fourth platoon in each rifle company rather as the British infantry platoons added a Lewis section to their three infantry sections. As the numbers of MG08/15s increased, they were integrated into the platoons, giving platoon commanders the ability to manoeuvre their rifle sections covered by the suppressive fire of the machine guns.

Men haul a *Granatenwerfer* on a handcart after the stormtroops during the battle of the Marne, July 1918. (IWM, Q55372)

GRENADE-LAUNCHERS

The German Army began the war with two types of rifle grenade in service. Both weighed just under a kilo and were fired from the Gewehr 98 rifle, using a special blank cartridge. Recoil was vicious and accuracy minimal, but once the trench lines were established, troops rigged up all manner of improvised mountings. By 1916 a purpose-built *Granatenwerfer* (grenade-thrower) had been introduced. It weighed 40kg (88lb), but broke down into two loads – the thrower (23kg/51lb) and the platform (15kg/33lb). It had a maximum range of 350m (383yd) and a minimum range of 50m (55yd). Infantry regiments had 12 each by 1916, and with them special 'rebounding' grenades were introduced. The latter carried a separate black powder charge so that when the grenade struck the ground, it was blown back into the air a fraction of a second before it detonated. The *Granatenwerfer* could also launch signal rockets. This handy two-man weapon could deliver an impressive hail of fire against enemy strongpoints; its ammunition was light, and if enough infantrymen carried forward sandbags full of grenades, the *Granatenwerfer* could support them with both direct and indirect fire.

MORTARS

After witnessing the success of Japanese improvised mortars at Port Arthur, the German Army ordered a series of purpose-built weapons for the pioneers. By 1914 the pioneers had three types of *Minenwerfer* at their disposal: the 7.6cm light mortar that threw a 4.7kg (10lb) bomb out to 1,050m (1,148yd); the medium 17cm mortar that fired a 49.5kg (109lb) bomb 900m (984yd); and the heavy 21cm mortar that delivered a 100kg (220½lb) bomb up to 550m (601yd). This last was originally intended for the defence of fortresses, and was the deadliest weapon on the Western Front. Its very high trajectory and heavy charges could bring about the collapse of whole sections

A *Minenwerfer* in action in the dunes on the Flanders coast, July 1917. (IWM, Q50665)

of trench. The mortars' noise, and slow, remorseless passage through the air added to the terror. New versions of all three mortars were introduced in 1916; these had much longer ranges and were capable of delivering gas-filled projectiles.

The trench mortars were assigned to the siege train in 1914, but although they remained nominally in the hands of pioneers, they were soon reorganized into independent mortar detachments. Their personnel were largely drawn from the infantry, and they were attached to the infantry on a basis of one *Minenwerfer Abteilung* per regiment. Each regimental detachment consisted of 12 7.6cm mortars and 24 grenade-launchers. The heavier mortars were grouped into Minenwerfer companies, with one normally attached to each division. Each company comprised three sections: one heavy (four 24cm or 25cm mortars) and two medium (eight 17cm mortars). There were also at least 13 Minenwerfer battalions as a reserve at the disposal of General Headquarters, that could be sent to support German attacks or to reinforce a hard-pressed sector. A Minenwerfer battalion had four companies, each equipped with six heavy and four light mortars.

Stormtroop battalions usually included a mortar company of their own. Independent *Sturmkompagnien* generally had a section of up to four light mortars.

FLAME-THROWERS

Soldiers from the pioneer units were already incorporated into the stormtroop detachments. On 18 January 1915 an all-volunteer formation of pioneers was created to operate the newly developed flame-throwers. By a curious twist of fate, the commander of the *Flammenwerfer Abteilung*, Captain Hermann Reddemann, was a former chief of the Leipzig fire brigade. He had been conducting experiments with flame weapons for several years before the war, and had collaborated with Richard

The light flame-thrower was operated by two men: one carried the tank of fuel and compressed nitrogen, the other aimed the hose. Early models had to be lit manually, which proved dangerous; later versions incorporated an automatic ignition system. (IWM, Q44155)

Fiedler, the man credited with perfecting the first operational flame-thrower. Two types were tested in combat: a man-pack version, the *Kleif* (short for *Kleines Flammenwerfer*), operated by two men, and a static version (*Grosses Flammenwerfer*) that projected a jet of flame for 40m (44yd). To operate the former, one man carried the fuel tank on his back, while a second man aimed the tube. Compressed nitrogen expelled fuel oil which was ignited as it left the nozzle. It was tested in February 1915 against the French near Verdun, and in June against the British. In both cases the terror inspired by jets of liquid flame enabled the German assault troops to capture their objectives with relative ease. No man was prepared to remain in a trench with blazing fuel oil cascading over the parapet.

The *Flammenwerfer Abteilung* became the 3rd Guard Pioneer Battalion. Initially composed of six companies, by 1917 it had expanded to 12 companies, a workshop detachment and a regimental headquarters. Each flame-thrower company consisted of 20 large and 18 small flame-throwers. A platoon (*Flammenwerfertrupp*) of between four and eight small flame-throwers was attached to most stormtroop battalions.

ARTILLERY

The Krupp 3.7cm cannon tested in 1915 had proved a disappointment, but the Germans remained convinced that the best counter to an enemy machine gun nest was a small field gun

The image of the stormtrooper exerted a powerful grip on German post-war politics. This grenadier carries regimentally made hand grenade sacks, a 120cm engineer's 'long spade' strapped to his shoulder strap, a slung Karabiner 98 and the M1916 'alert' gasmask container. (Nigel Thomas)

that used direct fire. The *Sturmkannone* was duly replaced by a mountain howitzer that could be manhandled across the battlefield. However, in early 1916 the stormtroopers received a specially converted field gun, the 7.62cm *Infanterie Geschütz*. This was the standard Russian field-piece with its barrel shortened from 2.28m to 1.25m, new sights graduated to 1,800m, and a low recoil carriage with wheels only 1.1m in diameter. It fired a 5.9kg (13lb) shell of German manufacture. By 1917 there were 50 infantry gun batteries on the Western Front; each stormtroop battalion included one, and the others were brought forward for the close defence of threatened sectors or as support for local offensives. They were also used as anti-tank guns. Batteries consisted of either four or six guns.

During 1917 the Germans supplemented the infantry gun batteries with another 50 or so 'close-range batteries' (*Nahkampf-Batterien*), each of four 7.7cm field guns on special low-wheeled carriages. Instead of being fixed directly on the axle, the gun was mounted on trunnions forward of it. These batteries had neither transport nor horses, and were used primarily as anti-tank guns firing semi-armour-piercing ammunition.

RECRUITMENT

Every German male was liable for military service from his 17th to his 45th birthday, but parliamentary opposition to the spiralling military budget helped ensure that less than half the young men eligible were actually called to the colours before 1914. Senior officers were also conscious that while the general population had increased by 50 per cent since 1870, the Prussian nobility had not bred as quickly. Expanding the army too rapidly would necessitate commissioning officers from outside the *Junker* class – an act so unthinkable that it was never fully implemented, even during the war.

In the three years before World War I, only 45 per cent of Germany's potential military manpower went into the army. In 1914 the German empire could mobilize an army of 4.9 million men from a total population of 67.5 million. France, acutely aware of its numerical inferiority, had trained all its young men but the disabled, and fielded 5 million soldiers from a population of just 39.5 million.

Between the ages of 17 and 20, German men were theoretically liable for service in the Landsturm. Service with the Regular Army began at 20 and consisted of two years' duty with the standing army and three for those posted to the cavalry or horse artillery. After completing regular service, men were assigned to the Reserve for four or five years respectively, and were liable to be called up for two weeks' refresher training each September. When a man reached 27, his liability for front line service was over, and he was transferred to the Landwehr. At the age of 39, men were re-assigned to the Landsturm, essentially a militia intended only for garrison duties. The high proportion of young men not selected for military service were not forgotten, but were assigned to the *Ersatz-Reserve* (supplementary reserve) for 12 years, and were theoretically liable for a little basic training. In 1914 this pool of untrained manpower provided a reserve of a million men in their 20s, and it was used to bring a succession of new reserve units to full strength.

DRAIN ON MANPOWER

The annual recruit contingent or class (*Jahresklasse*) consisted of all men who reached the age of 20 in a given year. During the war Germany's enemies closely monitored the arrival of each class in the front line, since the timing of each call-up revealed just how quickly German manpower was being expended.

Germany went to war in 1914 with the same passionate enthusiasm that gripped so many European nations. Thousands of young men volunteered for service ahead of their conscription class, and the German Army expanded beyond its anticipated strength. The class of 1914 was called up at its normal time – the end of September – but there was a delay of several months before all the recruits were taken into the depots. The men of the *Ersatz-Reserve* were being organized into new reserve divisions: the 75th to 82nd Reserve divisions plus the 8th Bavarian Reserve Division. Meanwhile the existing Reserve and Landwehr formations took their place in the German order of battle. The Landsturm was drawn upon to make up the losses, and was all but exhausted by the end of 1915.

The class of 1915 was called up between April and June 1915 (four months early). Yet this was not enough, and the class of 1916 was called up between August and November – a full year early. Nevertheless, each class received four to five months' training before being posted to the front line. When the German Army suffered over 300,000 losses during 1915, steps were taken to comb out more personnel; men previously rejected as unfit were re-examined under more stringent criteria, and many found themselves in uniform after all. The class of 1917 was called up from January 1916 (over 18 months early). Training time was reduced to three months as the holocausts of Verdun and the Somme shattered whole divisions. Writing after the war, several senior officers regarded 1916 as critical: the year the last of the peacetime-trained German Army perished.

The class of 1918 was called up from September 1916, and the first of these 18-year-old recruits were at the front by January 1917. Many of these young men were organized into new infantry formations: the 231st to 242nd divisions plus the 15th Bavarian. The class of 1919 was in uniform by the summer of 1917, but most of these teenage recruits were dispatched to the Russian Front to release more experienced soldiers for service in the West.

Many German soldiers ignored regulations and kept diaries, often filled with details about their own unit and those of their friends. But they were given official documents that told the Allies even more: their paybook showed which class they belonged to, and, from their company payroll number, the Allies could calculate how many men had been through a particular unit. Each soldier was allotted a number when he joined his unit, and if he was killed, captured or invalided out, his replacement would be given the succeeding number. It was very logical, but very useful for enemy intelligence. The British Army had an officer at General Headquarters whose sole duty was the analysis of captured paybooks. British records show that, for example, a company of the 202nd Reserve Infantry Regiment included men from the class of 1918 as early as April 1917. By September, the only members of earlier classes remaining in the regiment were returned sick or wounded.

Recruitment into the assault battalions was voluntary from 1915 until late 1917. Standards in the early *Sturmbataillone* were so high that when four Jäger battalions were converted to stormtroops, more than 500 men had to be transferred out as unsuitable. Although officers could be posted to a stormtroop unit compulsorily, men of other ranks were supposed to be under 25 years old, unmarried and with a good sports record. With Ludendorff's endorsement, the training role of the stormtroop battalions expanded. Soldiers, and especially NCOs, spent a limited period with an assault battalion before returning to their original unit.

REORGANIZATION FOR 1918 CAMPAIGN

The steady depletion of German manpower eventually frustrated Ludendorff's intention of raising all divisions to stormtrooper standard. In the winter of 1917/18, as he planned Germany's do-or-die offensive in the West, Ludendorff realized he faced an insuperable demographic problem: too many men in the ranks were in their 30s, or unable to meet the physical demands of the new tactics. His solution was to reorganize the army, concentrating the young and fit into attack divisions (commonly known as *Angriffdivisionen*). These received a disproportionately large share of artillery support, ammunitions, rations and training time. Ludendorff assembled them into an elite striking force that, in 1918, would achieve the first major breakthrough on the Western Front. However, for every attack division, there were now three trench divisions (*Stellungsdivisionen*) of marginal fighting value. An uninspiring mixture of the old and very young, they were less well equipped and certainly less motivated. Ludendorff's reorganization is the origin of the myth that stormtroopers were like the World War II special forces: elite units recruited at the expense of less glamorous line battalions. In fact the organization of the original stormtrooper battalions had not sucked the lifeblood of 'ordinary' regiments; they had been training units, and their personnel had eventually returned to their original regiments to pass on new ideas and methods and contribute to a constant 'levelling up' of tactical skill.

TRAINING

Ludwig Renn's novel *War* describes the experiences of a sergeant posted to a stormtroop battalion in the winter of 1917:

> We had to drag machine guns, fling bombs, advance along trenches and crawl without a sound. At first it was a severe strain on me. I sweated on every occasion and several times everything reeled around me, but only for a short time. Then, daily it grew easier. We were on duty from morning to night with only two or three hours of an interval at midday. I had no time for reflection and felt in good trim.

Renn's hero was not alone: a high proportion of the German Army was retraining that winter. As outlined above, the army was being reorganized into 'attack' and 'fortress' divisions; the fittest men were concentrated in the former, and the very best among them were posted to the stormtroop battalions.

Stormtroopers training at Sedan, May 1917. Note how one soldier carries a massive pair of wire cutters, one has a shovel and the soldier on the far left has a stick grenade at the ready. (IWM, Q55021)

THE FIRST UNITS

Captain Rohr's stormtroop detachment had effectively been a training unit since its inception. In December 1915 it hosted a cadre from the 12th Landwehr Division, instructing several hundred officers and men in the new tactics. The Landwehr troops learned how to fight in platoons and sections, rather than lining up each rifle company in a traditional skirmish line. They learned to use 1:5,000 scale maps of enemy positions, rehearsing their attacks on full-scale mock-ups of the French lines. For the first time, NCOs found themselves given a real job of leadership – making their own tactical decisions.

In 1916, after its performance at Verdun had proved the value of stormtrooper tactics, Rohr's battalion established a base at the nearby town of Beauville. It had barely begun a training programme for the four Jäger battalions scheduled to become stormtroop units when the Brusilov offensive and Rumanian declaration of war forced OHL to dispatch three of the battalions to the Eastern Front. Only the 3rd (Brandenburg) Jäger battalion was retrained, becoming the 3rd Jäger-Sturmbataillon on 4 August 1916, and 500 men had to be transferred from the battalion as unfit for the physical demands of the new role. The training programme involved repeated live fire exercises over dummy trenches, with flame-thrower, trench mortar and infantry gun detachments all in action.

The numerous stormtrooper battalions established in December 1916 were regarded primarily as training units. Selected officers and NCOs from each infantry division served brief tours of duty with an army-level stormtroop battalion, returning to their formation to pass on what they had learned. The stormtroop battalions did not spend their time in the front line, but remained at bases in the rear, though occasionally they would be brought forward to undertake trench raids or local offensives. Many assault battalions were allotted motor transport – a rarity in the German Army – so their transit to and from the battlefield was as rapid as possible.

The offensive at Caporetto was preceded by a period of specialized training in mountain warfare. Troops assigned to the operation were sent to the Fourteenth Army front in September

In October 1917 the Alpine Corps spearheaded the German offensive at Caporetto, one of the most comprehensive battlefield victories of World War I. The breakthrough was complete; 30,000 Italian troops were killed and 300,000 surrendered. (US National Archives)

1917 to acclimatize them; they undertook progressively longer marches in the thin Alpine air in preparation. Further weapons training was also required, as they were issued with three MG08/15s per company during that month. (The MG08/15 was nearly as complex as the full-size MG08, and almost impossible to keep in action without a fully trained crew.) The extra firepower was a blessing, but there was a constant shortage of trained machine gunners for the rest of the war.

RETRAINING THE INFANTRY

German infantry training altered during the war. The time allocated to recruits' basic training was reduced, but the content of their instruction became more relevant. General Ludendorff was not the pompous martinet he appeared. He had no time for the niceties of drill: it was irrelevant on the modern battlefield, and he likened it to dog training. (He had a similar regard for the sort of methods used to 'break in' recruits in more recent times.) Endless drill, he remarked, simply deprives young men of their personalities.

The infantry battalions of most major belligerents were taken out of the line for retraining at regular intervals. The catastrophic level of casualties made this essential: battalions often had to be flooded with new recruits to bring them back up to strength. When British battalions were withdrawn to the rear, their refresher training often took place at central depots, under instructors based there rather than under their own officers. French infantry were also trained by officers seconded from the General Staff. However, German infantry remained under the control of their own officers all the time, including training periods behind the lines. In both World Wars, the German Army ensured that its private soldiers had the strongest possible bond between them and their regiment. Each regiment was recruited from a particular town or district, and a small cadre of officers and NCOs stayed there at the outbreak of war, ready to train the new recruits. Throughout the war, officers and NCOs from the regiment would go back to the depot to supervise the training of new personnel. Returned wounded would be posted back to their old unit, returning to familiar faces.

The pre-war training of the German infantry was second to none. The veterans of the British Expeditionary Force may have been individually superior in many respects, but there were only six divisions of them. In August 1914 the German Army put 4 million men into the field. This was a tremendous asset that lasted Imperial Germany well into 1917. By then, many senior commanders were lamenting the end of the pre-war army, Ludendorff likening the German infantry of 1917 to a militia. However, although the overall quality of the battalions may have declined through the horrendous losses on the Somme, the German infantry remained better trained than all its opponents. Even by 1918, between a quarter and a third of the German front line infantry were pre-war trained (see Martin Samuels, *Doctrine and Dogma,* and Martin Middlebrook, *The Kaiser's Battle*). Few British infantry companies had more than one or two individuals with any pre-war experience by then. French infantry battalions no doubt had more, but their pre-war training was of little relevance: the elbow-to-elbow charges persistently attempted in 1915 simply gave German machine guns an unmissable target.

German infantry officers received new training as well. In the autumn of 1916 the Germans began to develop new defensive tactics, mainly as a response to the terrible power of the British artillery unleashed on the Somme. The traditional policy of packing the front line with troops and not yielding an inch had cost the Germans dearly. From September company commanders were

Next page:
Victory over Russia freed some 400,000 German troops for the 1918 offensive in France. But they needed retraining first: their equipment and tactics were out of date by the standards of the Western Front. (Private collection)

A stormtroop charge through woods towards open ground. Note the concentrated charge carried by the soldier in the right foreground. (Nigel Thomas)

sent on month-long courses at training areas just behind the lines. There they studied the new, elastic defences that were to prove so effective in 1917.

Comprehensive retraining began a second time in the winter of 1917/18. Infantrymen received extra training in rifle shooting – a skill that had been lost by all armies on the Western Front – and took part in endless route marches. By February 1918 battalions in the attack divisions were marching as far as 60km (37 miles) a day – the same sort of breakneck speed demanded of the German infantry in 1914. (In August to September 1914, for instance, the 35th Fusiliers marched 657km or 408 miles in 27 consecutive days, fighting 11 battles in the process.) By maintaining such a relentless pace, the Germans gave the Italians no time to recover after their front line was broken at Caporetto. However, the burden on the infantrymen had increased beyond all reason. A critical shortage of horses – and an almost complete dearth of motor transport – meant that artillery batteries had to make do with only four horses per gun, and at least half the infantry machine gun companies had to travel on foot.

The initial assault in March 1918 enjoyed the benefit of thorough rehearsal. Stormtroop battalions practised attacking full-scale models of their real objectives. Officers and senior NCOs had accurate aerial photographs to plan from. Live ammunition was used wherever possible, sometimes with unpredictable results. In his memoir, *Storm of Steel*, Ernst Jünger recalls the dangers of assault practice:

> I made practice attacks with the company on complicated trench systems, with live grenades, in order
> to turn to account the lessons of the Cambrai battle … we had some casualties … A machine gunner
> of my company shot the commanding officer of another unit off his horse, while he was reviewing
> some troops. Fortunately the wound was not fatal.

The tactical manual they employed showed that the training role of the stormtroops was now complete. The 1918 edition of the German infantry training manual was effectively a stormtroopers' handbook. There was no mention of dedicated assault units within the battalion – all German infantrymen were supposed to be trained in that way. The infantry squad was now the prime tactical unit, and where earlier editions had included diagrams showing long skirmish lines, there were now symbols representing rifle squads or machine gun or mortar teams. Six of the 18 squads in a company were designated light machine gun squads.

ORGANIZATION

There was no standard organization among the stormtroop detachments created in 1915/16. Most were simply infantry companies with a few added heavy weapons. Only with the establishment of army-level assault battalions throughout the West did a general structure emerge. The stormtroop battalions formed in December 1916 consisted of:

- headquarters: 10 officers and 32 men (although some were larger)
- 4 assault companies of about 4 officers and 120 other ranks
- 1 or 2 machine gun companies, each originally of 4 officers, 85 men and 6 machine guns, but expanded to 135 men and 12 machine guns during 1917
- 1 flame-thrower platoon of between 4 and 8 man-pack flame-throwers
- 1 infantry gun battery of between 4 and 6 7.62cm guns manned by about 80 men
- 1 mortar company with 2 officers, about 100 other ranks and 8 7.6cm mortars

This formation included up to 1,400 officers and men, and was the basis of German infantry organization during World War II. The number of infantry companies could vary from one to the

A posed photograph symbolizing the stormtrooper's heroism. Taking cover in a shallow ditch, the grenadier takes aim beside the half-buried body of a French soldier. (Friedrich Herrmann Memorial Collection)

five of Sturmbataillon Rohr. Their strength varied too: Rohr's companies were over 200 strong, and those of the 3rd Jäger-Sturmbataillon had 263. Compared to a standard infantry regiment, a stormtrooper battalion included many more heavy weapons.

German line regiments consisted of three battalions, each about 800 strong and organized as follows:

- battalion headquarters
- 3 infantry companies
- 1 machine gun company of between 6 and 12 MG08s
- 1 mortar detachment of 4 light (7.6cm) mortars
- 1 signalling detachment with 8 battery-operated signal lamps

Each infantry company consisted of three platoons, each divided into four 18-man sections. The latter were further sub-divided into two squads, each of one corporal and eight privates. This, the *Gruppe*, was the smallest unit, and was originally only an administrative arrangement that served no tactical purpose. The advent of light machine guns and the new tactics changed this forever. As noted above, during 1917 each company received three MG08/15s and many had at least six of them by the end of the year. The signalling detachments operated under the direction of the divisional signalling regiment; their largest lamps could be seen at up to 3,000 metres (1.9 miles) in daylight.

German battalions tended to be rather weak in manpower, but strong in heavy weapons. The 5th Grenadier Regiment defending the Menin road in September 1917 was typical, occupying a 730-metre (800-yard) front with one battalion in the outpost zone, one in support and one in reserve. Companies averaged two officers, ten NCOs and 68 of other ranks. The regiment's heavy

Stormtroopers engaged in assault training. (IWM, Q55483)

weapons comprised 35 MG08s, 32 MG08/15s and 12 light mortars. The 280 men in the foremost battalion were caught by the British bombardment on 20 September and only 20 survived to surrender.

Assault battalions were often divided into company-size battlegroups and sent to undertake special missions in support of line infantry divisions. For example, on 21 March 1918 the 3rd Jäger-Sturmbataillon was split into four: one infantry company, one flame-thrower platoon and two infantry guns were assigned to the 79th Reserve Division; one company, a flame-thrower platoon, two infantry guns, two mortars and a machine gun company went to the 50th Reserve Division; a similar-sized force went to the 18th Division; and one company and four mortars were held in reserve by the Second Army.

German stormtroops wearing gasmasks in action at Ploegsteert Wood. The Germans were driven from this position, 10km (6.2 miles) south of Ypres, in mid-1917, but although the British fortified it that winter, it was retaken by the Germans in April 1918. (IWM, Q56607)

FIGHTING SPIRIT

World War I imposed an unprecedented psychological burden on front line soldiers. Battles were no longer fought and won in a few days, but lasted for weeks and months. Men no longer fought a visible foe: the infantrymen of both sides buried themselves in the earth to avoid the pitiless hail of projectiles. It was a war of men against machines; flesh against steel. The battlefield doubled as a burial ground, with human remains frequently disinterred by shellfire as fast as they could be shovelled away. There was no martial glory for infantry. They never stood triumphant on a battlefield abandoned by the enemy, nor did they march into conquered cities; the front lines hardly moved. All they could do was to endure.

The stormtroopers were different: unlike ordinary infantrymen, they spent little time on the defensive, skulking in filthy trenches. Arriving at the front by lorry, they would filter into position after dusk and make a sudden assault on the enemy lines. By dawn, they would be on their way back to base, taking their prisoners with them – and leaving the infantry in that sector to face the inevitable Allied retaliatory bombardment. They were certainly used to shatter the 'live and let live' system (the informal truce arrangements sometimes arrived at by German and Allied infantry) and they were conscious of their status. They wore customized uniforms, carried whole bags full of grenades, and tucked coshes and daggers into their belts. Like fighter pilots and U-Boat crew, the stormtroopers became romantic figures to the German popular press – heroes to be emulated. The German war bond posters of 1914–16 featured a medieval knight, representing the German soldier; in 1917 the knight was replaced by a lantern-jawed, steely-eyed hero in a *Stahlhelm*, a gasmask dangling from his neck and a bag of grenades at the ready. This was the new face of the German warrior.

Stormtroop battalions also served to bolster the fighting spirit of the rest of the army. To become a stormtrooper was the aspiration of many keen young recruits, and, if the stormtroopers' trench raids sometimes upset the front line units in one sector, the reports of their deeds made welcome reading for German soldiers elsewhere. Men who had spent harrowing weeks under intensive Allied shellfire, unable to hit back, were heartened to hear of the stormtroops' exploits. Their raids were not just reported in Germany, but featured heavily in trench newspapers, one of which was even called *Der Stosstrupp* and carried a regular section entitled *Stosstruppgeist*, 'stormtrooper spirit' (Gudmundsson, *Stormtroop Tactics*).

As the Royal Navy's blockade of Germany began to take effect, so the German civilian population ran short of food as inflation eroded families' incomes. After the privations of the dreadful 'turnip winter' of 1916, anti-war feeling within Germany led to parliamentary demands for peace and to industrial unrest. Soldiers could not be isolated from this: while the army could censor their letters home, it could not edit the replies. Morale suffered as news from Germany filtered through the ranks. It had some curious side-effects, such as soldiers hacking off their jackboot heels and posting them home to family members short of footwear. (The soldiers then drew new boots from company stores.)

The morale of the stormtroopers was clearly higher than that of some units of the Regular Army. This division was formalized in the reorganization during the winter of 1917/18: the young, fit and keen were gathered into the 'attack divisions', and the less motivated were left behind. In the *Kaiserschlacht*, or 'Kaiser's Battle', this helped the Germans break through, but meant that casualties were concentrated among their best soldiers. The very success of this attack exposed the German High Command as liars: German propaganda had claimed that the enemy were on their knees, that Britain was being strangled by the U-Boats. But the size and content of the vast British supply dumps that were overrun that March told another story altogether: cases of coffee, chocolate, cigarettes – and the company rum. This proved all too tempting for hungry infantrymen in 1918, and looting slowed down the German advance. At the same time, even the least reflective stormtrooper became aware that he faced an uphill struggle. One soldier questioned in his diary whether the British were trying to make everything they could out of copper and brass, just to taunt the Germans, who were so short of vital metals.

LOGISTICS

Supplying troops in the trenches was fraught with difficulty. Supplies from the rear were likely to be unreliable; 80 troops going into the front line took at least five days' rations with them. Small cookers fired by solidified alcohol were used to warm food in the trenches, and large vacuum flasks were provided so that hot coffee or soup could be carried up. Ration parties were dispatched whenever hostile fire permitted, delivering food from ration depots established close to the positions. They were frequently delayed by enemy artillery fire or got lost in the pitch darkness, so the drinks were often cold by the time the soldiers received them.

Since most water in northern France and Belgium was undrinkable, the German Army was forced to organize local drinking water systems. Pipes were laid from existing waterworks or mains and new wells were dug and pumps installed. Breweries, sugar factories and other suitable buildings

Stormtroops gathered round a field kitchen in a French village, 1916. Stormtroopers enjoyed better rations than line battalions, and spent less time in the front line trenches, where hot meals were a rarity. (IWM, 56577)

were converted to water treatment plants. Drinking water was piped into villages as close to the front line as possible, and sometimes as far forward as the support trenches. This system broke down on the Somme, when the sheer weight of Allied artillery fire cut the pipes. The Germans resorted to mineral water, taking over existing factories and providing reserves of carbonated water close to the front. When soldiers entered the line, they took two water bottles and as many bottles of carbonated water as they could find.

FOOD SUPPLIES

In 1914, German field service daily rations consisted of:

- 750g bread or 400g egg biscuit or 500g field biscuit
- 375g fresh meat or 200g preserved meat
- 125–250g vegetables or 1,500g potatoes or 60g dried vegetables
- 25g coffee or 3g tea
- 20g sugar
- 25g salt

The meat ration was gradually reduced, falling to 350g at the end of 1915, and to 288g by mid-1916, when one meatless day a week was introduced. In October 1916 it was cut to 250g. Portions of preserved meat were cut to 150g. Soldiers not actually in the front line had only 200g of meat from June 1916.

Company commanders could order a daily ration of half a litre of beer, quarter of a litre of wine or 125ml of brandy, rum or arrack. The daily tobacco ration was two cigars or cigarettes or 30g of pipe tobacco.

In the front line trenches, soldiers often had to rely on their iron ration. They carried at least one iron ration, and usually more. It consisted of:

- 250g biscuit
- 200g preserved meat or bacon
- 150g preserved vegetables
- 25g coffee
- 25g salt

German infantry on the Western Front were compelled to abandon their trenches during the major battles of 1916. Their splendid deep trenches provided excellent protection, but they were conspicuous targets. Once British 9.2in howitzers obtained their range, the bunkers became death traps and the infantry were forced to fight from shell craters instead. Lurking in the surreal landscape carved out by the guns, the infantry were much harder for Allied forward artillery observers to locate. But it brought new hardships: ration parties failed to reach many units or took so long to find the soldiers that the food was ruined. Wounded men could no longer be evacuated along relatively safe communication trenches; instead they faced a hazardous journey across the wasteland, balanced on the shoulders of their comrades. More often than not, they had to wait until last light before any such movement could be attempted.

MEDICAL SERVICES

Each German infantry battalion had two medical officers, four medical NCOs (one per company) and 16 stretcher-bearers. The latter wore the red cross and were officially non-combatants. In the trenches, companies usually established a medical aid post just behind the fire trench. The regimental aid post was in the second support trench and usually in dug-outs or cellars designed to accommodate 30 wounded men each. They were provided with electric lighting, extra rations and stockpiles of dressings. The regimental aid post was staffed by three battalion medical officers and eight stretcher-bearers from the divisional bearer company (*Sanitätskompagnie*). A wounded soldier who required more treatment than the regimental aid post could offer was evacuated to a 'wagon rendezvous' (*Wagenhalteplatz*): a group of dug-outs about 4,000 metres (2.5 miles) behind the regimental aid post and manned by personnel from the divisional bearer company. Hot drinks and food could be provided here, and this post was connected by telephone to the main dressing station further to the rear. Wagons kept here were sent forward under cover of darkness to help the bearers bring back wounded soldiers.

The wounded were then evacuated to the main dressing station, usually situated in a shellproof shelter, probably in a village about 10km (6 miles) behind the front line trenches. Walking wounded were assembled into groups at the wagon rendezvous and sent back together. Wounded men were given medical cards that showed whether they were able to walk, were fit to be transported to the rear, or were too badly injured to move. Soldiers found at the main dressing station without a card or other authorization were sent back to their unit. Because there were never enough stretcher-bearers, wounded men were often carried back by their comrades, but every attempt was made to prevent stragglers slipping back to the aid posts and staying there.

EVACUATION PROBLEMS

Evacuating a wounded man was fraught with peril. Even if a stretcher party was not deliberately targeted by the enemy, there was more than enough random machine gun and artillery fire to strike them down. Gustav Ebelhauser helped carry back his friend across the battle-scarred landscape of the Somme: 'Every crater, every crevice, every hole unfolded new and more horrible pictures of death.

Stormtroops charging. (IWM, Q23770)

Opposite:
This study of German infantry
assaulting at Verdun in 1916
gives a good view of the M1916
assault packs, to which the two
lance corporals (first and second
right foreground) have strapped
120cm-long (47in) engineers'
spades. (Nigel Thomas)

One man they passed had his carcass torn to pieces, and was missing his head … Further on their feet dipped into the belly of another, causing the bowels to burst from the mutilated body.' They reached the aid post, where Ebelhauser's comrade died on the operating table (Ebelhauser, *The Passage*).

Most casualties – perhaps as many as 80 per cent – were caused by artillery. The shells burst into large chunks of razor-sharp iron that inflicted ghastly injuries. Although these soldiers often had the benefit of anaesthetic, it was difficult to evacuate them from a battlefield so often reduced to a sea of mud-filled craters. The sheer number of wounded frequently swamped the available medical facilities, condemning many men to a miserable death because they could not be treated in time.

GAS ATTACKS

By introducing poison gas, the Germans added a new dimension of horror to the battlefield, and if the Allies were slower to find such an evil use for their chemical industry, they soon made up for lost time. The French had a working gas shell by 1916; Haig badgered the British government for a gas shell too, and received a limited quantity for the latter stages of the Somme battle. By 1917 German soldiers were subjected to regular chemical attack, with the British specializing in saturation bombardments. One such attack struck St Quentin on 19 March 1918, just as the town filled up with troops for the German offensive: 3,000 drums of chlorine gas were fired from the British lines at 10pm, submerging the buildings in a thick greenish-white cloud. Respirators were of little help: the gas was in such concentration that no oxygen came through the filters. Fresh troops entering the area the next morning found the streets full of men coughing up the bloody remains of their lungs. One NCO from the 16th Bavarian Reserve Regiment would survive the Kaiser's Battle the following week, but end the war hospitalized after a mustard gas attack – Adolf Hitler recovered from his injuries but refused to authorize the use of chemical weapons in World War II. He believed the Allies would retaliate with even more deadly nerve agents than the scientists of the Third Reich could provide.

DISEASE

Until 1914, disease usually killed more soldiers than did the enemy. The first major conflict in which bullets claimed more lives than germs was the Russo–Japanese War of 1904–5. During World War I soldiers of all armies on the Western Front experienced the same phenomenon – partly due to improved medical care, and partly due to the unprecedented carnage on the battlefield. The single most important medical achievement of the German Army was to shield itself and Germany from the typhus epidemic that inflicted such terrible suffering on the Serbs and Russians. Frequent de-lousing of their own men and enemy POW kept the disease out of central and western Europe, while it destroyed the Serbian nation.

In October 1918 Germany was struck by the worst influenza epidemic of the 20th century. The 'Spanish Flu' was a virulent infection that struck across the whole world in the late summer of that year: it afflicted America, Europe and Asia simultaneously, but its effects were maximized in Europe, where civilian populations were already weakened by years of poor diet. Few German families escaped the soaring fever and hacking coughs that characterized the infection, and by November there were 400 deaths a day in Hamburg alone. When the disease vanished – as suddenly as it had come – it left 400,000 Germans dead. More people died in the latter half of

1918 than in the entire war. Militarily, it was a devastating blow for the German Army. Even the most die-hard stormtroopers could not fight with a temperature of 40 degrees (104°F).

The total number of German casualties during World War I will never be known exactly. It was controversial at the time: the High Command had resorted to deliberate falsification and many records were lost during the war. Approximately 2 million German soldiers died: roughly one in six of those mobilized. While in Britain the casualties sustained under Haig's command have attracted vocal criticism since the 1920s, it is worth noting that Germany's most successful offensive in the West, the great breakthrough in March 1918 and the subsequent assaults between April and June, cost the German Army 125,000 killed in action, 738,000 wounded and 104,000 missing or captured – a total of 963,000 casualties.

Combat Tactics

Prior to 1914, German infantry training was almost exclusively devoted to offensive tactics. Yet there was no consensus on how to attack across a battlefield dominated by quick-firing artillery, bolt-action rifles and machine guns. It seemed obvious that infantry needed to spread out to survive, but from the 1880s there was a sharp reaction against open order tactics; generals remembered the chaos that had ensued in many of the battles of 1870. At Gravelotte, for example, skirmishers became pinned down, unable to go forward or back, and whole battalions dissolved into disorderly mobs. Some officers came to believe that while closer formations might suffer more casualties in the short term, they were easier to control, and by retaining mobility, they would lose fewer men in the long term. This school of thought was rather discredited by the Boer War, when British infantry were frequently pinned down by long-range Mauser fire.

In the first years of the 20th century, German infantry reverted to widely spaced lines of skirmishers – 'Boer tactics' – only to return to closer formations as the difficulties of controlling such scattered units became apparent. An 80-man platoon spread over a 300m (328yd) front was impossible for its commander to manage. The commanders of the German corps districts had a free hand in the training of their men, which explains the patchy performance of German infantry in 1914: some divisions operated in thin skirmish lines, others came on in dense masses as if machine guns had never been invented. This lack of cohesion was punished with bloody finality in 1914: battalions attempting to close with the enemy in columns of platoons were cut to pieces. Even against the questionable marksmanship of the French and Russian armies, dense formations usually failed. Against the British Expeditionary Force (BEF) they were nothing short of suicide: witness the bloody repulse of the Prussian Foot Guards at Ypres.

Attacks With Limited Objectives

After the failure of the Schlieffen Plan, the German Army remained on the defensive in the West for the whole of 1915. Throughout that year the French Army expended hundreds of thousands of men trying to break through the German trench lines. British attempts in the spring and autumn were equally disastrous. However, the Germans were not entirely passive: divisional commanders frequently ordered 'attacks with limited objectives' (*Angriffe mit begrenzten Zielen*) to secure important ground or deny key terrain to the enemy. Pre-war German doctrine dictated that the methods by which such attacks were achieved were the responsibility of the local commanders, unlike their French counterparts, who were snowed under with tactical instructions from the General Staff.

By employing all the pre-war tactics of siege warfare German infantry were frequently able to seize French or British positions. The German Army had a far higher proportion of howitzers in its field artillery batteries, and this proved to be a crucial advantage. High-trajectory fire was much more effective against trenches than the flat-shooting field guns that made up the majority of British and French batteries. Howitzers, hand grenades and mortars enabled the German infantry to capture the front line enemy trenches, and helped hold them against a counter-attack. The vital high ground of Pilckem Ridge, the scene of their heavy losses in 1914, was taken by the Germans in April 1915 with the aid of 150 tons of chlorine gas, one attack with limited objectives that succeeded beyond expectation. Yet neither the artillery nor the new terror weapon enabled the infantry to make a major breakthrough.

'THE HELL OF VERDUN'

Attacking infantry faced two main obstacles – barbed wire and machine gun nests – and they had little time to deal with them. Defending artillery was likely to bring down a heavy barrage in No Man's Land the moment signal flares sailed into the air from the enemy trenches. When, in February 1916, the German Army returned to the offensive and attacked Verdun, the assault was

A German trench on the Western Front with a knocked-out British tank. (IWM, HU57859)

spearheaded by stormtroops and pioneers. While German artillery batteries suppressed the French guns with new gas shells, detachments of *Sturmtruppen* charged over the top to open gaps in the French wire. The concrete machine gun posts that dotted the gently sloping hills on the east bank of the Meuse were attacked by the flame-throwers of Reddemann's 3rd Guard Pioneer Battalion. Other stormtroop units raced to lob grenades into the French trenches. In some sectors, mountain guns with large steel shields were manoeuvred out of the German front line trenches to engage concrete strongpoints in direct fire.

The stormtroopers were followed by the line infantry, swarming forward in skirmish lines reminiscent of 1914. They occupied the French positions, overrunning any surviving bands of defenders. Succeeding waves of infantry brought forward the MG08s and box after box of ammunition to defeat the inevitable French counter-attacks.

The initial success at Verdun was not sustained after the first week. The French rushed in fresh infantry divisions and countless batteries of artillery – and German casualties mounted. Attacking German regiments continued to organize detachments of stormtroops to lead their assaults, but it proved harder and harder to coordinate the infantry rushes with the artillery support. Once beyond their original front line, the Germans were no longer working from accurate maps and aerial photographs. The French did not occupy such obvious positions, and many attacks came unstuck in hidden belts of barbed wire, or were decimated by previously concealed machine guns.

The initial German infantry attacks were supported by 1,600 guns, two-thirds of which were heavy howitzers. The devastation wrought by this unprecedented artillery concentration was incredible, but in a perverse way it led to a strengthening of the French defences. French infantry learned that digging proper trenches merely offered the German gunners a clear target. In the

Dead Germans found in the British wire after a night raid near Givenchy. The stormtroop battalions specialized in trench raids, often breaking up 'live and let live' arrangements which sometimes developed on quieter sectors of the front. (Private collection)

moonscape battlefield of Verdun, the defenders began to fight from shellholes, improvised positions within the tangled wreckage of the forests, and fortified basements among the ruined villages. To counter this more effective defence in depth, stormtroops tried to press on regardless of what was happening to their flanks, trusting to the succeeding waves of infantry to follow their progress. German artillery began to employ a 'rolling barrage', dropping a curtain of shells ahead of the infantry, although in practice the barrage often moved on too fast. As stormtroop detachments penetrated the network of French positions, they inevitably bypassed some of them: and this was the origin of 'infiltration tactics'.

DEFENDING ON THE SOMME

The Verdun offensive was called off in the summer of 1916 when the British Army launched its long-awaited offensive on the Somme, its first experience of continental warfare in the industrial age. For German infantry, obliged to sit in darkened bunkers reverberating under the tons of high explosive, the Somme was a nightmare. British accounts might praise the German fortifications, frequently remarking that the deep underground shelters were impervious to all but a direct hit, but this was small consolation when the monstrous guns of the Royal Garrison Artillery did score direct hits. Whole platoons were buried alive. Counter-attacks broke down as battalions lost half their men before they reached the start line:

> The English bombardment kept increasing in intensity at the turn of each hour. Even when night settled over the mutilated fields of France, there had been no let up … For three more days and nights it was for Ebelhauser and his comrades nothing short of hell on earth. Fire came crashing down from all directions … turning shellhole after shellhole into open and silent tombs. How many soldiers lay buried there, soldiers whose bodies would never be found? The earth shook night and day … The few remaining defenders of this section of the Western Front had become nothing more than crawling animals, seeking refuge in ever fresh-made holes. They slid from one crater to another in vain search for food as well as protection. But neither could be found. (Ebelhauser, *The Passage*)

German infantry regiments followed the unbending Prussian tradition of 'Halten, was zu halten ist' ('Hold on to whatever can be held'). The front line was packed with troops, offering a prime target to the British guns and their apparently limitless reserves of ammunition. (At the height of the battle, British artillery was delivering up to 500 tons of explosive per day on the frontage of a single division.) Officers who wished to do otherwise were given little incentive: some commanders who failed to regain lost ground were relieved of their command. General von Falkenhayn's words were of little comfort: 'The enemy must not be allowed to advance except over corpses.' German infantrymen did resist to the end, with the result that by August 1916 the German Army had lost as many men on the Somme in two months as in six months' fighting at Verdun. By the end of the battle, 138 German divisions had fought there, as opposed to the 75 that were engaged at Verdun; few of them had more than 3,000 infantrymen – less than half their original strength.

Like the French at Verdun, the Germans eventually found it impossible to maintain a proper front line on the Somme. They resorted to fighting from shellholes, occupying their front with mutually supporting outposts and machine gun nests. The bulk of the infantry were withdrawn several thousand metres, but stood ready to counter-attack. Throughout the Somme battle, the German infantry launched counter-attacks by day and night. Most were in battalion or regimental strength, although they did deliver an all-out effort against Delville Wood, prepared by four days' heavy shelling. The German High Command attributed their reverses on the Somme to the lack of depth of their defences, the excessive concentration of infantry in the front line and the Allies' superiority in artillery and aircraft. The latter advantage was keenly noticed by the infantrymen: 'French aeroplanes circled above our position and flew over our heads towards the base lines; but there was no sign of a German plane. We did not like our air force in any case, because of their swagger, and now we cursed them more than ever' (Renn, *War*).

It was extremely demoralizing to have Allied observer aircraft circling overhead. The Germans monitored the aircraft's radio transmissions, and were able to warn artillery batteries when their position had been compromised, enabling the gunners to get into their dug-outs or even evacuate the battery. But there was nowhere for the infantry to go, and no way to communicate with them quickly enough anyway.

ELASTIC DEFENCE

The Germans formalized their new defensive system during the winter of 1916/17. According to their new instructions for the defensive battle (*Führung der Abwehrschlact*) issued in December 1916, a forward zone of about 500–1,000m (547–1,094yd) was held by outposts only. This would keep back Allied patrols and disrupt the first stage of an attack. The main line of resistance was behind this – usually sited on a reverse slope, with up to three lines of trenches. Behind the trenches, stretching back for up to 2,000m (1.2 miles), were a series of well-camouflaged concrete strongpoints, arranged in a rough checkerboard pattern to provide mutual support. This was where the Germans intended to fight their defensive battle – out of view of Allied artillery observers and in plain view of their own. Waiting behind the main line of resistance were the German counter-attack forces, poised to attack the enemy just as they lost impetus; with their offensive stalled by heavy artillery and machine gun fire, Allied infantry could be overwhelmed by a judiciously timed counter-attack.

The new German defensive tactics placed great emphasis on counter-attacks, particularly those delivered from the flanks. Just as on the Russian Front in World War II where the Germans allowed Soviet tanks to break through, only to destroy them by a pincer movement, so in World War I the Germans wiped out whole brigades of British and French infantry by isolating them within the German defences. Attacking from the flanks, the Germans recaptured their forward positions, at the same time isolating Allied attackers who had penetrated to the German second- or third-line trenches. Unable to communicate with their artillery or bring forward ammunition, the would-be attackers were annihilated. This was the theory. On occasions, as at Vimy Ridge on 9 April 1917, or during the British offensives of 20 and 26 September and 4 October 1917 near Ypres, the attackers gained the upper hand.

The emphasis on infantry counter-attacks helped develop stormtroop tactics further. Aggressive infantry were the key to the German success, and during the defensive battles of 1917, the German infantry began to perfect the methods they would use in their own offensive the following spring. However, the defensive battles were not without cost: the *Materialschlacht* ('battle of material') pitted German infantry against the industrial might of the British and French empires. After their profligate expenditure of infantry in 1914/15, the French settled on the systematic pulverization of German trenches by massed heavy artillery and then occupied the lifeless ruins that remained. The British followed suit. At Messines, 2,266 British guns delivered 144,000 tons of explosive in support of a limited offensive that began with the detonation of massive mines underneath the German trenches.

The barrage that opened the great British offensive in Flanders was even worse than on the Somme. While the name of Passchendaele evokes a particular chill in British hearts, defending the Ypres sector in 1917 was a uniquely ghastly business for the German infantry, despite their advanced tactical ideas. The 'Hell of Verdun' was surpassed and the Flanders battle was called 'the greatest martyrdom of the World War'. There were no trenches and no shelters except the few concrete blockhouses, as described by General von Kuhl, Chief of Staff to Crown Prince Rupprecht: 'In the water-filled craters cowered the defenders without shelter from weather, hungry and cold, abandoned without pause to overwhelming artillery fire' (*The Official History of Operations in France and Belgium, 1917*).

MEN AGAINST TANKS

The battle of Cambrai began disastrously for the Germans, with whole units taking to their heels as hundreds of tanks ground over their positions. Despite Field Marshal Sir Douglas Haig's urgent pleas for more armour, the Tank Corps could only attack in penny packets during 1916, and the first major attack by French armour in 1917 had met with utter defeat. Some 82 Schneiders and St Armand tanks went into action on 16 April, but many got stuck trying to cross a landscape of lip-to-lip craters, and German artillery knocked them out one by one.

On the firm, level ground at Cambrai, it was a different story. The massed tank attack achieved surprise; the thunderous noise of so many tank engines was drowned by low-flying British aircraft, and there was no preliminary artillery bombardment. Fortunately for the Germans, the tanks of 1917 were mechanically unreliable, and the number of operational vehicles dwindled rapidly; by the time the Germans launched their counter-attack ten days later, there were not enough tanks to stem it, let alone to mount another armoured offensive.

On 30 November it was the turn of the German air force to swoop low over the battlefield. For the first time in the war, German aircraft were used in close support of the infantry:

Preceded by patrols, the Germans advanced at 7am in small columns bearing many light machine guns and, in some cases, flame-throwers. From overhead, low flying aircraft … bombed and machine gunned the British defenders, causing further casualties and, especially, distraction at the critical moment. Nevertheless, few posts appear to have been attacked from the front, the assault sweeping in between to envelop them from flanks and rear.' (*The Official History* …)

The phrase 'infiltration tactics' has been widely used to describe the German infantry's new offensive technique. It is therefore something of a surprise to find no mention of 'infiltration' in German sources. The expression is an understandable description of what the Allies thought was happening, but it was not the whole story. The new tactics were first encountered by the French after the failure of General Nivelle's offensive in April 1917. German counter-attacks were sudden, and very violent:

> They were heralded by very accurate artillery fire concentrated on the point of attack. The ground the Germans intended recapturing would be turned into a field of smoke and flame under a roaring, screeching sky that seemed about to collapse, forcing down the heads of the defenders; trenches would rock and cave under the violence of the explosions, then the air would buzz as the steel wasps of German machine gun bullets came over … Suddenly the range would lengthen and, looming out of the smoke of the last explosions, shadowy forms would rush forward, gesticulating wildly, enemy soldiers throwing grenades. (Spears, *Liaison 1914*)

What the Allies persisted in calling 'infiltration tactics' was described by the Germans as 'coordination' – of all the different weapons now employed by an infantry battalion. This is perhaps best illustrated by an example of small unit tactics from the battle of Cambrai. On 30 November, the 2nd Battalion, 109th Infantry Regiment, had penetrated the British front but was halted by machine gun fire approximately 500m (547yd) from Gonnelieu. Three separate machine gun positions were pinning the regiment down, and it proved impossible to communicate with the supporting artillery – a familiar problem on the battlefields of World War I. The 5th Company of the 110th Infantry Regiment had been following in reserve, and was now pushed forward to attack the main machine gun post that was blocking any further progress. Adjacent British positions were taken under fire by the

Stormtroops resting on the Western Front, May 1917. (IWM, Q80038)

regimental machine gun company, and a *Minenwerfer* was brought forward to a shell crater, and used to shell the 5th Company's objective. German artillery fire finally came down, shelling the immediate rear of the British machine guns. Dividing into squads, the 5th Company worked around the machine gun position, making a short rush from cover to cover each time the *Minenwerfer* dropped a bomb on the British. A squad led by Sergeant Gersbach reached the old trench line that led to the British machine gun, and bombed its way along the trench, lobbing grenades into each firing bay. The machine gun was captured and the advance of the 109th Regiment could continue. The whole operation, from the regimental commander ordering up the mortar and machine gun platoons to the storming of the trench, took about 2 hours. Combined arms tactics were essential in order to achieve success: 'The squad leader, supported by the fire of heavy infantry weapons and acting in conjunction with neighbouring rifle and machine gun squads, continues the attack from nest to nest, seeking always to strike the enemy resistance from the flank' (*Infantry in Battle*).

THE KAISER'S BATTLE

By the time the stormtroops led the great German offensive of March 1918, German infantry tactics had changed beyond recognition. The smallest 'tactical brick' was now the infantry squad, itself divided into a 'gun group' of one MG08/15 manned by two gunners and two ammunition carriers, and a 'rifle group' of between eight and ten men led by a corporal. Some other armies would take until the middle of World War II to accept this structure as the best way to achieve fire and manoeuvre within an infantry platoon.

Ludendorff's offensive was an all-or-nothing enterprise by which Imperial Germany would either achieve its war aims or be utterly destroyed. To this end, the stormtroops were ordered to push on at all costs. Whereas at Verdun they had gone firm on their objectives, which were then occupied by regular infantry, in 1918 they were to stop for nothing. They were to bypass those enemy positions that still held out, and keep advancing regardless of what was happening behind them or on their flanks. But this led to heavy losses during the first week of the offensive. Passing beyond the reach of German artillery, and leaving many of their own heavy weapons behind, the stormtroopers ran into enemy defences they could not overcome.

From March to June 1918 the stormtroop battalions led a succession of all-out attacks, and many were burned out in the process. They achieved unprecedented tactical victories, but enjoyed only local effects. In the end, the tactical excellence of the stormtroopers could not compensate for the political and strategic blindness of the German High Command. By holding out for unacceptable peace terms and concentrating on tactical warfare rather than grand strategy, it had condemned Germany to defeat. It was not the fault of the stormtroops; as one of their officers recorded: 'The brazen spirit of the attack, the spirit of Prussian infantry, swept through the massed troops … after forty-four months of hard fighting they threw themselves on the enemy with all the enthusiasm of August 1914. No wonder it needed a world in arms to bring such a storm-flood to a standstill' (Jünger, *Storm of Steel*).

Some historians argue that stormtroops were a flawed concept. By concentrating so much fighting power in elite formations, leaving others as 'squeezed lemons', it reduced the overall quality of the German Army. By contrast, the British did not follow this approach, but the events of 1918 showed that even average British divisions could be highly effective.

FRENCH POILU

Ian Sumner

When the French Army entered the war in 1914 it was just beginning to emerge from 20 years of disarray. A succession of political scandals – the Dreyfus affair (spying within the War Ministry), the *affaire des fiches* (the personal opinions and religious convictions of certain officers had been used to block their promotion), the disestablishment of the Catholic church (where the army had to intervene to keep the peace), and the use of the army in strikebreaking – combined with attempts to cut the two-year conscription period, or even replace it with a Swiss-style militia, had all left the army in an uncertain state of morale and training. Why, the Kaiser enquired of Tsar Nicholas in 1913, did he wish to ally himself with France when 'the Frenchman is no longer capable of being a soldier'?

Ironically, it was Germany's attempt to intervene in Morocco in 1911, the Agadir incident, that created a backlash of patriotism and anti-German feeling in France. Far from reducing the conscription period, the government increased it to three years in 1913. The army that went to war in 1914 still had many weaknesses – it was poorly trained and poorly equipped, particularly in heavy artillery. This hardly mattered to the politicians, however, for they expected the war to last no longer than six months at most.

JOINING UP

The French Army was manned by conscription, and every 20-year-old male was liable for three years' service with the colours. Until 1905, not every man of the qualifying age was called up: selection was by ballot of those eligible to serve, and there were many exemptions. After that date, nearly all the exemptions were abolished, and service was virtually obligatory.

Every January, a list of men eligible for service by age was posted in each *commune*. Those listed had to appear before a board consisting of a general officer, the departmental prefect and other representatives of local government. Every man was measured and weighed by a medical officer: some had their call-up immediately postponed because of lack of stature, and more were then excluded on grounds of congenital infirmity. Others were rejected on more arbitrary grounds – a tattooed face could be sufficient. In January 1915, one board was considering a man who was covered in tattoos from head to foot. Rejecting him, the medical officer remarked jokingly that 'there was no more room'; the man, who had already seen service with the brutal Bataillon d'Infanterie *Légère d'Afrique* (BILA), replied, 'There's room for a bullet', and he was passed fit for service. He was soon proved right about the bullet, too; he was wounded at Carency just four months later. Convicted felons were called up along with the rest. Those who found themselves in prison when their call-up was due were allowed to serve out their sentence and were then sent to the BILA.

In a tradition which dated almost from the beginning of conscription at the end of the 18th century, those selected by ballot for service each year were given a big send-off by their home town

Opposite:
A sergeant of the 3e Bataillon de Chasseurs à Pied, from St Dié. (Ian Sumner)

CHRONOLOGY

August 1914	Battle of the Frontiers	24 Oct–15 Dec 1916	First Verdun offensive
7–11 August 1914	Battle of Alsace	16 April–10 May 1917	Second battle of the Aisne (Chemin des Dames)
20 August 1914	Battle of Sarrebourg		
20 August 1914	Battle of Morhange	17 April 1917	Battle of Les Monts
21–23 August 1914	Battle of Charleroi	31 July–10 Oct 1917	Second battle of Flanders
22–24 August 1914	Battle of the Ardennes	20 Aug–8 Sept 1917	Second Verdun offensive
24 Aug–16 Sept 1914	Battles of the Haute–Meurthe and the Grand Couronné	23–27 Oct 1917	Battle of Malmaison
24 Aug–6 Sept 1914	First battle of Guise	21–31 March 1918	Second battle of Picardie
25 Aug–11 Sept 1914	Battle of the Mortagne	4–16 May 1918	Third battle of Flanders
27–28 August 1914	Battle of the Meuse	27 May–1 June 1918	Third battle of the Aisne
27 Aug–8 Sept 1914	Battle and siege of Maubeuge	9–11 June 1918	Battle of Matz
6–13 September 1914	First battle of the Marne	15 July 1918	Fourth battle of Champagne
15 September 1914	First battle of the Aisne	18–29 July 1918	Battles of Soissonais–Ourcq
15 Sept–19 Oct 1914	Race to the Sea	18 July–6 Aug 1918	Second battle of the Marne
21 Sept–13 Oct 1914	Battle of Flirey	29 July–8 Aug 1918	Battle of Tardenois
30 September 1914	First battle of Picardie	8–17 August 1918	Battle of Montdidier
18 October 1914	First battle of Flanders	8–29 August 1918	Third battle of Picardie
22–30 October 1914	Battle of the Yser	17–29 August 1918	Second battle of Noyon
29 Oct–15 Nov 1914	Battle of Ypres	29 Aug–20 Sept 1918	Advance to the Hindenburg Line
17 Dec 1914–5 Jan 1915	First battle of Artois	26 Sept–15 Oct 1918	Battle of Champagne–Argonne
20 Dec 1914–16 Mar 1915	First battle of Champagne	28 Sept–10 Oct 1918	Battle of the Crêtes de Flandre
5 April–5 May 1915	First battle of Woëvre	28 Sept–11 Nov 1918	Second battle of Belgium
9 May–18 June 1915	Second battle of Artois	14–15 October 1918	Battle of Roulers
25 Sept–14 Oct 1915	Third battle of Artois	20 Oct–11 Nov 1918	Battle of Lys–Escaut
25 Sept–16 Oct 1915	Second battle of Champagne	29 Sept–30 Oct 1918	Battle of Oise–Serre–Aisne
21 Feb–4 July 1916	Defence of Verdun	1–5 November 1918	Battle of the Chesne
1 July–26 Sept 1916	Battle of the Somme	5–11 November 1918	Advance to the Meuse

or village, dressed in distinctive costumes with ribbons and flowers, and given a special flag to carry. Although this custom did not die out completely in the era of universal liability, it did become rather more muted. Yet it never disappeared entirely, even during wartime. Captain J. C. Dunn, in his book *The War the Infantry Knew*, notes in March 1918, 'Going on leave, I saw in Steenwerck the latest class of French conscripts leaving home for their depots. Dressed in their Sunday best, beflowered, beribboned, beflagged, befuddled, they were calling at every friend's house and being given liquor. Poor boys.'

Most men went into the infantry. Restrictions in size and weight limited those who could serve in the cavalry, whilst service in the artillery and engineers was normally reserved for those who had worked on the railways or in public works, shipyards and telecommunications. The infantry was, therefore, composed primarily of men from an agricultural background, although 20 per cent were shop assistants, small craftsmen and factory workers, and a further 5 per cent clerks or teachers. After their service with the 'active' army, conscripts passed into the Reserve for a period of 11 years. On mobilization, each infantry regiment, and each light infantry (*chasseur à pied*) battalion, raised a Reserve unit, which was intended to take the field, but only to man garrisons and lines of communication. In the event, these Reserve divisions had to take their place in the line alongside those made up of serving soldiers. As Joffre said in 1915, 'There is no such thing as Reserves.'

On completing his service in the Reserves, each man passed into the Territorials for a further seven years, and then into the Territorial Reserves for a final seven years, making 28 years' service in total. The Territorials were intended purely as local defence units and were only recalled to the colours in times of war. In an emergency, as during the Race to the Sea in September 1914, some Territorial

A squad of the 29e Régiment d'Infanterie (RI), whose depot was at Autun in Burgundy. The length of the rifle with its bayonet fixed is quite apparent. Note the roll on the greatcoat shoulder, to support the straps of the pack. (Ian Sumner)

A trainload of foreign volunteers (note the Swiss flag on the left) leave a major city, perhaps Paris, for their depot. (Ian Sumner)

regiments saw action as well, but for most of the war, those not guarding lines of communication were used as works battalions – making and maintaining trench systems, roads and railway lines.

Regiments were created on a local basis. Every regiment drew its recruits from a specific number of local government areas (*arrondissements*), while divisions and army corps were formed from regiments from the same Military Region. Like the British Pals battalions, this provided a source both of strength and of weakness. Soldiers were able to serve with men from their own immediate locality, an advantage at a time when country accents could be difficult for any outsider to understand. However, heavy casualties would have a disproportionate effect on a relatively small area, and there were other disadvantages to this system. In 1907, the 17e Régiment d'Infanterie (RI), whose depot was in Béziers, was ordered to quell unrest amongst the local wine growers. Faced with men who undoubtedly included friends and relatives, the regiment mutinied, and over 500 soldiers were sent to Tunisia as punishment.

Peacetime training was conducted almost entirely within the regiment. A shortage of large training grounds, and a shortage of money, meant that field exercises were few. Larger formations conducted manoeuvres on a four-yearly cycle. In the first two years exercises were conducted at brigade level; in the third year at army corps level; and in the fourth year at army level. The result was that no conscript would ever serve through the whole of the training cycle. The training provided for reservists was even more limited. They were recalled for only 40 days each year, in two periods, the first of 23 days, the second of 17; and a shortage of suitable exercise grounds meant that much of this time was spent in barracks, rather than in the field. The Territorials had one nine-day training period a year; the Territorial Reserves, one day only.

Mobilization was ordered on 1 August 1914. The classes of 1896 to 1910 (men between 24 and 38 years of age) were called up immediately, and some 4,300 trains transported them to their depots and war stations. The classes of 1892 to 1895 followed in December 1914, those of 1889 to 1891 in March–April 1915, and those of 1886 to 1888 in the following year. Calling up the older classes, destined for service in the rear areas, was designed to allow fit young men to be sent to the front. Yet that alone would not be enough. The class of 1914 was called up early, in August of that year, and

Every cavalry division included a battalion of chasseur cyclists. When in action, the bicycle was folded in two and carried on the rider's back. (Ian Sumner)

the class of 1915 followed in December 1914. The class of 1916 was called up in April 1915, that of 1917 in January 1916, that of 1918 in April–May 1917, and finally that of 1919 in April 1918.

In addition to the metropolitan army, which served almost wholly on French soil (conscripts were prevented by law from serving abroad in peacetime), a number of regiments which garrisoned French possessions abroad, particularly in Africa and Indochina, could also be called upon to serve in France. Most importantly, these regiments were unique in having combat experience, albeit only of colonial warfare, and had thus attracted officers and volunteers who were unwilling to serve in a dusty mainland garrison town and had instead sought out active service.

Some of these regiments were raised for service in North Africa – in the infantry, the zouaves, tirailleurs and Foreign Legion. The tirailleurs were raised from the indigenous peoples of Algeria and Tunisia, the zouaves from Frenchmen. Only the zouaves were raised from conscripts; the other regiments were all made up of volunteers. During the war, these regiments had to maintain a garrison in Algeria, Tunisia and Morocco, and consequently sent to France only individual battalions, grouped together as provisional *régiments de marche*. The North African regiments also included a small number of cavalry units – *chasseurs d'Afrique* and *spahis*.

The other, larger, group was that formed by the Colonial regiments. Raised from French citizens and, in contrast to the metropolitan army, all made up of volunteers, these regiments served as the garrisons of French colonies, largely in western and central Africa and in Indochina. They were originally part of the navy, only transferring to army control in 1900, and retained a separate administrative structure throughout the war (indeed, until 1958). Their main depots were in the principal French naval ports – Cherbourg, Brest, Toulon, Rochefort – and so they were on hand to take the field in 1914. Battalions of indigenous African and Indochinese troops also formed part of the Colonial organization. These units were not present during the opening campaigns in France, but as casualties mounted it became impossible to ignore them; indeed, the manpower crisis that occurred in the later stages of the war forced the introduction of conscription in West Africa.

All armies and corps contained a significant cavalry component whose intended role was quickly rendered insignificant by trench warfare. Over the winter of 1914–15 most cavalry

A squad of zouaves on patrol. All are carrying their full pack, including cooking vessels – a practice which started on campaign in North Africa. The sergeant on the right wears a marksmanship badge on his sleeve. (Ian Sumner)

regiments had created a squadron for service on foot. But, by 1916, the infantry needed more men to replace casualties, and the artillery needed horses, so six cuirassier regiments, with drafts from other mounted troops, were converted to infantry, forming two divisions of *cuirassiers à pied*.

The peacetime army had a strength of 817,000 men, augmented on mobilization to 2,944,000. In all, some 7,800,000 served with the colours during the war, around 80 per cent of a total population of 9,697,000 men of eligible age. To these can be added 229,000 volunteers and 608,000 Colonial troops.

In addition to these fighting troops, workers were brought in from abroad to act as replacements in industry or as works battalions in the rear areas; around 200,000 men from the colonies (including 50,000 Indochinese) as well as 100,000 foreigners (including 13,000 Chinese) and some 82,000 prisoners of war were employed in one way or another.

JOINING THE REGIMENT

Every infantry regiment comprised three peacetime battalions of four companies each, numbered 1 to 12. At mobilization, calling up the reserves enabled the formation of a Reserve regiment of two battalions, which took the number of the parent regiment plus 200 (thus the 1er RI formed the 201e). Its battalions were numbered 5 and 6, and its companies numbered from 17 to 24. A peacetime recruit, joining his regiment in October, would spend around two months learning the basics of military life. Training at squad level began around the middle of December of each year. Exercises in company strength followed in mid-March and continued until the summer, and the manoeuvres season.

All the men of the five field armies had been assembled by 10 August, the Reserve divisions by the 13th, and the units charged with defending Paris by the 15th. Recalled reservists were processed in the shortest time: Abel Castel, for example, reporting at the depot of the 35e RI at Belfort on the morning of 1 August, was on his way to join his regiment that same afternoon. The 275e RI at Romans was assembled in two days, issued with its food and ammunition the next day, and on its way to the front within the week. But these were men who had completed their service only recently and were expected to have retained at least some of their training.

The class of 1914 was thrown into the field quickly, probably too quickly, in order to replace casualties. In the 74e RI, a report of late 1914 noted, 'Instruction in combat is very rudimentary. Information on the present conflict appears to be totally unknown at the depot. The men claim that they only fired their rifles once a week. The volunteers from Alsace do not know how to shoot.' Roland Dorgelès managed to join the 39e RI without any training at all, simply by insisting that he be sent directly to the front.

For new recruits in subsequent classes, the process was slower. The 'missing' companies of each regiment (13 to 16) became the regimental depot, and were used for the basic training of recruits. Further companies, numbered from 25 to 28, formed a 7th Battalion, which occupied camps situated in the countryside around the depot towns, and conducted field exercises. With this part of his training complete, the recruit then transferred to the 9th Battalion (there was no 8th Battalion) of a regiment from the same Military Region, formed by combining drafts from the local regiments; until 1916 these were also known as Divisional Depots, and then Divisional Instruction Centres. These 9th battalions were stationed in the rear areas. They helped acclimatize new troops to service at the front (usually through providing working parties), and also provided specialist training, for example as signallers, pioneers or machine gunners. From here, the trained soldier would be sent to the front as part of a draft of reinforcements.

The experience of Henri Latécoère is typical. After reporting to his depot (that of the 107e RI in Angoulême) when the class of 1917 was called up in January 1916, he spent five months in barracks

Some senior officers, notably General Mangin, enthusiastically supported the extensive use of black African soldiers on the Western Front. However, they were not suited to the conditions, especially in winter, and had to be supported by white battalions. Some battalions had to be retained in West Africa (here, Fort Bonnier in Timbuctoo), serving in German West Africa and against the Senussi Revolt. (Ian Sumner)

and two months in a camp completing his basic training, before forming part of a draft for the front in August 1916. His first posting was not to a combat regiment, but to a training unit, the 9th Battalion of the 138e RI, another infantry regiment in his division. Here, he underwent his advanced training, to make him ready for the front. In November 1916, he was posted as a replacement to a Divisional Depot of the 3e DI, a completely different division. In Latécoère's case, he then had to wait a further four months until the class of 1917 was considered old enough to serve at the front.

As Latécoère's story shows, a recruit was not necessarily posted to his local regiment, but was sent where the need was greatest. While many regiments managed to maintain at least a regional, if not a purely local, character throughout the course of the war, this was impossible for those with depots situated in the towns and cities of the north and east, by then under German occupation. By 1917, for example, a typical squad in a nominally Picard regiment, the 128e RI, was led by a corporal from just outside Paris, who commanded two Charentais, from western France, a Picard, a Norman, a Breton, and one man from the Ardennes.

Serving soldiers, reservists or conscripts all received a big send-off when their regiment or draft left the barracks, usually for the local railway station. With the bands playing famous old tunes like '*Sambre et Meuse*' or '*Chant du Départ*', cheering crowds gathered, offering the soldiers flowers or even kisses, sometimes singing the '*Marseillaise*' or the popular song '*Quand Madelon*'. The soldiers responded in kind, or, in the case of the chasseurs, with their own song, '*Sidi Brahim*'. This remained common practice, even in 1916. 'A moving moment,' recalled Latécoère. 'We are greeted with cheers by bystanders. The bugles at the head of the column sound the march.'

UNIFORM

In the late 19th and early 20th centuries, the army, as an institution, had come under attack from both Left and Right. In consequence, much needed reforms had often been sacrificed on the altar of political expediency. Several attempts to design a camouflage uniform for the army had all failed. The first of these, the bluish-grey *tenue Boër* of 1902–03, complete with slouch hat, was rejected on the grounds that its colour was too close to that worn by the Italian Army; the second, the *beige-bleu* uniform of 1903–06, and the third, the grey-green *tenue réséda* of 1911, were turned down because they were too like German uniforms. To complicate matters further, any proposal to abolish the red trousers of the infantry, and replace them with something more suited to modern warfare, was condemned as somehow un-French. A project that included a blue-grey uniform, promoted by the military artists Edouard Détaille and Georges Scott, got no further than the artist's drawings.

Evidence from the Balkan Wars, however, showed just how vital a camouflage uniform had become, and a fourth trial was undertaken in 1912. On this occasion, the cloth involved was *drap tricolore*, a fabric composed of alternate blue, white and red threads, and it was judged successful until it was noticed that the manufacturers of the red dye used in the material were all German. Nevertheless, the project went ahead – without the red threads – and, in the summer of 1914, the famous horizon blue (a mixture of 35 per cent white thread, 15 per cent dark blue and 50 per cent light blue) was born.

Deliveries had not yet begun by the outbreak of war, and the French Army entered the conflict wearing a uniform little different from that of 1870. This was the uniform that became the

Next page:
Preceded by the regimental band, flowers in their buttonholes and in the muzzles of their rifles, a regiment march off to war from their garrison town in the Touraine. (Ian Sumner)

scapegoat for French defeats – the red trousers were too visible on the battlefield, it was claimed, making the soldiers easy targets. The autumn and winter of 1914 saw a number of measures rushed into service, replacing the red trousers with patterns in blue or dark brown. However, the more likely explanation for French losses lay in the tactics employed and in structural weaknesses in the army as a whole – lack of reconnaissance, too few officers and NCOs, insufficient artillery support – rather than simply in the clothing worn by the soldiers.

With preference allotted to front line units, horizon blue made its debut in the early spring of 1915. The first items to be made in the new fabric were greatcoats, followed by trousers and then the tunic. The new uniform was similar in appearance for all arms of service, the only difference lying in the collar patches of both tunic and greatcoat, and in the piping down the outside of the trouser leg. Rank was displayed in short coloured strips on the cuffs. The trousers were tucked into puttees.

Headgear consisted of a képi. The original pattern of 1914 was worn under a cover of blue cotton to reduce its visibility, but this too was replaced by a version in horizon blue. The steel Adrian helmet made its first appearance towards the end of the same year, replacing a steel skull cap worn under the képi, but it was not widely used until 1916. In reply to an officer who had proposed that a helmet be introduced, Joffre wrote optimistically, 'We will not have the time to make them, I will break the Boche within two months', but his prediction proved sadly wide of the mark. The first examples of the helmet were painted with a gloss finish, but a matt version was introduced in late 1916. For off-duty wear, the helmet was replaced by a horizon blue *bonnet de police*.

Colonial and African units, however, wore a khaki uniform. The ready availability of khaki cloth from the UK may have played a part in this decision, but as the war progressed, French- and

A column of infantry, encumbered by their packs, march through a town early in the war. (Ian Sumner)

'*Les poilus de la 51e*': the photo is dated 1916, but none of these men have been issued with the full horizon blue uniform. The two men in the light-coloured uniform in the back row are wearing the canvas jacket and trousers adopted as a fatigue uniform. Regimental bandsmen served as stretcher-bearers, but buglers remained with their companies. (Ian Sumner)

American-made items were also introduced, with the result that three slightly different shades of khaki were all eventually in use.

'Everything made for the soldier,' grumbled Henri Barbusse, famous for his novel *Le Feu*, and a member of the 231e RI, 'is ordinary, ugly and of poor quality.' So it is hardly surprising that the soldier supplemented his regulation uniform with all manner of items, dispatched by loved ones or obtained by the man himself by fair means or foul. Sheep and goat skins, even rabbit or hare, woollen scarves, balaclavas and pullovers in different colours, waterproofs, rags wound around the boots for warmth – all were adopted with enthusiasm. 'Yesterday's man about town is no longer recognizable in this hairy, bearded combatant, plastered in mud and filth, infested with fleas, covered by sheepskins, and wearing deep trench boots,' as one army doctor observed.

Cold and rain always posed problems. In the hills of the Vosges, winter temperatures could fall so low that even the wine and bread froze. The winter of 1914–15 was particularly hard, since a trench system, with its sheltering dug-outs, had not yet been fully constructed. However, later winters were little better. 'We struggled against the cold the best we could,' recalled one soldier. 'Our cap protected our ears and forehead; a scarf was wound around the lower part of our faces; only our eyes were visible. On top of this heap of cloth was perched our helmet, a shaky tin roof, and over that, where possible, a blanket, which fell across our shoulders, making us look like a sentry box.'

Rain meant mud: *boue, mélasse, gadoue, gadouille, mouise, mouscaille* – there were so many names for the substance that was central to the life of every front line soldier. 'Communications trenches are little more than sewers of mixed water and urine. The trench little more than a sheet of water. Its sides collapse with a wet, sliding noise as you pass. And we are all transformed into clay statues, with mud up to our mouths.' Mud got everywhere, but it was particularly dangerous when it penetrated into the breeches of the infantry's firearms. In the wet spring of 1915, Maurice Genevoix recorded that two trenches were lost to the enemy because the mud had put so many rifles out of action.

Water was scarce in the front line, and water for shaving scarcer still. The alleged hairiness of the soldiers gave rise to their most enduring nickname, '*poilu*' ('hairy one'), but in the front line, this was

Another colour party, this time of the 57e RI, which recruited in Libourne and Rochefort. All the escort have been decorated with the Croix de Guerre. Eventually, the regiment would receive the same honour, with a green and red lanyard decorating the colours, and worn by the men on their left shoulders. (Ian Sumner)

regarded as yet more journalistic nonsense in a war that had already seen too much. The traditional nickname of the infantry was '*les biffins*' – 'rag-and-bone men'. To each other, they were '*les bonhommes*' – 'the lads', or, as war weariness overtook them, '*les pauvres cons du front*' or 'PCDF' – 'the poor bastards at the front'.

The Croix de Guerre was introduced on 8 April 1915, as a distinction for all men Mentioned in Orders. The ribbon bore a bronze star for a mention in regimental or brigade orders, a silver star for divisional orders, a gilt star for corps orders, or a bronze palm leaf for army orders. Five bronze stars were exchanged for a silver palm leaf. Awards could also be given to any regiment which had received sufficient citations, in the form of a lanyard in the colours of the ribbon of the Croix de Guerre, Médaille Militaire or even the Légion d'Honneur. The rationale behind these distinctions was to provide a tangible reward for men who had distinguished themselves on active service. But, some wondered, where lay the value of a reward that could just as well be given to a soldier for a bold feat of arms under fire, as to the man who simply set up the army's Camouflage Service and never got near the front line?

EQUIPMENT AND WEAPONS

In the army of 1914, experience of campaigning in Africa and elsewhere in the colonies had created the tradition that a soldier carried as much as possible on his person. The leather straps of his personal equipment supported three leather cartridge pouches (one either side of the belt buckle, and a third in the small of the wearer's back), a leather pack and a bayonet frog; across his shoulders was a canvas haversack and a one-litre water bottle (later replaced by a two-litre version). In addition to his own equipment, each man carried one of the squad's six cooking pots, or one of the company's tools (pickaxe, spade, shears or axe). Depending therefore on what he was carrying, and whether or not he was carrying a tent section, the total weight lay between 25kg (55lb) and 28kg (62lb).

It was units of the Tenth Army in the Ypres sector that, in April 1915, suffered the unfortunate distinction of being the first to experience a gas attack. At that time there was no defence against its effects, and an enemy breakthrough was halted only at great cost. By August, however, a mask was being distributed to front line troops. The mask itself, the P or P2, was rudimentary, consisting of nothing more than a treated cloth pad worn over the nose and mouth and secured to the head by cotton tape. This was sufficient for up to 2 hours' protection. A separate pair of goggles was also issued. Both mask and goggles were kept in a small waterproof package which could be attached to the wearer's personal equipment (also useful for storing tobacco!). They were supplemented in some units by hoods of treated fabric, but technical and manufacturing problems meant that these were not universally adopted.

Soldiers found the P2 difficult to put on quickly and hard to adapt to the contours of the face – factors held to account for the near success of a German attack south-east of Rheims in October 1915. Nor was it of any value against phosgene, first used on 26 November 1915, near Verdun, and from January 1916, a new mask, the TN, was introduced. The TN consisted of a conical shaped mask with elasticated straps and a separate pair of goggles. They were carried in a small oval tin, suspended from the waist-belt, and provided protection for up to 4 hours against chlorine gas, and up to 5 hours against phosgene. A further modification, making the goggles part of the mask, was then introduced in the autumn of 1916, and this new version, the M2, remained the standard pattern until 1918. The performance of the M2 improved on that of the TN, making it possible to survive for more than 4 hours against chlorine, and also making it better than contemporary German masks. From February 1918, the M2 was finally replaced by the ARS 1917, which was closer in appearance to German patterns, but included improved filtering.

PERSONAL WEAPONS

The basic infantry weapon was the 8mm Lebel rifle, originally designed in 1886, and modified in 1896. Although generally a robust and accurate weapon, the Lebel suffered from one major defect – the design of the magazine. This was filled by pushing a maximum of eight single rounds down

A group of graduates of the Machine Gun School at Le Ruchard; all are northerners, from the 85e (whose pre-war garrison was Cosne-sur-Loire), 87e (St Quentin), 89e (Sens), 91e (Mézieres) and 95e (Bourges) Régiments d'Infanterie. The courses run by the school were intended for officers and NCOs who would command machine gun detachments; the training of machine gun crews took place within the regiment. (Ian Sumner)

Machine gun training on the unsuccessful St Etienne. The high firing position of the gun was a definite disadvantage. The firer wears a special reinforced baldric to help him support the weight of the gun when on the move. (Ian Sumner)

a tube bored in the fore-end. As each bullet was consumed, the Lebel's centre of gravity changed, requiring every shot to be carefully aimed. Reloading was necessarily slow, and the gun was over-long. The Lebel was an obsolescent weapon, much inferior to the Mausers and Mannlichers carried by the enemy.

From 1915, it was replaced by the 1907 Berthier. This was a lengthened version of the standard cavalry carbine, originally intended for Colonial troops. The particular advantage of the Berthier was that its ammunition was loaded in three-round clips, and a change to five-round clips in 1916 brought further improvement. It took some time to introduce the Berthier because so many Lebels were already in stock, but the class of 1917 was armed with the new weapon from the beginning. Lebels, rather more robust than the newer Berthiers, continued in use with rifle grenades (see below); others, with a telescopic sight attached, were used by snipers. A small number of fully automatic FA17 rifles were also issued in 1917–18, but they suffered from a number of defects that severely restricted their actual use.

In 1914, each man carried 88 rounds on his person: 32 contained in four paper packets, in each front pouch, and 24 in the rear pouch. However, the regiments belonging to the 6e, 7e and 20e corps, stationed near the eastern frontier with Germany, were issued with 120 rounds per man. In wartime conditions, this tended to be the general level of issue, although the regulations for the Berthier specified only 84 (i.e. 28 three-round clips). The company baggage held a reserve of a further 112 rounds per man.

Accompanying the rifle was an 1886 pattern bayonet. This weapon was long (45cm/18in), of cruciform cross-section, and very slender, which meant it had a tendency to snap. The bayonet was the object of much mythologizing, and even acquired a nickname, 'Rosalie', from a popular song of the first August of the war. The bayonet charge, with colours flying and bugles sounding, remained a gleam in the eyes of those, journalists and others, who never saw the front. Jean-Norton Cru, who served with the 250e RI, and later made an extensive study of wartime memoirs, was dismissive of the notion. In a typically grumpy aside, he noted that, since bayonets were routinely fixed prior to combat, there was no more reason to call an attack a bayonet charge than a puttee attack. There was little hand-to-hand fighting during the course of the war; the bayonet was more useful for opening tins, or as a hook from which to hang equipment.

Officers (as well as cadets and *adjudants*) carried a pistol, either the regulation 1892 revolver, or one of any number of makes such as Colt, privately purchased. Swords were normally left with the company baggage, particularly after the first few months of the war, although an account of the 221e RI at Verdun in July 1916 describes a captain trying to launch a counter-attack, sabre in hand. Many officers replaced their sword with a walking stick, British-style, but since this still rather obviously identified their status, they continued to suffer heavy casualties. Some junior officers carried the same rifles as their men, but that was a personal decision.

HAND GRENADES

The nature of combat at the front saw the hand grenade come into its own. At the outbreak of war, the regulations governing the use of hand grenades dated from 1847, while the grenade itself still came with an exterior fuse. The first attempts at replacements consisted of nothing more than small explosive charges attached to pieces of wood. A more modern-looking weapon was the Besozzi grenade, approximately the size and shape of a lemon, introduced in early 1915. But the Besozzi still used an exterior fuse, which had to be lit with a slow match (or, more often,

French bombers, 1914–15. The private on the left holds an 81mm spherical bomb. The centre figure smokes a pipe to provide an instant source of flame for his improvised *pétard raquette*. On the right is a warrant officer armed with the unusual Danish-invented Aasen Type C 'parachute grenade' – a shrapnel grenade armed by pulling a long cord from the handle as it was thrown. (Adam Hook © Osprey Publishing Ltd)

the bomber's pipe!) – a task requiring some concentration in the middle of No Man's Land. The Besozzi was replaced by the F1, lit instead by striking the exterior fuse. However, the cardboard tube that contained the fuse provided little protection from the damp of the trenches, and the grenade all too often failed to explode. The F1 was quickly followed by the pear-shaped P1, whose explosive content was too weak to shatter the shell effectively. Three more P-series grenades, numbered 2 to 4, were then produced. They were closer in design to German stick grenades, with long handles and ribbons to help stabilize them in flight.

It was not until 1916 that an efficient grenade, the Billant (a modified version of the F1), was finally produced. This retained the lemon shape of the Besozzi, but was fired, like the British Mills bomb, by pulling a wire pin and allowing a lever to rise and thus ignite the fuse. However, the French habit of carrying these grenades loose in a haversack, allied to poor-quality workmanship, meant that the levers and pins easily became entangled and premature explosions were common.

A small number of special grenades were introduced in 1916 for clearing trenches and dug-outs. These contained either tear-gas, phosphorous or 'calorite', a compound that burnt at nearly 3,000°C, and was used to destroy anything metallic. None of these special grenades, however, was produced in any quantity.

More significant was the introduction of the Vivien-Bessières (VB) rifle grenade. A number of earlier 'home-made' attempts, involving catapults, had been made to find a method of projecting grenades into enemy trenches – none of them truly successful. The VB was a 'bullet through' weapon. Once a grenade had been placed in the special muzzle cup, and the rifle placed with its butt on the ground, a fired bullet struck the grenade and ignited the 8-second fuse. The maximum range of the VB was 170 metres (186 yards), much further than a man could throw, and it became a centrepiece of the new platoon tactics of 1916.

MACHINE GUNS

The first machine gun introduced into the French Army was the 1897 Hotchkiss. Problems with overheating led to the development of a number of competitors, but none could match the Hotchkiss, and one, the 1905 Puteaux, was markedly less effective. Attempts by the Government Arsenal at St Etienne to improve the Puteaux succeeded only in over-complicating it, making a poor design worse still. Nevertheless, it was introduced into the army as a replacement for the Hotchkiss. Exposed to the conditions of the Western Front, the weapon quickly revealed its shortcomings, and it was banished to the colonies, to be replaced by the faithful Hotchkiss.

The Hotchkiss was not fed by rounds held in fabric belts, but instead employed short aluminium trays containing 24 rounds each. On grounds of economy, it used the same 8mm

A group of the 55e RI pose with their Chauchat. Some men wear a horizon blue 'alpine' beret that was briefly issued in 1916. It was unpopular with the Alpine troops, who did not like to see their distinctive headgear worn by the whole army, and it was unpopular with everyone else because it was so big, and so difficult to stow away. It was replaced by the fore-and-aft *bonnet de police*, which several other men are seen wearing here. (Ian Sumner)

rounds as the Lebel rifle. Its rate of fire was between 400 and 600 rounds per minute, with a range of 1,800m (1.2 miles) direct and 4,000m (2.5 miles) indirect. Even though it was air-cooled, and did not therefore include a water jacket, the Hotchkiss was not a light weapon – the gun itself weighed 24kg (53lb), and its tripod base about the same. The ammunition was carried in wooden boxes, each containing 12 strips (i.e. 288 rounds), weighing 12kg (26lb) each.

The result, although weighty and cumbersome, was an excellent weapon. At Verdun, one section of two guns was isolated by the German advance and held off the enemy for ten days and nights, during which the two guns are supposed to have fired in excess of 75,000 rounds. Both were in excellent order when relief finally arrived, and, almost as importantly for their crews, had not used any of their precious water.

The Hotchkiss and St Etienne were too heavy to carry into the assault, so the French had also looked to develop a weapon that would incorporate the machine gun's volume of fire into the attack in a more easily portable form. The result was the Chauchat.

The Chauchat (more properly the Chauchat-Sutter-Ribeyrolles-Gladiator, after its inventors and manufacturers) was developed as part of a pre-war programme to produce an automatic rifle rather than a machine gun. Chauchat conceived his new weapon as something analogous to an artillery piece, able to lay down a barrage of fire at enemy targets. Indeed this volume of fire was considered almost more important than the shot-by-shot accuracy of the weapon.

To produce the barrage required, the weapon was designed to be fired at the walk, with the firer and his number two side by side. To keep up the volume of fire, the number two had to know when to change magazines with the minimum of delay, so the magazine was made with openings on the side, allowing him to keep an eye on the ammunition consumption. This may have worked well on a test range, but in the field it was disastrous. The difficulties of maintaining accurate fire while walking under fire over broken ground are obvious. Mud and dust entered the gun's firing mechanism; the magazines were too easy to damage when carried in their pouches; the spring was

The accurate and powerful 37mm infantry gun, here shown in a post-war photograph. Wheels could be attached for moving over rough ground, and there was also a gun shield, but the weapon was heavy enough without the extras. (Ian Sumner)

French infantry with 58mm trench mortar, Verdun, 1916. A mortar man (centre) adjusts the 58mm trench mortar during a quiet spell behind the first line positions. On the right, a gas sentry waits to bang his shell case alarm gong at the first whiff of gas. The soldier on the left carries about 25–30kg (55–66lb) and is armed with the 8mm Berthier rifle. (Adam Hook © Osprey Publishing Ltd)

too weak. Moreover, the bipod was flimsy, the sights were poorly placed and aligned, and an awkward prone firing position was needed to avoid being hit in the face by the gun's long-recoil action.

A survey ordered by General Pétain in May 1917 shows that many units were only too aware of these shortcomings; however, it also revealed that when the gun worked, it worked well. Citations for medal winners show that the Chauchat could be used as its inventor had envisaged:

> Soldat Carpentier, 20e RI, near Nogentel, Oise, 31 August 1918 ... he advanced on the enemy, firing while walking, the rest of the platoon led by Sergeant Berthault. He succeeded in manoeuvring around the flank of an island of resistance and in capturing, with his comrades, four machine guns and twenty-five German gunners.

Carpentier received the Croix de Guerre with palm.

TRENCH ARTILLERY

The main French field gun, the 75mm 1897, although excellent in open country, had proved itself incapable of destroying well-constructed trenches or barbed wire entanglements. Indeed, the French Army had no modern howitzers at all in its inventory; when the need for a weapon of this type became clear, all that was available was 15cm mortars, veterans of the Crimea!

These obsolete weapons were replaced in the trenches by a number of experimental types, including some pneumatic models, but these were all superseded in April 1915 with the introduction of the 58mm Second Pattern mortar, which fired a bomb of around 20kg (44lb), stabilized by fins, to a range of some 1,200m (1,312 yards). Other, heavier, types also saw service, including a monstrous 240mm weapon, but the 58 became the standard. A number of examples of the British Stokes mortar also saw service.

Trench mortars, nicknamed *crapouillots*, from a word meaning 'toad', were served by the artillery, the batteries numbered as 101 to 107 of a number of field artillery regiments. In February 1918, these batteries were amalgamated into five trench artillery regiments (175e–179e). The batteries consisted of 12 tubes each, and they were distributed in such a way that every infantry division could call on the services of a half-battery.

There may be duckboards at the bottom of this trench, but there is no revetting on the sides. British troops who took over French sections of the line were sometimes appalled by the 'relaxed' attitude to trench construction shown by their allies. The officer on the left is from the *chasseurs à pied*, as revealed by the hunting horn badge on his helmet, and the dark blue trousers. His *vareuse* has an integral belt. (Ian Sumner)

For many soldiers, tobacco was one of life's pleasures, and much off-duty time was devoted to carving a pipe. (Ian Sumner)

There was one further close-support weapon: the 37mm cannon, based on a naval pattern, and crewed by infantrymen. The first examples reached the front in April 1916. It was an excellent weapon if served well, but its components were too heavy for the crewmen to carry for any distance, which limited its effectiveness. The shield (28kg/62lb) was carried by the sergeant-commander; the tripod (38kg/84lb) by two numbers, and the barrel (48kg/106lb) by the gun layer and the loader. These five men were armed with a pistol, while the remainder of the section carried a cavalry carbine. Ammunition was carried by other numbers. One former gunner recalled that, in 1917–18, 'our superiors placed us at the end of the column, so we frequently lost touch'.

INTO THE TRENCHES

Early in 1915, Maurice Genevoix, a lieutenant in the 106e RI, observed a column of troops passing through a village. At first he thought they were a working party from a territorial regiment, but an old friend reveals that they were in fact a new draft from the class of 1914:

> They are wearing greatcoats that are too big for them, and slide off their shoulders. They are carrying their packs too high, which chafes the backs of their necks; they rub the area while their eyes stare fixedly ahead, some pale with empty eyes, others red in the face with great beads of sweat, despite the cold. [His friend remarks] 'They're willing, and that will get them so far ... but it's not enough, and will soon run out ... Too young; far too young.'

New personnel had to adapt quickly when they arrived at their new unit. In his novel *Les Croix de Bois*, Roland Dorgelès, who had served with the 39e RI, describes the arrival of three newcomers:

> We were all on our feet, and formed a curious circle around the three bewildered soldiers. They looked at us, and we looked at them, with no one saying anything. They had just come from the rear, they

had just come from the cities. Only yesterday, they were walking the streets, looking at women, trams and shops. Only yesterday, they were living like men. And we looked at them amazed, envious, like travellers arriving in a fantasy land.

It required all the leadership skills of squad, platoon and company commanders to blend the new faces into one unit.

It was the squad that would quickly become the soldier's world. There were 16 squads (*escouades*) in each company, organized into four platoons (*sections*). Each squad consisted of 15 riflemen, commanded by a corporal. The new soldier soon learned that his regiment was the best, particularly when compared to other arms of service. Certain regiments had acquired an elite reputation even before the outbreak of the war, each with its own traditions and *esprit de corps*. The light infantrymen of the *chasseurs à pied*, for example, whose peacetime uniform was dark blue, disdained the colour red as the symbol of 'mere' line infantry; the 'r-word' could only be spoken in three specific connections – the colour of the French flag, the colour of the ribbon of the Légion d'Honneur, and the colour of the lips of one's beloved. Everything else was *bleu-cérise* – 'cherry blue'. The chasseurs tried to maintain their distinctive uniform for as long as possible after horizon blue was introduced, simply to emphasize their difference, and thus 'superiority'.

Some units and formations acquired a heroic reputation during the course of the war: the most notable of these was perhaps the Régiment d'Infanterie Coloniale du Maroc. Originally created from a number of battalions that happened to be serving in Morocco at the outbreak of the war, it became a formidable regiment, acquiring more citations than any other (indeed, a new distinction, in the form of a double lanyard, had to be invented just for them). Other celebrated formations included the 'Iron Division' of Foch's 20e Corps, the 'Aces Division' (the 14e DI), the Breton regiments of the 10e and 11e corps, and the northerners of 1er Corps, whose towns and villages were right in the front line.

A line of Schneider PB2 buses, commandeered from the City of Paris, waits on a road in the forest of Compiègne. While some buses were used to transport troops, many more were converted to carry fresh food. (Ian Sumner)

As the war progressed, squad organization changed, due in part to manpower pressures, and in part to technical innovation like the introduction of the Chauchat automatic rifle and of specialist bombers, armed with either hand grenades or the Vivien-Bessières rifle grenade. In 1916, the fourth company of each battalion was withdrawn to form the divisional depots, and three machine gun companies were created within each regiment. At the same time, changes were made to the platoon organization of the rifle companies, so that one half-platoon consisted of a bombing squad and a Chauchat squad, whilst the second consisted of two squads of riflemen, each with two VBs. The first platoon was commanded by the senior lieutenant, the second platoon by the third senior, the fourth by the second senior, and the third platoon by the *adjudant*.

Squad organization changed once more in September 1917. Now both half-platoons contained a bombing squad and a Chauchat/VB squad, and this remained the case for the remainder of the war. A further reorganization was introduced in October 1918 – each platoon was now to consist of three combat 'groups' of 13 men, each in turn made up of a Chauchat team and a bombing team – but it was too late to see service.

The machine gunners formed separate companies within the regiment; administratively these were part of regimental headquarters, but in practice one served with each battalion. Like their counterparts in the British Army, French machine gunners saw themselves as an elite. According to Lafond, 'They feel somewhat superior to – or at least different from – the ordinary companies.' Yet their own high opinion of themselves was not always reciprocated by their comrades in the infantry battalion. Machine gunners were frequently dismissed as 'dug-outs' (*embusqués*) – soldiers who served well away from the front line and its dangers. They were excused standing watch, and so generally got a good night's sleep, unlike the ordinary rifleman; and because they were obliged to stay near their weapons at all times they were also excused from working parties. Privileges like these were unlikely to endear them to the ordinary infantryman.

Like many of his comrades, Georges Demonchy, of the 4e Régiment de Zouaves, had a finely honed sense of who was, or was not, a dug-out:

> Corporals and soldiers were not dug-outs: they manned, and suffered in, the trenches; they occupied advanced posts and went on patrols. But sergeants were dug-outs, as were machine gunners, artillerymen, officers, the regimental transport, and staffs at regimental, brigade and divisional level. In addition, heavy artillery, engineers, aviators, drivers, and all the services at the rear were thought of as dug-outs by the division, and even more so by those at the front.

This seems a little hard on the engineers, at least. All army signallers were part of the 8e Régiment de Génie, serving in small detachments along the front, and they suffered many of the same hardships as the infantry. Despite the best efforts of the signallers, communications between units remained difficult because repeated bombardments broke telephone and telegraph wires. This put an extra burden on the company runners, many of whom were killed. Engineers also engaged in mining operations along most of the Western Front, but particularly at the hilltop villages of Les Eparges in the Woëvre, south of Verdun, and at Vauquois in the Argonne. Both villages disappeared in the frequent explosions, and the summit of the crest of Vauquois was reduced in height by 18 metres (20 yards). The field artillery remained unpopular with those in the front line, for many could quote examples of friendly batteries firing too short into their own men, despite the frantic

The Villa Monplaisir, built on a reverse slope somewhere in the Woëvre. Despite its homely nature, the writer of this postcard, a cavalryman serving with the hussars, was looking forward to coming home on leave. (Ian Sumner)

use of signal flares. Trench artillery, on the other hand, was respected for its work in defence, but soldiers knew that if the trench artillery was suddenly reinforced, then an offensive was in the air.

Non-commissioned officers (in the French Army, the term was applied only to those with the rank of sergeant and above; corporals counted as 'Other Ranks') were all promoted private soldiers. The number of NCOs had been severely depleted by the two-year conscription period introduced in 1905. The return to three years did not take place until 1913, and it was only in their third year that prospective NCOs found their feet. The best of the men who looked to the military for a career tended to become officers; and of the remainder, many sought out a comfortable administrative post, with a view to the civil service post that became their due after 15 years' service. Consequently the number of trained NCOs at the outbreak of war was low. Each sergeant commanded a half-platoon of two squads.

Some officers were products of the Academy at St Cyr, but French government policy ensured that perhaps as many as 60 per cent were recruited from the ranks, after a one-year course at the school at St Maixent. In 1914, applications for St Cyr were falling, following the Dreyfus affair and the official disfavour that subsequently hung over the army; as many as 1,000 posts for lieutenants stood vacant. Most junior officers were drawn from the professional classes – teachers and small businessmen – particularly after mobilization. The casualties inflicted on officers from every regiment during the Battle of the Frontiers meant that their ranks contained a much larger proportion of promoted NCOs than had previously been the case. In November 1914, 15 of the 21 second lieutenants of the 39e RI fell into this category, in addition to three of the company commanders. By 1916, in the 129e RI, only two of the 12 captains, three of the nine lieutenants and two of the 16 second-lieutenants had pre-war experience.

At the outbreak of war, a soldier's pay stood at one franc a day. And, during the war, an extra franc a day was paid as a 'trench allowance' (of which half, 50 centimes, was retained as an end of service gratuity). But even a packet of tobacco cost 40 centimes, so soldiers had little money to spend. Promotion would certainly mean a pay increase – a sergeant, for example, could earn just over two francs a day in basic pay. Promotion to the rank of corporal or sergeant lay in the hands of the company commander; further progression, to the ranks of *sergent-major, adjudant* or *adjudant-chef*, was a decision for the colonel.

Officers messed together, as did the NCOs. Pierre Chaine, who served with three different infantry regiments, noted that 'Officers talk about women, non-coms about pensions and promotion, but the soldiers talk about wine.' And then he added, 'But love is rare, wine dear, and promotion only seldom.' The difference between the ranks was noticeable in other areas as well, with signs that spoke of 'lavatories for the officers, toilets for the NCOs, and latrines for the men'.

FOOD

Two ration scales were in operation, depending on the type of activities currently occupying the regiment. Both included a daily ration of 700g of bread, 600g of fresh meat and 300g of tinned meat, 50cl of wine, or 1l of beer or cider, or 6.25cl of spirits. The main difference between the two scales lay largely in the provision of extra potatoes, pasta, sugar and coffee. Tinned sardines in oil were often substituted for the meat portion. In Muslim regiments, rations contained no pork and no alcohol.

Every regiment had a reserve of food, sufficient for several days – tinned, stringy beef in gravy (known sardonically as 'monkey'), a dozen pieces of hardtack per man, packets of sugar, coffee tablets and packets of dried soup – but, naturally, the men preferred to eat something fresher, if at all possible. A small sum of money, administered by the *sergent-major* (the NCO in charge of company administration), was available for each company to spend on local produce, where it could be obtained, to supplement the food provided by the army. In some rear areas, cooperative shops were set up, where soldiers could also buy extras for themselves.

The main meal of the day was supposed to be served at 10am for other ranks, 10.30am for the NCOs, and half an hour later for the officers. The colonel ate at midday, and generals often later

The prospect of a hot meal attracts a hungry audience, transcending any language barrier. Cooks were often categorized with the 'dug-outs', since they were always stationed in the rear, perhaps 500–600 metres behind the front line. Nevertheless, they were often the target of enemy bombardments, as the smoke of the cooking fires gave away their positions. (IWM, Q10865)

A photo reputedly depicting French troops in action, but probably taken on peacetime manoeuvres. The firing line has been formed, with the men in pairs, lying in scrapes behind the excavated earth, which has been reinforced by their packs. In the background, a platoon waits its turn to be fed into the firing line. (Ian Sumner)

than that. But this was not always possible during a relief, or a more permanent move, nor, all too frequently, during attacks: 'We ate whenever we could, in case we couldn't eat when we wanted to.'

The company's mobile cookers were stationed in the second line of trenches, or even further to the rear, and the food had to be carried up to the front line, by working parties drawn from each platoon or squad. This was by no means an easy duty to perform. At Verdun, a party from the 18e Bataillon de Chasseurs à Pied (BCP) took all night to do so: 'they returned, dropping with fatigue, at dawn, the last hundred yards under enemy machine gun fire. Exhausted by the strain, they declared they would rather starve to death than do that again; but in the evening, moved by a sense of duty and comradeship, they set off again across the cratered ground.'

Some men were appreciative of the efforts of the cooks in turning out meals under difficult circumstances; others, like Jacques Meyer, a lieutenant serving with the 329e RI, were less impressed:

> The main meal of the day, called 'soup' no matter what it was, consisted of meat, either with a rubbery lump of pasta or rice, or with beans, more or less cooked, or potatoes, more or less peeled, in a brown liquid, only just distinguishable from a slick of congealing fat that lay over it. There was no question of green vegetables, nor of vitamins …

To wash it down came milky, well-sugared coffee and red wine.

If mud was a major part of soldiers' lives, it was so from necessity; wine, however, played a major role from choice. The wine, *pinard*, was simple *vin ordinaire*; nevertheless, it was a true lifter of men's spirits, despite the constant suspicion it had been watered down by the company cooks. Many battalions in rest areas found a pretext for sending a party to visit a nearby village, complete with 20 or 30 water bottles, to fill up with wine. The canny soldier would have made sure to fire a blank round into his water bottle for just such an occasion; the gases from the discharge expanded its capacity beyond the standard 2 litres. As one trench newspaper put it, 'Water, the ordinary drink of the soldier; wine, the extraordinary drink of the soldier'. Spirits, in the form of an *eau-de-vie* called *gnôle*, were sometimes distributed before an attack or in extremely cold weather, at the rate of one-eighth of a litre for each squad. Since the same ration of wine and spirits was issued to a squad, no matter how many men were present on duty, the true skill of a corporal lay in his ability to divide up the liquid into equal portions.

Throughout the war, many soldiers received parcels, sent either from home or from a penpal. These included knitted gloves and scarves in a variety of surprising colours, food and tobacco. Food was always the most highly prized since for many men it came from their own, or a neighbouring, farm – hams, sausages, pâtés, *rillettes* and *confits*, or cakes. Shared with the rest of the squad, following the unspoken rule, these always provided a welcome supplement to the regulation diet. For men without family, or those from the south and far from home, acquiring a female penpal (*marraine de guerre*) provided a human element, an evocation of peacetime normality, lacking in the front line. Some of these relationships prospered and, at the end of the war, became permanent; but even if that were not the case, a penpal could still be a reliable source of home comforts.

During the day, perhaps one-quarter of the unit were on duty at any one time; at night, one-half spent periods of 2 hours as sentries. Much of a soldier's day (and night) was taken up with working parties. During the day, there were old trenches to repair, new ones to dig, gabions to make and fill, and details to bring up supplies – wire, sandbags, ammunition – from the reserve lines. At night, it was possible to work on the trench defences, repairing the wire and, in the early days of trench warfare at least, clearing long grass from No Man's Land; stretcher-bearers could venture out to retrieve the wounded, and parties went off to bring up food and water.

Many dug-outs, particularly those in the front line, were simply 'funk holes', scraped in one wall of the trench. Philippe Barrès, serving with the dismounted 12e Régiment de Cuirassiers, offered this advice to the prospective trench dweller: 'Don't stick your legs outside your scrape, it's raining; don't lift your eyes up, or the rain will get in them; don't move your arms, or freezing water will run under your blanket ... but don't forget to move or you'll freeze. And don't fall asleep.' More permanent dug-outs were constructed, if there was any timber about, with the aid of a tent section to catch the water. In the rocky countryside of the Vosges, soldiers could sleep in small wooden huts they built themselves, placed on the reverse slopes. Soldiers fighting

Another posed photograph. The men are all wearing their packs; the sergeants are not. Note the reserve ammunition pouch, worn in the small of the back. An officer kneels behind. (Ian Sumner)

in the chalk hills of the Vauquois, like André Pezard, serving with the 46e RI, may have thought themselves luckier than those further north: 'Along steps that went down 15 metres [16.4 yards] below ground level were bunk beds which took up half of the passage. It was our dormitory, our living room and our dining hall. Its occupants gained in security what they lacked in ventilation.'

'Torn from his regular job, from his home and his family,' wrote a contributor to the newspaper of the 227e RI in 1915, 'the French citizen is from one day to the next a warrior, ready for anything, or a builder, engineer, bricklayer, marksman, bomber, machine gunner, cook.'

But of all a soldier's skills, the most prized was the ability to sleep. Sentry duty and bombardments quickly disrupted normal sleep patterns; added to this was the fatigue brought on by working parties, so soldiers had to learn to snatch sleep where they could. As one soldier recalled, 'I quickly learned how to sleep in wet boots, because you couldn't get them back on once you'd taken them off, to sleep for four hours in a sodden greatcoat, in the middle of explosions, shouting and foul smells.' Jean-Louis Delvert, in the trenches of Verdun with 101e RI, complained, 'Impossible to have the briefest rest. We are devoured by fleas – when we're not under fire, you can feel them biting. That Saturday, I noted in my diary that I hadn't slept for nearly 72 hours.' Some fleas were so persistent that many French soldiers were convinced they had been decorated with the Iron Cross for their contribution to the German war effort.

Rats were equally disruptive to a good night's sleep, as Jacques Vandebeuque, serving with the 56e BCP in front of Les Eparges, found:

Rats, rats in an incalculable number, are the true masters of the position. They multiply in their hundreds in every ruined house, in every dug-out ... I've spent some terrible nights: covered by my galoshes and greatcoat, I've felt these awful beasts working on my body. There's fifteen to twenty of them to every one of us, and after eating everything, bread, butter, chocolate, they start on our clothes. Impossible to sleep in these conditions: a hundred times a night, I throw back my blanket and the fright I give them with a light is only temporary. Almost immediately, they're back, in even greater numbers ...

This photo follows on from the previous two. Having imposed their will on the enemy, the men rise and deliver a charge. If this is indeed representative of what took place in 1914, then such a mass of men would have provided an easy target for the enemy, whatever the colour of their uniform. (Ian Sumner)

IN ACTION

The reality of war came as an enormous shock to the men of 1914. 'We were not paper soldiers,' wrote Jean Galtier-Boissière, a corporal serving with the 31e RI, 'but all most of my comrades knew of war came from patriotic prints.' His comrades were soon to be disillusioned. On 24 August 1914, they were in action. Just as bayonets were fixed, the sun came out to illuminate a 'moving forest of bayonets':

> In front of us was a completely empty hillside: not a tree, not a wall, not a fold in the ground ... Bullets whistled, shrapnel burst; big shells burst in huge pillars of earth ... Deafened, ears ringing, you couldn't hear orders being shouted ... Deaf, mute, stupefied with dust and noise, I walked on hypnotised. One single thought, one idea ... Forward! Forward!
>
> [The bugler sounds the charge.]
>
> Now we are moving forward in bounds, following a signal from the adjutant ... you run straight ahead, your pack weighing you down, burdened by pouches, water bottle, haversack, which all wrap themselves around your legs ... then throw yourself onto the ground ... men are tripping over, others are hit in the head as they get up. The bullets arrive in storms, very low down ... 'We're being crucified by machine guns,' my neighbour says, before collapsing.
>
> Another bound! ... The enemy that is machine-gunning us is still invisible. We haven't even fired a single round yet. There's only about a dozen of us now ... I'm huddled behind two piles of earth. Listening to the machine guns clatter: tac-tac-tac. The bullets whistle past: what a hellish din. Every shot I hear, I think, 'This one's mine.'
>
> How long are we there? ... Why is no-one giving any orders? And what is our artillery doing?
>
> Suddenly someone shouts, 'Fall back!' Wonderful ... The adjutant points us towards a small field of potatoes. On my knees and elbows, I start off, my face nearly on the boots of the man in front. Made it! Bullets are landing all around me, cutting off leaves ... we're about twenty metres from a main road with trees running along the side of it ... The ditch is safety. But it means crossing an area swept by fire. Tricky moment! One man leaps up, takes a few steps, then collapses, face on the ground ... Another goes, and gets halfway before rolling like a shot rabbit, holding his stomach, shouting, 'Oh! Oh!' A third man tries, suddenly stops and turns, his face all bloody, and collapses, crying for his mother ... I'm last, I run as fast as I can and throw myself into the bottom of the ditch: safe!
>
> Our losses are very high. The lieutenant-colonel, the battalion commander, and three-quarters of the officers are out of action ... Everyone looks downcast, and talks in hushed tones. The regiment appears to be in mourning.

The nature of these early battles was essentially linear, as envisaged by pre-war theorists such as Grandmaison and Foch. Each battalion moved to contact by throwing out skirmishers, whilst holding the remainder of its men in columns in reserve. Each platoon of 50 men was spread out over 100 to 200 metres (109 to 219 yards) of ground, with the men in pairs – far too widely spaced for effective command. Once contact had been made, troops were fed into the firing line with two objectives – to suppress enemy fire and, with the support of the field artillery, to inflict sufficient casualties to make the opposing line waver. Then, once the enemy lost the desire to continue the

firefight, a bayonet charge was supposed to deliver the *coup de grace*. Victory would result, therefore, not from superior tactics, or even superior weaponry, but from the imposition of superior will. Attacks of this type failed for several reasons: the strength of defensive firepower was underestimated, coordination with the artillery was poor, with assaults frequently launched without waiting for the guns to come up, and the lack of heavy artillery and howitzers meant that the enemy could make themselves safe by taking cover behind any kind of crest.

Although at grass-roots level artillery and infantry tactics were continually evolving in response to battlefield experience during 1915, the French lacked the material preponderance and tactical sophistication needed to subdue the equally dynamic German defence. Instead of 'fire and movement', with infantrymen covering each other by rifle fire as they moved in alternate groups, the whole line advanced together, keeping as close to the barrage as possible. The enemy, it was hoped, would be so disorientated by the bombardment that the infantry could simply occupy the ground conquered by the artillery. Each failed attack resulted in a bombardment more powerful than its predecessor, yet the artillery barrage remained ineffective. A persistent shortage of heavy artillery forced the army into reliance on a weapon – the 75mm field gun – which was actually incapable of destroying wire entanglements.

The introduction of the Chauchat and the VB rifle grenade in 1916 prompted something of a rethink. Each assault now consisted of a number of waves. A first wave formed by the rifle/bomber half-platoons, accompanied by engineers with wire cutters, was followed by a second wave made up of the bomber/VB half-platoons. A third wave followed 30 metres (33 yards) behind, again consisting of bombers and riflemen, with the role of clearing the captured trench. And behind them came the remaining two platoons of the company, with the VBs on the flank and in the centre, acting as a reserve.

The role of the first wave was to capture the first line of enemy trenches, and then move on – with their main objective to gain ground; the second wave acted as a reserve, and could pass through the first in order to maintain the impetus of the attack. The moppers-up of the third wave took possession of the trench, bombing their way along the traverses, and reducing any strongpoints. Formations for the assault were kept flexible. The first two waves might be in extended order, with four or five paces between each man, but the third and fourth could be in columns of squads, to make it easier to manoeuvre quickly. Yet, all too frequently, the pace and form of attacks were ruled by a rigid timetable that left insufficient discretion to local commanders to exploit success.

Virtually from the onset of trench warfare, French soldiers, in common with those of the other armies on the Western Front, were carrying out tactical experimentation and innovation. By 1916, the French Army were moving towards tactical methods that emphasized concentrated firepower and the flexible use of infantry. In 1916–17 Nivelle and Pétain refined this method, attacking limited objectives with the heavy artillery concentrations necessary to ensure success. During the battle of Malmaison, in October 1917, General Franchet d'Esperey, the commander of the Sixth Army, successfully introduced specially trained squads of infantry whose role was to accompany the tanks, in advance of the main infantry assault, and direct them towards their targets. By 1918 the French Army had, like its British ally and German enemy, reached a peak of tactical sophistication.

In a series of instructions in 1918, Pétain sought to achieve greater cooperation between air power, artillery and tanks, all acting in support of the assaulting infantry, measures which bore fruit in the counter-offensives of summer 1918. Drawing on his experience of the battlefield of Verdun, where men frequently lost touch with their command posts, he proposed greater emphasis on marksmanship and self-reliance amongst the infantry – concepts previously absent from French training.

Earlier in the year, the French had still been on the defensive. To reduce casualties from enemy bombardment, Pétain ordered that the front line should be only lightly held, preferring a more flexible defence in depth, featuring strongpoints with overlapping fields of fire. Where the commander followed Pétain's orders, as did General Gouraud, the commander of the Fourth Army, then the German offensive, Operation *Reims*, in July 1918, failed completely. But by no means all of Pétain's generals agreed with his tactics, emotionally committed to the idea that they would not concede a single metre of French soil. During the German Operation *Blücher* on the Chemin des Dames in April 1918, the regiments of the Sixth Army, now under the command of General Duchêne, were caught by the bombardment, taking heavy casualties, and were forced to give up ground so painfully won during the previous April.

However neat and tidy a diagram might look in the training manuals, an attack was still a frightening and confusing affair. Chevallier's novel *La Peur* records impressions of an assault in 1917:

We are waiting for Zero Hour, to be crucified, abandoned by God, condemned by Man ...

Suddenly, the artillery thunders, obliterates, eviscerates, terrifies. Everything explodes, bursts and shudders. The sky has disappeared. We are in the middle of a monstrous whirlpool; clods of earth rain down, comets meet and shatter, throwing off sparks like a short circuit. We are caught at the end of the world. The earth is a building in flames, and the exits have been bricked up.

'Ready, we're going!'

The men, pasty white, numb, shuffle a bit, checking their bayonets. The NCOs growl out a few words of encouragement. Lieutenant Larcher is in the middle of us all, tense, very conscious of his rank and his position. He climbs onto the firing step, looks at his watch, turns and says, 'Ready, we're going ... Forward!'

The line shudders, and the men hoist themselves up. We repeat the shout 'Forward!' with all our might, like a cry for help. We throw ourselves behind our shout, every man for himself in the attack ...

Men fall, bunch up, split up, disappear in pieces. ... You can hear bullets hit others, hear their strangled cries. Every man for himself. Fear has almost become an asset. A machine gun on the left ... which way now? Forward! That way safety lies. Flat on the ground, flames, rifles, men. 'The Boche! The Boche!' The Germans waving their arms, escape down a communications trench ... Some, mad, fire after them ... 'Damn, I'll get you!'

Set piece attacks like these were in fact the exception. Much more frequent were patrols and trench raids. The staff were constant in their demands for information, particularly on the comings and goings of the enemy. Prisoners, especially those wearing the tunic that bore their regimental number, or those carrying their personal papers, were what was required. That such actions might bring down retaliatory shelling onto the heads of those that took part was of little account. Parties were normally between four and ten men in strength, accompanied by a corporal or sergeant; on important occasions, an officer might join them. Raiders were always volunteers; in some regiments, they became a semi-permanent sub-unit, a *corps franc*.

Actions of this type were common where there was a 'fire-eating' officer. However, many men took the attitude that they would not engage in combat unless directly ordered to do so, or unless provoked by the enemy. A Christmas Truce certainly took place in the French lines in 1914, as it did in the British (one account, from the 99e RI in Picardy, suggests that hostilities were unofficially suspended for the whole of the Christmas season, from Christmas Eve to Twelfth Night). It is difficult to establish how typical this was, because many soldiers chose not to reveal such incidents to their superior officers. Paul Rimbault, of the 74e RI, recalled a quiet sector on the Chemin des Dames in July 1917, where the German listening posts were only 8 metres (26 feet) from those of the French, and where 'the Boche, sitting on the parapet, smokes his pipe, while the French soldier writes a letter in the same position'. But this seems to have been an extreme example.

Many men saw the enemy soldier as a fellow sufferer, equally afflicted by poor living conditions and a callous staff, and were unwilling to make life worse for anyone by gratuitously opening hostilities. Certainly when trenches were only around 20 metres (22 yards) apart, artillery fire was just as likely to hit friendly as enemy trenches, so it was in the interests of everyone to maintain a tacit truce. Attitudes like these were deplored by the High Command, a view echoed by men like Antoine Redier, an officer who served with the 338e RI, before joining the staff of Fourth Army: 'Actually, most of our men, disoriented by the war, do not seem to recognize that the German is their hereditary enemy; they dislike him simply as an opponent, but that is not enough ... We must fortify the soldier against this ridiculous idea – that the Germans are just men like us.' In his post-war study of combatants' memoirs, Jean-Norton Cru dismissed Redier as a man ignorant of the opinions of the ordinary soldier, and as one who kept or acquired the prejudices of the rear, and argued that his views did not accurately represent the attitudes prevalent in the front line. Whatever the truth of the matter, Redier, whose home was in Lille and thus under German occupation throughout the war, remained a resolute and vocal German-hater throughout the 1930s.

The men of 1914 had gone to war with enthusiasm, to drive the enemy from France and to liberate Alsace and Lorraine. But that attitude quickly wore off after the Battle of the Frontiers and the failed offensives of 1915. Writing on the second day of the Somme offensive, Second Lieutenant Louis Mairet thought that the soldier of 1916 was fighting not for Alsace, nor to ruin Germany, nor for his country. He was fighting because he could not do otherwise, with resignation on the one hand, but also with an honesty and pride which helped him acquiesce in the sacrifice he was making. Glory – *la gloire* – much discussed as the motive for fighting (although only in the newspapers) was dismissed. 'Glory,' noted one artillery officer, 'was not as pleased with mud as we were ... We did not know her; she did not know us. We asked her for nothing; she promised us nothing.'

The soldier, observed Chaine, goes through several stages at the front. First comes the recruit who has never been under fire, and, prey to his imagination, is beset by nerves. Then, after emerging unscathed from a number of engagements, he loses his fear of combat. He starts to thinks that shells will not touch him and that bullets whistle harmlessly by. After a while, however, he begins to realize that this might simply be a lucky streak that will soon come to an end. He becomes cautious and tries to calculate the risk in everything he is about to do. After that follows the final stage, one of sheer hopelessness, when the soldier resigns himself to certain death. The modern version of courage, Chaine concludes, is not to recoil from an invisible and inevitable death.

DISCIPLINE

By no means everyone willingly consented to being placed in uniform, or under discipline. In September 1914, the normal court-martial procedure was suspended and replaced by a system of summary courts-martial, where the sentence would be carried out within 24 hours, without any right of appeal. It was in this fashion that, over a two-day period (17–18 October 1914), Fourth Army was able to condemn 31 men to death for self-inflicted wounds, of whom 13 were actually shot. Soldat Bersot of the 60e RI, whose case was reviewed in 1932, was shot for refusing to obey an order to don trousers soaked in the blood of one of his dead comrades. These summary procedures were abolished and the pre-war system reintroduced in April 1916.

From the autumn of that year, the number of desertions began to grow. The return to a more regular system of courts-martial meant that, rather than face summary execution, those found guilty of desertion were placed in the front line as punishment. Where, wondered those already serving there, were *they* to go as punishment? To the rear? Finding themselves equated with criminals did nothing to help morale, already low after the heroic sacrifices of the battles of Verdun and the Somme. The failure of the Chemin des Dames offensive in April 1917 provoked a paroxysm of indiscipline amongst the unhappy troops.

The mutinies of 1917 were not protests against the war itself, nor against war in general; rather they were protests against the conduct of this particular war, against the way in which the soldiers saw themselves as sacrifices on the altar of futile offensives. The mutinies began not during the Chemin des Dames offensive itself, but during the subsequent succession of consolidation attacks ordered by Pétain upon taking up command; those involved were the units which were moving up to the front, and not those already there. Losses amongst officers and NCOs undoubtedly played their part in this, since they had led to a shortage not only of commanders within each unit, but

As in Britain, the number of men under arms allowed women to take jobs previously done by men. Here the craftsmen and -women of the depot of the 26e Régiment d'Artillerie, at Le Mans, pose for a photo. (Ian Sumner)

also of commanders at brigade, division and even corps level – of men of experience and judgement who might have been promoted in the field.

During the course of war, approximately 2,300 men (an estimated figure, since one-fifth of the relevant archive has been destroyed) were sentenced to death, of whom 640 were shot (by comparison, the British executed 306 men, the Germans only 48). Only 27 French soldiers were executed for mutiny, and 60 per cent of all executions actually occurred between 1914 and 1915.

The measures introduced by Pétain when he took command in 1917 – the use of offensives with limited objectives, his compassionate response to the mutinies, the introduction of improvements in living conditions and the reintroduction of leave – undoubtedly helped the army recover its morale; yet while some regiments were able to perform well in 1918, others remained shaky to the end.

OUT OF THE TRENCHES

CASUALTIES

The losses suffered by the French Army were enormous. Of those men serving in 1914, a quarter did not return. By November 1914, the 74e RI had already received 1,175 replacements, out of a complement of 2,700; in the same period, the 129e RI had received 1,345 men – nearly 50 per cent of its effectives – as replacements for casualties incurred during the battles of that summer. In the same division (the 5th, commanded by the 'thruster' General Mangin), the same regiments also lost heavily at Verdun. In a two-day attack on Fort Douaumont on 22–24 May 1916, the 74e lost 1,964 men and the 129e 1,334; the four regiments of the division lost a total of 5,359 men. The fort remained in German hands. The following April, the 146e RI, serving in the Chemin des Dames sector again under General Mangin (by this time an army commander, and nicknamed 'Butcher' by his men), lost 41 officers and 1,900 men in one day. In the same offensive, after only five days of battle, a report from General Headquarters noted that 24 divisions were worn out, and 17 needed to be withdrawn from the front line immediately.

During the course of the conflict, 1,350,000 men of the French Army were killed. A further 3,200,000 were wounded in some way, and about one-third of those would be crippled for life. Men killed in the trenches were frequently buried close at hand because there was simply no opportunity to do anything else. Jacques Arnoux, serving with the 116e RI in the trenches at Perthes-les-Hurlus in September 1915, noticed in the side of the trench fragments of crosses, which bore fragmentary inscriptions: 'Under a scrap of red képi, I read, "Here lie soldiers of the 10e RI. Show respect." Next to it, "Here lie fifteen brave men of the 11e RI. Show respect."'

The men of the regimental band acted as stretcher-bearers in the front line. Battlefield casualties were taken first to collecting points in the front line, and from there were carried to the regimental dressing stations, which normally lay in the reserve trenches. Here the regimental medical officer, assisted by an auxiliary (usually a medical student) and four medical orderlies, performed the first triage. Every division also included eight *ambulances* (in the French use of the word, a medical unit, and not a vehicle); these acted as back-up to the regimental posts. These units treated everyone who could be dealt with immediately; everyone else who had a chance of recovery was sent to an evacuation hospital.

Evacuation hospitals were located some kilometres behind the front line. Here men were held, either in tents or huts, until they could be evacuated to the rear. A small surgical unit was attached to each. Of the hospitals in the rear, only a relatively small number were under military control; the remainder were run by civilian organizations under army supervision, of which the largest was the *Société de Secours aux Blessés Militaires*.

The army's medical services were caught unprepared for the large number of casualties, and at first lacked sufficient quantities of even the most basic equipment – for example, sterilizers, large well-lit and heated tents, and vehicles that could accommodate stretchers. It was only with the importation of Ford light lorries that evacuation by motor transport became possible. Trains and canal barges were eventually used, but it was not until 1917–18 that they became truly effective.

Convalescent leave normally lasted 30 days but had to be taken at a pre-designated address. Some men, too far from home to return there easily, stayed instead with their penpal, many of whom were surprised to find that their correspondent spoke with a thick country accent, or was even a black African.

Fifteen days in the trenches were supposed to be followed by eight days in reserve. The relief was always eagerly anticipated, even if it did not always go smoothly. As Louis Mairet, of 127e RI, described:

Don't you know it's the relief? We wander around in the night, splashing through the mud. Flares go up, pickets fire; German patrols are out in No Man's Land, their heads are kept well down. The rain is torrential. Finally, the relief begins. Packs on! We set off, stumbling around in the downpour. Squeeze to one side to let a squad pass. Start off again. Arrive at a crossroads, and wait for the 1st Platoon, but they don't arrive. Off again; go to meet the captain on the road. We wait for the captain, packs still on our backs in the rain. He arrives, we set off again, muddy and sodden. Stop at Cauroy. Arrive at Hermonville at two in the morning. Mud, filth. Not a dry stitch on. Tired. Exhausted. We throw ourselves down onto some straw. If you have never done a relief, you will never know what it's like!

'Small' rest periods (*petit repos*) were spent in the reserve front line; longer periods (*grand repos*) were taken further away, a trip by lorry or train. The quality of the accommodation provided for the troops varied from sector to sector. In some, the cellars of a village or town provided a safe haven, particularly when the village was far enough away from the front line for many of its inhabitants to have stayed behind. In others, all that could be offered was a pile of flea-infested straw in the corner of a barn. Where no accommodation could be found, engineers were supposed to build barrack huts, but this rarely happened, certainly not before 1917. And rest periods were not always restful. 'Coming from the trenches,' wrote Georges Pineau after the war, 'there were inspections of arms, clothing, boots, hair, feet, field dressings, reserve rations and cartridges; you mounted guards, got vaccinated, scrubbed potatoes, cleaned the huts, washed your clothes, listened

The widespread introduction of motor ambulances speeded up the evacuation procedure enormously. This particular vehicle, taken at Epernay-sur-Marne, appears to be driven by a British woman driver. (Ian Sumner)

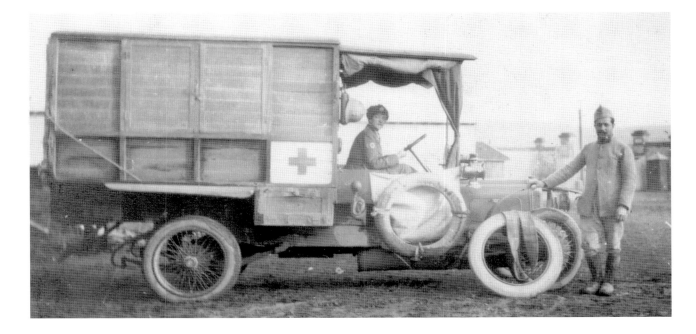

Unloading an ambulance at a
military hospital in or around
Perpignan. Note the stretcher on
the left, which includes collapsible
legs. (Ian Sumner)

to lectures on the machine gun or how to wear a gasmask, took part in parades, reviews and ceremonies with drums a-beating, and, just to keep your hand in, went on exercise.'

Leave was a precious commodity, all the more so because of its rarity. In 1915, men who had served at the front for one year were entitled to a period of six days' leave every four months. But leave, of course, was cancelled on the eve of any major attack; indeed, such was the nature of French strategy in 1915, with attacks taking place all down the line, that leave was unofficially cancelled in its entirety, and was only reinstated when Pétain took charge in 1917. Unfortunately for the man going on leave, his six days began from the time he left his unit and not on arrival at his destination. One real complaint during the mutinies of 1917 was the length of time it took to get anywhere after leaving the front. Restrictions on railway services in wartime were compounded by the layout of the network itself; there were few cross-country trains, and most lines led into Paris and out again. Soldiers from the south or from Corsica might be away from their unit for as long as three weeks. And the problem was actually made worse by Pétain's reforms; once he reintroduced leave, so many trains were going into Paris that the lines became blocked, and men spent hours waiting by the lineside. In response, special leave camps were erected in the Paris suburbs, with accommodation and food. Local politicians were quick to protest about this sudden influx of soldiers, an attitude that did nothing to reassure the men that they were fighting in a just cause.

The sheer number of men called up had also led to manpower problems in civilian life. Over the winter of 1914–15, so many engineering craftsmen had been conscripted that it adversely affected munitions production, and the men had to return to their factories. The shortages also affected agriculture: from 1915 onwards, leave to help with the harvest was given to any conscripted farm worker currently serving at regimental depots, and to anyone serving in a Territorial unit. In 1917, this was extended to include any recently conscripted soldier with an agricultural background.

The gap between the reality of trench life and the way that life was portrayed at home became all too quickly apparent to the ordinary soldier. Paul Boissière, writing for the benefit of his fellows

The regiment marches off to meet its new fate. (Ian Sumner)

in the trench journal *Le Crapouillot* in 1917, describes a visit to a cinema, where he could not contain his amazement as he watched 'the groups of enthusiastic actors who cross barrages as if they weren't there, and show the credulous how to die with a smile on your lips and your hand on your heart while the orchestra plays a waltz'. Men on leave were asked by curious, but hopelessly naïve, civilians, 'Do you fight when it rains?', or even, 'Do you fight on Sundays?' As men of all nations discovered, their experience of warfare was so different from the life of a civilian that their experiences had to be disguised behind a series of clichés. In 1927, Paul Vaillant-Couturier wrote, 'The divorce between the Front and the Rear did not only stem from the inequality of risk. It was more an expression of the gap between classes – the class of the sacrificed, and those responsible for the prolongation of that sacrifice.'

Sooner or later, every rest period had to come to an end. Paul Tuffrau, an officer of the 246e RI, recorded some impressions of his regiment's departure from the village where it had been stationed:

> Men run hither and thither; a quartermaster announces that the coffee is ready and everyone can fill their water bottles; the machine gunners' mules shoot out of a side street ... the young washerwomen of the village, who have been eyeing up the soldiers since they arrived, put down their irons to watch ... this sudden departure to battle; men buckling on their packs whilst holding their rifle between their knees, while they watch and tease them.

Departure often called for some ceremony. Pierre Mac Orlan, a machine gunner with the 226e RI, wrote: 'the company marker flags were uncovered, the drums took the lead, followed by the CO, his runner and the battalion following. One blast on the whistle, the bugles ready themselves with a flourish, and all at once, the regimental march crashes out with all the power of brass and drums. The battalion, in step, arms at the slope, marches off to meet its new fate.'

BRITISH TOMMY

Martin Pegler

World War I was a watershed in British military and social history, and even now its repercussions can still be felt. Women's suffrage, the rise of the Labour movement, and an increasingly vociferous anti-military stance by politicians and populace were the results of those years of terrible conflict. No town or village in the British Isles escaped their casualties, and the loss to society was incalculable.

Germany was a formidable industrial power, politically bent on colonial expansion, and it posed a direct threat to British interests worldwide. Britain was as keen to protect its interests as Germany was to expand, and the will to wage war was strong on both sides. Britain had not fought in a European war since the defeat of Napoleon in 1815, but Germany had learned much from the Franco–Prussian War of 1870. The use, or more accurately misuse, of modern technology during that conflict had left its mark upon the minds of the Prussian generals. At the outbreak of war, their larger army had double the number of machine guns than Britain had, as well as a prepared strategy (which fortunately was not adhered to), an understanding of the devastating power of massed artillery, and defensive capabilities of entrenched troops against attacking infantry.

The stalemate for which the war became infamous had set in by winter 1914, and lasted until spring 1918. During that time, a continuous line of fortifications stretched from the Belgian coast to Switzerland. Over 5 million Englishmen were in uniform, drawn from all social classes, and the conflict cost Britain £7.5 million per day. Impressive though these figures are, they do not convey fully the true cost of the war on the people of the embattled nations, for this was total warfare, with civilians far removed from the front line becoming targets. Poison gas, flame-throwers, tanks, radio communications, even the indiscriminate bombing of civilian targets became an accepted part of warfare. By 1918 not only had the political map of Europe changed; so too had the psychology of warfare.

ENLISTMENT

It is a fact of life that men join armies for a multitude of reasons in peacetime. However, the outbreak of war in England in 1914 provoked a huge upsurge of patriotism that to modern minds is difficult to comprehend. It is therefore possible to generalize about the reasons for enlistment with perhaps more accuracy than would normally be acceptable.

Britain's professional army was small, around 247,000 men. As casualties mounted it became clear that this was insufficient to meet the needs of a European war. The Territorial Force, formed in 1908 from the Volunteers and Yeomanry, provided a stopgap of trained manpower to reinforce the British Expeditionary Force, but even this was rapidly proving inadequate. Field Marshal Lord Kitchener's call for 100,000 volunteers was met with such an overwhelming response that the War Office could not cope. From July to November 1914, 253,195 men voluntarily enlisted in Great Britain. Never before had the War Office had to deal with such numbers of recruits. The problems caused were manifold, not only logistically but socially, as classes who had hitherto only ever rubbed shoulders found themselves eating, sleeping and training together.

Why did so many young men rush to join the colours at a time when the reputation of the army was still an unsavoury one?

The answer appears to lie in three root causes: boredom, poverty and patriotism. Many veterans like Clarrie Jarman, 17th Battalion, the Queen's (Royal West Surrey) Regiment, recall the excitement generated by the war and the frustration of young men like himself stuck in futureless, poorly paid jobs:

I was 16, and working as a sales assistant at a big hardware merchants in Woking. I earned six bob [30p] a week, and worked from 7am to 7pm six days a week. I gave most of my money to my mother. I hated being at home, and the job wasn't exciting. When the recruiting sergeants and bands came round they seemed like the most interesting thing that ever happened in Woking.

Opposite:
A young Territorial artilleryman proudly wears the Imperial Service badge on his right breast, signifying that he has volunteered to serve overseas in the event of a war. (Mike Chappell)

CHRONOLOGY

PRINCIPAL BATTLES

23 August 1914	Mons	31 July–6 Nov 1917	Third Ypres/Passchendaele
26 August 1914	Le Cateau	20 Nov–7 Dec 1917	Cambrai
6–10 September 1914	Marne	21 March–5 April 1918	Somme
3–28 September 1914	Aisne	9–29 April 1918	Lys
10–31 October 1914	La Bassée	27 May–2 June 1918	Aisne
19 Oct–21 Nov 1914	First Ypres	15 July–4 Aug 1918	Marne
10–13 March 1915	Neuve Chapelle	8–12 August 1918	Amiens
22 April–24 May 1915	Second Ypres	21–31 August 1918	Bapaume
9 May 1915	Fromelles	26 Aug–3 Sept 1918	Scarpe
15–25 May 1915	Festubert	12–18 September 1918	Epehy
25 Sept–15 Oct 1915	Loos	27 Sept–5 Oct 1918	Cambrai
1 July–17 Nov 1916	Somme	28 September 1918	Flanders
9 April–16 May 1917	Arras	6–12 October 1918	Le Cateau
7–14 June 1917	Messines	17–25 October 1918	Selle
		1–11 November 1918	Sambre
		11 November 1918	Mons recaptured
		11 November 1918	Armistice signed

Although underage, he looked old enough to be the required 18, and enlisted with two chums in the Queen's Regiment for the princely sum of 5/- (25p) a week. Tens of thousands of other young men did the same.

Poverty was a big motivating factor. Many working-class men lived on or under the breadline, trying to support their families on minimal wages. Army doctors in 1914 noted that malnourishment was rife amongst applicants, some 44 per cent of whom could not attain the minimum 36in (91cm) chest size. For these men, the army offered a regular wage, better food and some excitement. Fred Wood, an unskilled labourer from working-class Sheffield, commented that although his companions complained about the food, in the first six weeks of training he put on 8lb (3kg). Like most recruits he enlisted for 'The Duration' – that is, until the war ended. His army enlistment was the best thing he ever did. He comments, 'The longer it went on, the happier I was.'

Sometimes motives were mixed. Fred Dixon, who joined the Surrey Yeomanry, spoke for many in explaining why he enlisted: 'All of us were terrified that it would all be over before we got there. We all prayed that the war would continue until we had a chance to do our duty.' Therein lay the clue for the third reason for joining up. Publicity about the plight of 'poor little Belgium', stories of atrocities and the spread of 'Hun frightfulness' aroused a genuine anger in many. Fearing German expansionism and the threat to Britain and its empire, men felt that it was their duty to fight, to 'do their bit'; this sense of patriotic outrage prompted many to join up. Fred Wood recalled his feelings at the time:

> People then were very naïve … we believed the newspaper reports, and one evening my chum Ginger said, 'We shouldn't let them get away with it.' We all agreed, so four of us went to the recruiting office and signed up. I was the only one who came back alive in 1918, though.

The procedure for enlisting was straightforward enough. Local recruitment centres were set up in Territorial Force drill halls or local town halls. Volunteers were given a basic medical examination, and if they passed swore an oath of allegiance, accepted the King's shilling, and returned home to await their call-up. The minimum age was 18, but recruiting officers turned a blind eye to many well-built

A sergeant and a corporal of the 1/16th (County of London) Battalion (Queen's Westminster Rifles), London Regiment, Territorial Force, pose for a camera before departing for France in 1914. (Douglas Honeychurch)

youths, as in the case of 15-year-old George Dawson, a railway engine cleaner, who enlisted in the 1st Battalion, Lincolnshire Regiment, and was serving in France at the age of 16. However, with so many enlisting, recruiting officers could afford to be rather more choosy in 1914 than they could later in the war.

If there was an overwhelming surge of patriotism amongst many men, there was an equal lack of interest amongst others. In many instances this was due to the belief that the war would not last for more than a matter of weeks, but there was a strong core of pacifists who did not believe in war as a means of solving political disputes. Many were imprisoned for their beliefs, but others like George Wells opted to join the Royal Army Medical Corps (RAMC) as orderlies. He commented, 'I believed then, as I still do, that there was no possible justification for killing, but I had no objection to saving lives. Many of my Quaker friends suffered because of public abuse, but I escaped all that because of being in uniform.'

Older men with settled careers and families were more reluctant to join up. They were not so swayed by lurid tales of German atrocities, and far less inclined to leave secure jobs for glory or excitement.

Many men were in jobs deemed vital for the war effort, and were refused permission to enlist. This was not a happy state of affairs for those who saw the army as a means of escape from a tedious job, and large numbers of men joined under assumed names to escape detection by irate bosses who could ill afford to lose skilled labour. Tom Setchell was a machinist making parts for engines. After two applications to his manager for permission to enlist were refused, he joined up under a false name and never went back to his old profession. He said that 'never once did I regret the choice. I ended up in the Engineers, and became a professional soldier after the war.'

By July 1915 the National Registration Act had recorded all men aged between 18 and 41, and in October of the same year the Derby Scheme created a system of short-term enlistment, with men then being placed on reserve until called up. Single men who were fit enough to serve were becoming a rare commodity by the end of 1915, so in January 1916 conscription was introduced. This meant all single men up to age 41 could be conscripted, and this was then extended to all married men later in the year. So scarce was manpower by

Arguably the most famous poster of all time. The stern gaze and accusing finger of Earl Kitchener of Khartoum left little doubt in the minds of patriotic Britons as to where their duty lay; the reputation of the great man was unassailable in 1914. (Mike Chappell)

1918 that the age for service was increased to 51. Up until February 1916, 2,631,000 men had volunteered. Conscription increased the number by another 2,340,000.

By whatever means the government ensured that men joined the army, there was no doubt that the world the men entered was unlike anything they had ever experienced before.

TRAINING

RECRUITMENT

Enlisting was a relatively straightforward process in 1914 providing one had plenty of patience. Huge crowds surrounded the temporary recruitment offices, with the police attempting to keep some semblance of order. For the new recruit, the process of taking the King's shilling was as much a matter of having patience as of possessing a good constitution and his own teeth. Once inside, a form of attestation was filled out: the biggest problem for many was the age factor (18 being the minimum). Many hopeful 16-year-olds were eyed speculatively by a regular sergeant and told, 'Hop it, and come back tomorrow when you're 18', followed by a conspiratorial wink.

The medical examination was not detailed. A doctor would check for obvious defects in eyesight, teeth and chest. TB was still endemic amongst working-class men and any sufferers would be summarily rejected. Those considered sound of mind and body were told to return home, where they would be given instructions in due course. Many who were rejected simply went to other recruiting stations where standards were known to be lower. Fred Wood, at 5ft 6in (1.7m) and with a 32in (82cm) chest, was turned away with the suggestion he 'got a bit bigger'. He therefore went to another area in his native Sheffield and was accepted without question.

Joining instructions for training battalions arrived at varying times. Some men received them within a week; others began to think the army didn't want them at all. Most were told to report to

Training in England. Men of a New Army infantry unit performing 'physical jerks' under the supervision of an instructor from the Army Gymnastic Staff, a corps of athletes dedicated to training units of the British Army to the peak of fitness before sending them off to fight. (Mike Chappell)

their local training depot. Clarrie Jarman was marched straight out of the recruitment hall to Stoughton barracks, home of the Queen's Regiment. The following day all the new recruits were sent by train to Purfleet in Essex, where they lived in tents from August 1914 to April 1915.

Training was designed not so much to teach the men the art of war as to toughen them. Drill, bayonet fighting, musketry and French digging were all taught. For men who were urban dwellers, the constant physical exercise was tough. Private Jarman recalled a typical training exercise: 'We marched from Colchester to Ipswich, 18 miles, where we stayed one night, then in five days we covered 150 miles over the Suffolk moors, living rough. We arrived back at Ipswich at 10pm. We were then roused at 11pm and made to march all night back to Colchester.'

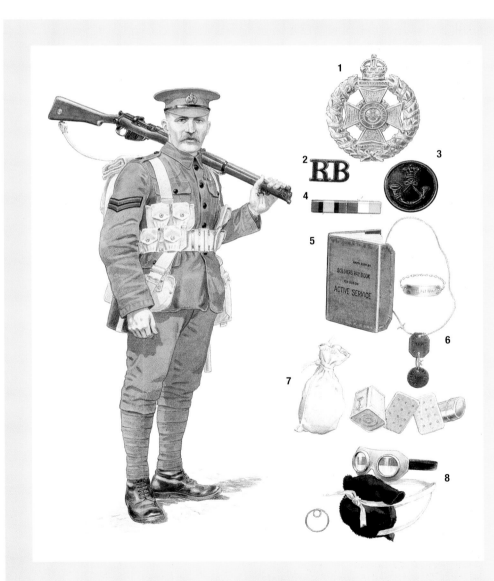

Corporal, Rifle Brigade, 1914
The NCO depicted is a typical 'Old Contemptible' regular of the original British Expeditionary Force serving with the 1st Battalion of his regiment in the 11th Infantry Brigade, 4th Division. He wears the 1908 pattern infantry equipment 'marching order', which contains 150 rounds of .303in rifle ammunition, water bottle, entrenching tool, bayonet, greatcoat, ground sheet, mess tin and rations, as well as personal items, etc. He carries a Short Magazine Lee-Enfield rifle Mk III. The insignia on the right includes the cap badge (**1**); the shoulder title (**2**) and black button (**3**) of the Rifle Brigade; and the ribbons of the Boer War (**4**). Also depicted are a record and pay book containing personal details (**5**); identity discs (official) and bracelets (unofficial) (**6**); a ration bag and emergency 'iron ration' tin (**7**); and a primitive gasmask (**8**). (Mike Chappell © Osprey Publishing Ltd)

LOGISTICS

The organization of food, clothing and billeting for the new volunteers was a massive and time-consuming undertaking. All over the country, Kitchener's new recruits were despatched to temporary billets, often miles from their training areas, and into the hands of redoubtable landladies, some of whom were less than pleased to have soldiers foisted upon them. There were wildly varying conditions dependent on area. Soldiers who joined locally raised units could find themselves treated as heroes by the populace, with free beer in the local pub and landladies who took to them as if they were their own sons. Fred Wood, by then in a Northern Cyclist battalion, found the opposite:

> We seemed to be nobody's children. We had no uniforms, so wore a khaki armband, and had to buy our own food. Pay was very irregular, and we had to walk four miles to be on parade at 6am. We got old Metfords [rifles] in February 1915, then spent all our time doing bayonet charges.

With army pay of 5/- (25p), rations allowance of 14s 7d (73p) and a retainer from their old firms, usually of half their weekly wage, some recruits had never been so well off. If their finances were improved, their humour was not: army discipline and the monotonous training exercises devised before the Boer War were rigidly adhered to as late as 1917. The concept of the machine gun was largely ignored, and soldiers were instructed in the art of marching in open formation towards 'the enemy' with the sole intention of 'getting to grips with the bayonet'. Fred Dixon wryly commented that 'most instructors were elderly regulars, who never heard a shot in anger. They bullied us, threatened us, but taught us nothing that was of any use in France. You learned that when you got there, if you lived long enough.' Much training consisted of endless drilling, intended to turn a man into an order-obeying machine. The more intelligent soldiers found this offensive, and some officers felt it robbed men of their initiative. This was particularly the case in the huge holding and drafting camps which sprang up around the coastal regions of France. As the demand for men increased, so did the need to speed up the passage of new recruits to the front. Many of these depots became notorious for the bullying that went on, and few men had a good word to say for them.

When not drilling, fatigues were the order of the day. Men had little spare time or energy for relaxation whilst training, and bitterly resented the dozens of sometimes pointless tasks devised for them by NCOs. Aside from guard and cookhouse duties, these could include polishing every conceivable article of military hardware, such as hobnails on boots, horse shoes, mess tins and bayonet blades. Some men accepted this as part of an inevitable process; others, particularly the better educated middle-class volunteers, considered it demeaning and unnecessary. The length of time spent training varied from unit to unit. Clarrie Jarman's unit trained from August 1914 to November 1915, although his observation on this was that they were taught nothing of any great relevance about trench warfare.

Until the early months of 1917 training followed a set pattern. Men were taught to drill, march and drill some more. Private Jarman, then a keen athlete, quite enjoyed the physical demands of training, but was sceptical of its practical value: 'We went on route marches, cross-country runs and were drilled like guardsmen. Sometimes we would have bayonet practice against a straw dummy and two or three times we went to the ranges, but that was as close to fighting training as we got. We had to learn that at the front.' After the Somme, there was a move towards informing men as to objectives (men were shown models of the proposed battlefields, for example), as well as closer cooperation between artillery and infantry, and the proper use of timing where mines were to be used.

Indeed, combat training was conspicuously lacking from the 1914 *Infantry Training* manual, written as it was in the days of open warfare. Men were instructed never to lie down and seek cover when advancing, but to walk steadily towards the enemy. Even pausing to fire was frowned upon, official thinking being that given the slightest excuse men would fling their weapons away and retreat, traits which the men of the Great War rarely exhibited. The appalling casualties inflicted brought about a gradual change in thinking by the close of the Somme campaign. It had become clear that the war could not be sustained if losses continued at the same rate. One estimate suggested that by mid-1918 16-year-old boys would have to be conscripted merely to continue the war effort at its current level. The entry of the United States proved this to be a pessimistic forecast; nevertheless, there was no doubt that lives could no longer be expended at such a rate.

As described in the first chapter, Germany had evolved a system of attack using shock troops (*Stosstruppen*), well-armed but lightly equipped units which would spearhead an assault, striking at strongpoints, machine gun positions and observation posts, robbing the enemy command of its defensive capability then moving on to let infantry units clear up. Although the Allies never entirely adopted the same system, a much more flexible approach to infantry assault had become evident by 1917. Fred Mowbray, who enlisted in 1917, recounted the following:

> We were taught things like advancing in short rushes and giving covering fire. As a Lewis gunner, I was told how to target pillboxes to make the Germans keep their heads down whilst the infantry went in with grenades. It all seemed very real and frightening. Not like I thought soldiering was going to be.

The tactical doctrines of pre-1914 had to change, in the same way that the technology of the war had changed.

UNIFORM AND EQUIPMENT

For the front line soldier, the issue uniform did not change to any great extent during the war years. The Kitchener recruits faced an acute shortage of almost everything, and were initially issued with blue serge uniforms until a supply of khaki arrived. Once it did, the soldier could expect to live, sleep, fight and die in it. The service dress comprised a hip-length four-pocket jacket, with a collar that buttoned up to the neck. The trousers had provision for braces on the outside and vertical slash pockets in the side seams, and were of the same rough woollen serge cloth as the tunic. Worn with the issue long drawers, long-sleeved vest and heavy flannel shirt, they caused the wearer to become unbearably hot in summer, as Private Jarman recalled: 'In summer on long route marches, the boys would be running with perspiration, and some of the new recruits, who weren't as fit as us, fainted from the heat. Even in shirtsleeve order it was hot. We wore the same uniform summer or winter.' An unofficial but popular summer modification to the trousers was to cut the legs off to make shorts.

In addition, B5 ammunition boots with hobnailed soles were standard issue at the start of the war. They were made from reversed hide (undyed), had steel plates on the toes and heels, and were heavily greased. Woollen puttees were wound around the lower legs. Fred Wood was reduced to helpless laughter by the attempts of his fellows to tie the puttees neatly: 'Some chaps had them tied from ankle to knees, others wound them round and round their calves like bandages. We were saved by an older man who had served in the Boer War, who showed us the trick. They were awful

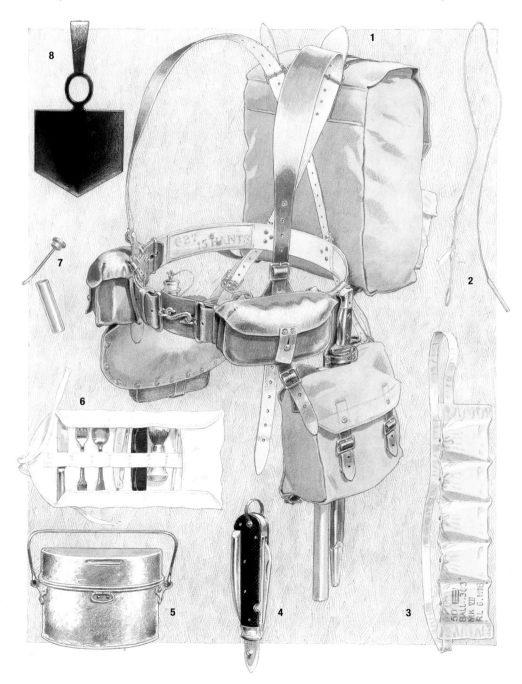

British infantry equipment, 1914–18. This shows the 1914 pattern leather infantry equipment (1), assembled in its full 'marching' configuration with the pack buckled to the back and the haversack on the left side. Other items carried include a whipcord 'pull through' for cleaning the rifle's bore (2); extra ammunition carried in a cotton bandoleer (3); a jack-knife (4); a mess tin (5); a 'holdall' for items such as cutlery, razor, comb, lather brush, toothbrush, etc (6); an oil bottle (7); and a mattock-head of an entrenching tool (8). (Mike Chappell © Osprey Publishing Ltd)

things.' In subsequent trench warfare, it was found that tightly wound puttees restricted the blood flow to the feet to such an extent that trench foot and even gangrene could occur in the constant wet and muddy conditions.

Headgear was a simple soft peaked cap, which soon had its wire support removed to give it a battered look. Later the 'Gor blimey' (a soft cap with ear flaps) was issued, to be replaced by a soft cap without flaps. This new trench cap had a more military appearance than the 'Gor blimey' and could be rolled or folded and put away when the shrapnel helmet was worn. The trench cap was standard issue from 1917 onwards. However many soldiers retained their 'Gor blimey' caps where possible for use in winter weather.

There were several types of personal equipment in use at this time. Regular and territorial battalions were issued the 1908 pattern web equipment. New army units (those raised under the Kitchener volunteer system) were usually issued the 1914 pattern leather equipment. Will Wells, who arrived in France with the 'Manchesters' early in 1916, noted, 'We were told to hand in our old leather equipment, and were given salvaged sets of webbing. Mine was stiff with dried blood, and I swapped it for a decent set as soon as I could.'

1908 pattern equipment comprised a pack and a haversack, a set of ammunition pouches holding 150 .303in rounds of ammunition, an entrenching tool, a water bottle and a mess tin. The pack and haversack might contain spare socks, a shirt, underwear, a greatcoat, a blanket, emergency rations and a washing and shaving kit. A popular army joke featured a small boy asking his father, 'What are soldiers for?' 'To hang things on' was the reply. The latest addition to His Majesty's Army found it too true to be funny. A full set of equipment could weigh in excess of 70lb (32kg), about the same as a medieval suit of armour.

The most instantly recognizable symbol of the British Tommy was, of course, the steel helmet. These were issued on a trial basis late in 1915, and were officially referred to as 'shrapnel helmets'. So effective were they in preventing fatal head wounds (a reduction of 80 per cent was calculated) that full-scale production was authorized by the government, and by the end of the war over 7.5 million had been manufactured. Initially, many soldiers found them irritating: 'I had worn a soft hat since the start [of the war] and the steel helmet felt like a lump of lead on my head. I hated it until a lump of shrapnel knocked me senseless at Cambrai. It saved my life, and I regarded it with some fondness afterwards' (J. Dalton, Tank Corps). The helmet was designed so that the chin strap retaining rivets would shear in the event of the helmet being blown off: this would avoid garroting the wearer or breaking his neck. Experienced soldiers in action wore the helmet tilted slightly forward for maximum protection.

Another vital piece of headgear was that potent symbol of the war, the gasmask. Early lachrymatory and sternutatory gases had the same effect as tear gas, although they rarely proved fatal. The first masks were simply cotton wool pads soaked in neutralizing chemicals, or urine if no chemical was available. These were replaced by the P and PH helmet (so called because the fabric of the helmet was impregnated with a chemical solution, Phenate Hexamine). The wearer breathed in through the nose, drawing air through the material of the hood and out through the mouthpiece, which was a simple non-return valve.

In late 1916 the box respirator was introduced. This was a rubberized mask with a long tube attached to a filtration unit. Jim Marshall had reason to be grateful for his. Whilst carrying their Vickers gun into position at Arras, his team came under sudden bombardment:

Next page:
British troops blinded by tear gas wait outside an Advance Dressing Station, near Béthune. Each man has his hand on the shoulder of the man in front of him, in an image reminiscent of John Singer Sargent's painting *Gassed* featured on the front cover of this book. (IWM, 11586)

Our sergeant noticed that some shells were not exploding, and called, 'Gas, gas!' We dropped everything and pulled our masks on, but not before we had taken a whiff of it. I was coughing something terrible, but daren't take the mask off. We had to lug the guns into position, mount them and stand at readiness, all with the masks on. It was a couple of hours later that an officer came up and asked why we still had our masks on, as the all clear had been sounded ages before. Our sergeant felt a right fool, but we reckoned better safe than sorry. We were all frightened of gas.

Once an effective means of combating gas had been introduced, its use as a practical weapon diminished, but it still exacted a steady toll of casualties throughout the war.

As with any army on a period of long active service, issue clothing was modified, adapted or discarded according to need and conditions. It became clear that the service clothing was deficient in some respects. Greatcoats were not waterproof, and once weighed down with rain and mud soon became unwearable. Boots and puttees were impractical in sodden trenches, and the tunic was not warm enough in winter. Men often added their own clothing sent out from home or purchased locally, and most wore home-made sweaters, scarves and socks. The problem of supplying warm clothing that did not hamper movement was addressed by the War Office, and in 1915 goatskin jerkins were issued. Private Dalton, initially sent to Flanders with the Royal Marines, noted that although 'they were quite warm, they stank to high heaven when they were wet and soon became clogged with mud'. In late 1916, a sleeveless leather jerkin with a blanket lining was issued. This proved both comfortable and durable, and remained in service for numerous years afterwards. For wet weather there was a rubberized cape (introduced 1917), with a collar and a button-up front. Although hot to wear, it was genuinely waterproof, and could also be used as a groundsheet, or attached to another to form a shelter. Prior to this soldiers used a rectangular groundsheet, which was draped over the shoulders.

Protection for the legs was more difficult. Wrapping empty sandbags around calves and thighs gave additional warmth and to a certain extent protected against the mud. Thigh-length waders became an important part of trench clothing. These were issued as fixed stores and would be inherited by each battalion upon taking over a new trench. They were only effective up to a point, as Harry Wood experienced:

On our way we passed a man stuck to his waist in a drainage sump. We gathered round and got some trench timbers under his arms to give him support. We pulled him out eventually but he left behind his waders, boots and trousers. He was so exhausted he had to be stretchered to an aid post.

There was less latitude with headgear, particularly in view of the necessity of wearing a steel helmet for protection. In winter, a cap comforter was often worn underneath. This was a simple woollen tube which doubled as a hat or scarf. Soft caps were invariably worn out of the line.

Many tests were carried out with bulletproof waistcoats, and a number of types were privately purchased. Examples such as Dayfield, BEF, Wilkinson and Pullman were a few of those available. In 1917 the EOB (Experimental Ordnance Board) was issued officially on a limited basis. Like most of its type it was heavy at $9\frac{1}{2}$lb (4.3kg) and hot to wear, but it could stop a service .455

pistol bullet, or a rifle round providing it was not travelling at more than 1,000 fps, about one-third of its initial velocity.

On the whole, British clothing was solidly made and there were few shortages, which, considering the number of men to be clothed, is quite remarkable. Some of the logistical statistics are quite mind numbing. For example 45,351,488 pairs of boots and 137,224,141 pairs of socks were supplied in four years! It is worth noting that few soldiers were ever seen wearing items of pilfered German clothing, whereas, by 1917, British boots, jerkins and groundsheets had become prized booty amongst German troops.

WEAPONS

THE RIFLE

The outbreak of war saw the British Army equipped with the Short Magazine Lee-Enfield (SMLE), but soon the old Long Lee-Enfield and a variety of other weapons were pressed into service.

With the introduction of the SMLE in 1903 Britain became the first major power to abandon the idea of issuing carbines to cavalry units and rifles to infantry. The SMLE was issued to both. It was shorter and lighter than any other current service rifle of the time and usefully, as it turned out, was easier to wield than the Mauser in the close confines of a trench.

It took some skill to master, and most young recruits developed a healthy respect for the recoil, as Fred Dixon remembered:

A 9.2in gun on a Mk I railway mounting in action at Maricourt, September 1916. Chalked or painted on the side of the mounting is 'The Big Push', the name by which operations astride the River Somme were commonly known. (IWM, Q4297)

> We were taken to the ranges in Colchester and issued with 25 rounds of .303 [ammunition]. The instructor went through the safety routine, then told us to fire 10 rounds aimed. I didn't hold the butt tight enough into my shoulder, and when I pulled the trigger I was sure I'd broken my collar bone. Firing the rest was agony, and I was black and blue for a week after.

Many soldiers were shipped to France having barely mastered the art of shooting, and the skill at arms of the pre-war Regular Army had vanished by 1916. For trench fighting, the rifle was really not the most practical weapon, particularly when 17in (44cm) of bayonet was attached to it. It was, however, extremely powerful, the bullet being capable of penetrating 18in (46cm) of oak and 36in (91cm) of earth-packed sandbags, as well as a double thickness of housebricks at 200 yards (185m). In skilled hands, hits at 1,000 yards (925m) were quite feasible, the bullet having an extreme aimed range of over double that distance.

PISTOLS, HAND GRENADES AND TRENCH CLUBS

For close combat work, infantrymen often obtained pistols (captured German Lugers were a great favourite), particularly when patrols or trench raiding were called for. Although not officially issued to infantrymen, revolvers were carried by specialists, such as machine gunners, despatch riders, tank crew and Royal Engineers. The three most commonly issued types were all in service .455in calibre, and comprised the Mk V or VI Webley, Colt New Service, and Smith & Wesson Hand Ejector. All were difficult to shoot well without considerable practice, although the heavy bullets were effective. Perhaps the skill required to master the rifle and pistol was one of the reasons for the popularity of the hand grenade, more of which were issued than any other form of weapon. Over 61 million were produced, of which the most effective type was the No.5, commonly known as the Mills bomb. It had a simple spring-actuated fuse mechanism, and could be thrown quite accurately to about 30 yards (27m). It had a tendency to break into irregular fragments on detonation, due to the offset (as opposed to central) position of the explosive. The Mills bomb was extremely effective and survived long into the post-World War II era. Corporal James Allsop testified to its efficiency in a raid in June 1916:

> We had to get prisoners, so we had a big 'do' set up. I was one of the mopping up party, to make sure the Jerries didn't come out of their dug-outs behind us. Well, we put up a barricade in the [German] trench and as our chaps headed back with prisoners, Jerry came at us. We couldn't hold them back, and they brought a Maxim up, so I lobbed a bomb and ducked behind the traverse. When the smoke cleared there were six Jerries on the ground. The rest hid, they wouldn't argue with a Mills.

Home-made and issue trench clubs were also handy weapons in a fight, and came in a variety of shapes and sizes.

Entrenching tool handles studded with nails, cut-down machine gun barrels and sprung steel coshes all made an appearance. Issue clubs usually comprised a length of stout wood with a rough cast-iron head or steel cap. All were crude, but effective enough, as were the trench knives used. Sheath knives, cut-down bayonets and a number of proprietary knives such as the Robbins punch dagger and bizarre Pritchard revolver bayonet were all carried, although little evidence exists of their use in action. As one wit dryly remarked of the bayonet, 'It has no place in warfare except as a candleholder, in which capacity it excels.'

Officers had abandoned their swords after 1914, but not so the cavalry, who were issued with the pattern 1908 sword. Designed for thrusting, its clean lines and slim blade made it an effective weapon. The cavalry of 1914–18 could function in a traditional role or, increasingly, as mobile infantry. Most ended the war as dismounted infantrymen, armed with the universal SMLE. Ironically, with the return of mobile warfare in 1918, the BEF suffered from a shortage of horsed cavalry.

MACHINE GUNS

At platoon and battalion level, machine guns had begun to dominate tactics by 1915. Most were based on the Maxim design, and, although reliable, they were costly to manufacture, complex to operate (it took ten intensive weeks to train a Vickers gunner) and very cumbersome. A loaded Vickers weighed about 100lb (45kg) and consumed huge quantities of ammunition. In a long-range barrage, a single gun could easily fire 100,000 rounds, with some companies recording nearly a million fired rounds over a 24-hour period. Although it was extremely efficient, it was clear from early in the war that a lighter automatic weapon was needed, and this came in the form of the American-designed Lewis gun.

The Lewis was the first effective light machine gun issued, although 'light' was a relative term, as a loaded one weighed an impressive 29lb (13kg). With its 550rpm cyclic rate it gave a squad of infantry the equivalent firepower of a section. Its 47-round drum magazine produced a distinctive football rattle clatter when the weapon was fired, and although it was prone to a bewildering number of stoppages (one manual lists 33), it was well liked. Fred Mowbray, a private in the King's Royal Rifle Corps, was a Lewis gunner, and liked its solid build quality as well as the effectiveness of its firepower. His section, held up by a pillbox during the advance of 1918, called him forward to deal with the defenders. He emptied two drums through the firing slit and rushed the box. Although he had knocked out the Maxim crew inside, a second gun hidden behind the pillbox caught him with a sweeping burst. Hit across the arms and stomach by six bullets, the impact lifted him off his feet, flinging him and his gun into a shell crater. With bullets through his left hand and right elbow, his war, but not his life, was over. He was still alive because the solid steel receiver and breech assembly of the Lewis absorbed the impact of the other rounds. He had hated the weight of the Lewis, but commented wryly that 'the old Lewis gave me as much protection as a suit of armour. Mind you, it was nearly as heavy.'

OTHER WEAPONS

The trenches were a breeding ground for weapons, many of them bordering on the bizarre. Some were designed as a response to a specific need, whilst others appear to reflect the short-sightedness of the inventor. Some, like the West bomb-thrower, were theoretically quite sound. It was no more

Men of the Machine Gun Corps operating a Vickers machine gun and (background) a captured German Maxim gun near Mouquet Farm, the Somme, September 1916. This is in fact a posed scene – neither gunner has raised the backsight on his gun. (IWM, Q1418)

than a small steel-framed variant of a medieval trebuchet, relying on several very strong coil springs to provide power and fling a hand grenade several hundred yards. However, the springs proved so strong that several operators were injured when the machine fired itself prematurely. Others flung live grenades into the parapet of their own trenches.

The problem of grenade-launching was soon solved by either attaching a short rod to a Mills bomb, or fitting a steel discharger cup to the muzzle of an SMLE, both of which would safely launch a grenade.

The service rifle was often the means by which less than practical inventions were introduced to the luckless infantryman. Two ideas that were issued in some quantity offered solutions to the problem of wire cutting. One comprised a spring-loaded pair of jaws that required the rifle to be used as a lever, forcing the cutting edges together and (theoretically) severing the wire. This required the hapless soldier to stand upright, unwise when in full view of the enemy. The other was a forked bar that clamped onto the rifle's muzzle, which was then pushed over the wire strand, and the trigger pulled. The bullet then cut the wire. As many belts of wire were yards deep, the amount of ammunition one man would have to expend is best left to the imagination.

Other weapons were more practical. Trench mortars, invaluable for their almost vertical trajectory, were an area in which Britain at first lagged behind Germany. The first British pattern fired a 60lb (27kg) spherical cast-iron bomb, nicknamed the 'toffee apple', attached to a steel shaft. On firing, the shaft often snapped, leaving the eventual destination of the bomb uncertain, and a direct hit

30 July 1916: the battle of Pozières Ridge on the Somme – an 18pdr RFA gun crew pose for the camera near Montauban. (They would not be firing with horses to their front.) All the ammunition lying ready is high explosive shell which, with less than a pound of explosive, was less destructive than a 3in mortar bomb. Clearly visible is the pole trail which limited the 18pdr's elevation and thus its range. (IWM, Q4325)

improbable. However, from this early design of projector emerged the highly successful Stokes mortar, which in turn was the model upon which the majority of modern mortar designs are based.

Trench warfare also revealed the deficiencies in service weapons. A rifle and bayonet were too cumbersome for trench fighting, but, curiously, Britain made no attempt to produce a practical semi-automatic rifle or sub-machine gun, unlike Germany and France. The US Army introduced the eminently practical Model 1897 Winchester pump-action shotgun decried by the War Ministry as 'un-military'. Semi-automatic pistols did make a significant appearance, however, as mud often clogged service revolvers, an occurrence to which semi-autos were relatively impervious. In addition, they were quicker to reload, had a greater cartridge capacity, and found favour with both officers and other ranks. Jim Marshall had a rare Webley .455in semi-automatic:

> I got it from an Aussie, who had got it from a pilot. It was a lovely gun, and during the big retreat in 1918 I used it in anger several times. I modified my holster to carry it, and nobody said I couldn't. The only trouble was ammunition, as it took special .45in cartridges. It was very powerful, and quite accurate. I shot a Jerry machine gunner, and one of my section gave me his helmet. The bullet had gone clean through, and I measured the distance afterwards at 45 yards [41m].

ACTIVE SERVICE

TRENCH LIFE

Few recruits had any real concept of the realities of life 'at the front'. For most recruits, their first taste of the war was an audible one, as Clarrie Jarman recalled:

> We arrived at Amiens by train, and could hear a rumble in the distance, which was the artillery. We marched to Dornancourt and went into the line for the first time. The bullets whizzed and cracked, and made us duck. The shells whined overhead, but we learned quickly when to take cover and when not to.

The trenches varied greatly in construction and comfort. In Belgium, the high water table prevented deep trenches being dug, so breastworks of sandbags with wooden retaining supports were constructed. In France, the chalky soil lent itself well to deep trenches, with high parapets built up with sandbags giving some cover against sniping. Deep dug-outs gave protection to headquarters and resting soldiers, and during heavy bombardments. However, for most a 'funk hole' scraped into the facing wall of the trench and lined with rubber capes was the best that could be expected. It was not the policy of the General Staff to encourage British troops to make themselves too comfortable, as it was felt that it discouraged 'the offensive spirit'. The Germans had no such qualms, and built concrete-lined dug-outs as deep as 60ft (18m) beneath the ground – impervious to the heaviest shelling. Trench routine was physically demanding. 'Stand-To' was at dawn, where all troops would man the trench in expectation of an enemy attack. Wet weather was universally hated. In Flanders, the poor drainage often forced both sides to abandon their trenches for higher ground, as water levels rose to waist height. A tacit truce was usually observed. The chalk

Men of the 13th Battalion, Durham Light Infantry (23rd Division), rest in a communication trench before the attack on Veldhoek, one of the battles of Third Ypres (Passchendaele), September 1917. In addition to their personal arms and equipment, they are encumbered with picks and shovels, rolls of sandbags, Lewis gun magazine panniers, 'bombs' and bandoliers of extra small-arms ammunition. Note that not all the ground fought over in this campaign was the rain-sodden marshland so often described. (IWM, Q5965)

of the Somme clung in 10lb (4.5kg) balls to men's feet and exhausted even the fittest of men. Such conditions meant that a 500yd (460m) journey could take several hours. If the line was being shelled, or under sniper fire, then those manning the trenches were effectively trapped until nightfall. Winter conditions reduced the line to a series of sludge-filled ditches, from which there was no escape, save leave or a wound. But if winter was grim, it was more than compensated for by spring and summer. The shell-churned soil became ablaze with poppies, cornflowers and a host of other species. Larks, unaccountably still resident, would hover, trilling in the sky. Few soldiers forgot the beauty that sprang up amidst the desolation, even in the face of battle. Some never had the chance to adapt to trench life. Curiosity was a killer, and any who risked a look over the parapet seldom lived to repeat the experience. Sixteen-year-old Private George Dawson was shot in the head on his first day in the trenches, dying shortly afterwards. Until 1915 German snipers, who had learned their trade hunting in the vast German forests, dominated the trenches, but by 1916 Britain was producing well-trained men more than capable of controlling No Man's Land.

Occupation of the trenches depended upon conditions. A usual tour of duty was four to seven days in the line, the same in reserve and a week at rest. At Ypres in 1917, torrential rain and broken drainage ditches turned the ground into a swamp, and 24 hours was the maximum men could stand such exposure. After major battles, particularly hard-hit units would be placed in quiet sectors, where unofficial 'live and let live' policies ensured that front line service was not too arduous. That being so, average casualties in 'quiet' sectors would be 40 per month. There was no such thing as a safe place at the front, as Jim Marshall of the Machine Gun Corps had learned:

> We had just come out of the line, and were heading back to our billets when Jerry dropped a couple of shells in front of us. We didn't take any notice, they were always doing it, when there was an almighty roar and flash. Next thing I was lying in the road yards away. I had my tunic ripped off and the tripod [for the Vickers gun] vanished. I was completely deaf, but not hurt much. They never found two of my chums and the other died at the aid post.

As many soldiers saw it, trench life was '90 per cent routine and 10 per cent terror'. The hardest thing to endure was shellfire. There were no means of retaliation for the ordinary infantryman, who had no option but to seek the deepest shelter possible and endure it. The older men held up better under fire than the young ones, whom they would try to encourage. Jim Wooley of the West Yorkshire Regiment recalled a 4-hour bombardment in a dug-out full of shell fumes, with dirt falling from the creaking roof timbers: 'We had a new lad, who'd not been with us long. After a bit he started sobbing, and one of our chaps who had a young son moved next to him and put his arms round him. After a bit the lad began to recover. Things like that often happened.'

Trench mortars were also a feared hazard, but could be beaten. In trenches known to be targeted, a lookout would watch for the tell-tale black speck of a mortar bomb rising from the German lines. He would then blow a whistle to alert men, and if he was experienced enough shout 'Left!' or 'Right!' to indicate the direction they should run to escape the blast. The explosive effect from the bigger mortars was devastating, and those caught in the proximity stood no chance. Fred Wood was one of a working party called to find survivors after such a detonation. Ten men were missing, but only sufficient remains were found to fill two sandbags. If the site of the mortars could be pinpointed, calls were placed to the artillery for emergency retaliation, which invariably raised a cheer from the British lines. In extreme cases, the artillery could also be called upon to deal with a persistent sniper.

For much of the time, trench life was a regime of monotonous routine with dangerous overtones. The stress of living under the constant threat of sudden death or wounding affected men in different ways. Some simply couldn't take the strain and went absent, risking a capital sentence from a court-martial.

Others found ways of disabling themselves, the most common being using a rifle to shoot themselves through the hand or foot. Some would deliberately expose an arm or shoulder above the trench to encourage a sniper's shot. Such self-inflicted wounds, if discovered, were severely dealt with by the army. The soldiers themselves took a less judgmental view. Fred Wood, a sergeant by then, spoke for many:

> By 1918 those of us who had survived were sick to death of the war. We reckoned we'd done our bit, and it was up to the shirkers who'd avoided the war to have a go. I was very fatalistic by then. I didn't think I could survive, and wondered how I had managed up till then. When a chum of mine, who'd been out since 1915, reported to the MO with a bullet through the hand we knew it hadn't been an accident. But we didn't blame him at all. Many times I wished I'd had the courage to do the same.

Hot food could be brought up to the men in forward trenches in insulated containers – very large vacuum flasks – such as these being inspected at Arras in winter 1917. Note that the man under inspection seems to wear a long-sleeved sheepskin jacket. More often, rations were simply carried up in sandbags. (IWM, Q4832)

FOOD

Predictably, the soldier's main preoccupation was with his stomach. The official rations for British soldiers in the line would have raised a cheer had they always been issued – 1½lb fresh meat or 1lb salt meat, 1lb biscuit or flour, 4oz bacon, 3oz cheese, ½lb tea, 4oz jam, 3oz sugar, 2oz dried or 8oz fresh vegetable, 2oz tobacco and ½ a gill of rum per day. Front line troops were frequently hungry, as rations failed to reach them through shelling or improper allocations. Private Jarman noted that 'our main food in the line was bully stew. We shared one loaf between four men. Sometimes a ration of cheese or butter would arrive, usually when we had no bread. Tins of biscuits were always there to eat. They were like dog biscuits.'

The ubiquitous hardtack biscuit was the colour and consistency of concrete, 3½ x 4in (90 x 100mm) and could crack teeth if bitten into. When pulverized by a rifle butt and mixed with bully beef, it could be fried, or soaked overnight and mixed with currants and dried fruit and boiled into a duff. In cold weather, when no charcoal was available, it also burned satisfactorily. Some soldiers even believed that attached to an entrenching tool handle, it would make a fearsome club. Fred Wood's opinion of the rations is largely unprintable:

After 'stand-to' we'd cook breakfast. This was usually some old bacon with bits of sandbag stuck to it, fried up in a Dixie. The only things we ever had plenty of to eat was bully, biscuits and plum and apple jam. Out of the line we spent all our money on food. If the carrying party could get through the shells, we'd have hot stew for lunch. If not it was bloody bully stew again. Sometimes we'd have Maconochie [a brand of tinned stew which was quite popular] or cheese and raw meat, [which would arrive] all mixed in the same sandbag. I never once had eggs or fresh fruit. Once I got a loaf that was all bloody, but we scraped the worst off and ate it. We were treated like beasts, and I never thought it was fair.

The issue of a rum ration was a saving grace, especially in the winter months. At breakfast time an NCO with a large earthenware jar marked 'SRD' (Service Rations Department) would carefully dole out a measure to each man. It was Navy rum, not diluted, and its strength caught many unawares, leaving them watery-eyed and coughing. After a freezing night men insisted that they could feel its warmth spreading out into their fingers and toes, and if they exaggerated the physical effect, then it was certainly worth its issue for boosting morale.

Also eagerly awaited were the parcels sent from home. Packed by mothers, wives, sweethearts or simply collected by local people and sent en masse, their contents were a welcome diversion from the basic food rations. Sometimes, though, the contents were not so useful. John Dalton once received a parcel from a schoolgirl in his home town that consisted of 'three pairs of very small socks, boiled sweets, a crushed fruit cake, a bible, a tin of vermin powder and a tract exhorting the reader to give up alcohol'. For many men at the front, parcels provided a lifeline with home, with small comforts such as tobacco, underwear, books and a host of other small items improving the lives of the recipients.

Soldiers were past masters at 'scrounging', and many a meal was supplemented by fruit from nearby orchards, vegetables from garden plots, and even fresh meat if a farmer was unlucky to have an ex-butcher amongst the men billeted with him. After a Scottish battalion had left a well-stocked farm near Arras, the farmer claimed for the loss of '32 chickens and one pig'. Officially the CO

An elderly woman serves coffee to British troops at a French *estaminet* behind the lines at Croix du Bac near Armentières. The *estaminets* of the Western Front were one of the first ports of call for troops just out of the trenches. (IWM, Q635)

determined that they had been lost through enemy action, and his men were not responsible. Roast pork was served in the officers' mess for three days afterwards. Incidents such as this occurred throughout the front lines.

RELAXATION AND LEAVE

Not all of the reinforcements sent to the Western Front in 1918 were callow boys; here men of the 1/5th Battalion, Devonshire Regiment, take their ease, July 1918. They had recently arrived in France via Marseilles having spent the years since 1914 in India and the Middle East. (Mike Chappell)

Once out of the line, there were few places for soldiers to go. The most popular were the *estaminets* found in every village. A cross between a café and a pub, they were the focal point for most off-duty soldiers. Wine and beer were cheap, and *oeufs et pommes frites* were usually available, especially in exchange for a few tins of bully beef or jam. French women were less inhibited than their British counterparts, and many fond liaisons were formed. Most of the larger towns had red light districts, but social taboos were not easily shaken off. Will Wells spoke for many when he recalled his attitude towards the 'pleasure parlours': 'They were used by a certain sort – none of my friends would have dreamed of it, although we were curious. A lot of Australians and Canadians went there, but they had a different upbringing and of course they were paid more.' Money was always in short supply.

The majority of men allocated most of their pay to wives or parents, which left little for having a good time. The mere fact of being out of danger and in convivial company was enough to cheer up the most dour soldier. A few weak French beers added to the moment, and evenings would be spent singing, telling tall tales and being cheeky to the young girls who always seemed to inhabit the *estaminets* and bars.

Home leave was a rare commodity, and once every 14 months was an average. Usually no warning was given, simply a 'chit' detailing 'seven days leave, starting immediately'. Soldiers would arrive home filthy, lousy and exhausted, but it was worth it. Fred Wood spent five days sleeping, having the luxury of a hot bath whenever he felt like it, and reading. Others enjoyed a more hectic social life, frequently in local pubs. Married men preferred the comfort and companionship of their families, and most found leaving them to return to the front a terrible ordeal. As much as anything, the sudden removal from peace and safety to a life of death and destruction was hard to reconcile. George Wells, upon arriving back in France, commented that within two days of his return to the front line, he was embroiled in a savage and major battle: 'The life I had left behind was as remote to me as the moon, and I felt that the front was all I had ever known. Nothing else seemed real.'

This was an attitude that became more acute the longer a man served and that was common among all soldiers, enemy or ally. The life of comparative safety that existed in Britain seemed totally unreal compared to front line service. A soldier's friends, their shared daily experiences and constant exposure to death in a multitude of forms was the reality that mattered. It was almost impossible for a man to convey the reality of life at the front to family or friends, even if social convention had permitted such frank discussions.

When Harry Wood was on leave, having a quiet drink in his local, a family friend came up and slapped him on the back, commenting, 'I suppose you've been having the time of your life, young fellow.' Years later, Harry said, 'What I wanted to do was tell him what it was like to watch a man sniped in the head die, or collect up the parts of someone caught by a shell. But it just wasn't done, so I drank up and walked out.' It was a gulf that grew wider as the war progressed, and which never closed. As one veteran said, 'Either you had been at the front, or you hadn't. That was all there was to it.'

For the vast majority of soldiers who had never before been abroad there were a multitude of attractions in the larger French towns, where the oddities of French life proved a constant source of fascination. Cafés, patisseries, restaurants and souvenir shops soon exhausted carefully hoarded funds, and evenings saw groups of men in varying stages of intoxication weaving unsteadily back to outlying billets before their leave passes expired, leaving them open to a charge.

Although gambling was officially forbidden, there wasn't a regiment that didn't have its resident clique of near-professional gamblers. One of the most popular games was 'Crown and Anchor', which, although discouraged, was seldom officially prohibited. Card games of all sorts were popular. Some of the Irish soldiers in particular gained a popular reputation for their willingness to bet on anything, and one tale tells of two men standing in the open during an intense artillery bombardment, betting on when a particular landmark would be hit. When a flying splinter badly injured one, his friend insisted on carrying him back to an aid post. Refusing congratulations for his bravery, he insisted, 'If I hadn't brought the old devil back I'd never have got the five bob he owes me!'

Religion was an important social factor, most men having been brought up with some form of belief. The army catered for the major denominations, with Catholic and Anglican clerics attached to most battalions. Out of the line, church parades were compulsory, but the minority religious groups were left pretty much to their own devices. Men who entered their religion as atheist to avoid church parades usually found themselves doing extra cookhouse fatigues instead.

In the shared dangers of the line, belief was a common bond, not a division as it so often became in peacetime. It was not uncommon for prayers to be heard during lulls in particularly heavy bombardments. Thousands of men took great comfort in the facilities provided at Christian centres such as Toc H in Poperinghe, or the numerous YMCA rest rooms. Quite often they were the only place that men could relax in a civilized manner, and read or write. Tea, chocolate and food were always available at modest prices, and the dehumanizing effect of the trenches could temporarily be thrown off.

DISCIPLINE

There was a strong tradition of repressive discipline in the army of 1914. The Regular Army was used to dealing with tough men, often ex-labourers, unskilled and poorly educated. The men of the New Armies were a different breed. Willing volunteers, they came from a wider social cross-section, and many were of officer material. They expected to be treated as civilized men, not cannon fodder, but few exceptions were made for them except in New Army and Territorial units, where a looser disciplinary system could often be found, especially in the earlier years of the war.

Even for the best behaved soldier, it was difficult to avoid some form of punishment, albeit for a trivial offence. During the retreat from Mons in 1914, it was declared a punishable offence to 'steal fruit from the trees of a friendly nation'.

Army regulations list 27 punishable offences, from 'War Treason' down to 'False Answering'. Most soldiers fell foul of the rules at some point. Private Wood noted that 'thieving was common, and if you had your cap or shirt pinched, well, you had to pinch another or get crimed for it'. Punishments meted out depended on a number of factors. If a regiment were in the line, then minor crimes tended to be treated with less severity, but the general conduct of a soldier and the testimony of his officer or senior NCO would count for a great deal. Many good soldiers in the line had reputations as troublemakers out of it. Private Marshall recalled a sergeant who was regularly reduced to the ranks after picking drunken fights with the detested 'Redcaps', the Military Police. Once in the line, his coolness and authority always earned him back his stripes.

Others were punished more severely. During the war over 300 men were shot for offences ranging from cowardice to sleeping on duty. Less drastic was 'field punishment No.1', which involved being tied to a gunwheel or T-shaped frame and having to remain on public view for a set number of hours each day, no matter what the weather conditions. Although not painful, it was certainly uncomfortable and humiliating.

The experienced NCOs took into account the strain of warfare on their men, and exercised a paternal control over them. When, after two days without rest, 18-year-old Jimmy Hughes dozed off when on sentry, he was shaken awake by his company sergeant-major, who told him, 'If Jerry

came over now he'd shoot you. That's nothing compared to what I'll do if I catch you asleep again.' He then gave Hughes a sip from a flask full of rum, leaving him very much awake. Not all were so lucky. During the retreat from Mons, two guardsmen, who had not slept for five days, were found asleep on sentry. Both were court-martialled and shot.

The relationship between the men and their officers was crucial in forming efficient fighting units. Men tended to admire 'traditional' officers, who possessed all of the upper-class public school values of their genre. Not only should they be able to command, but they should also be gentlemen. Scorn was poured upon officers who were drunkards, profane or uncaring about their men. This attitude mellowed as the war progressed, when lack of suitable officer material saw large numbers of men being promoted from the ranks. Private Dalton (himself a pre-war volunteer who became a captain) commented that 'by 1918, soldiers would accept orders from officers that the 1914 regular would have made mincemeat of'.

It is a great credit to the selection process that so many competent officers were produced during the war. Many other ranks developed strong bonds with them, often going to extreme lengths to assist an officer in trouble. Countless medals were awarded to soldiers who risked their lives to bring 'their' officer back when wounded, even at the cost of their own lives. When Private Marshall's captain was left wounded in a shellhole, a member of his Vickers team, never noted for his love of authority, made three attempts to locate him, having to be forcibly restrained when about to try a fourth time. Commanders realized the value of good officers, and any who showed a lack of fibre soon found themselves returned to depot or assigned to menial duties.

A subaltern of the Irish Guards checks the gas helmets of his platoon, September 1916. Flannel hoods soaked in chemicals – like these P helmets – were later replaced by the more familiar respirator. (IWM, Q4232)

The battle of Arras, May 1917: men of a divisional pioneer battalion carry forward screw pickets, sandbags and barbed wire. Wire obstacles were invariably set up under cover of darkness when screw pickets could be fixed in silence. The hammering of driven pickets, by contrast, attracted enemy fire. (IWM, Q5258)

There were many other ways in which men could incur the wrath of the army. Contracting venereal disease was classified as a 'SIW' (self-inflicted wound), exactly the same as for a man who had shot himself. Soldiers convicted of such acts could be put in prison, though some were given the option of returning to the front line, with additional fatigues when out of it, army reasoning being that they should not be spared the dangers that their comrades were facing. Some men simply fell foul of bullying NCOs, and although no ex-soldiers would openly admit to participation, there are several tales of unpopular NCOs being fatally shot or simply disappearing in action in strange circumstances. Authority was no guarantee of safety. Persistent offenders would be sent to military prison – the 'glasshouse'. Renowned for their brutal discipline, the prisons took most of the toughest cases, overseen by the Military Police.

As far as most men were concerned, the 'Redcaps' existed solely to make life for the average soldier as miserable as possible. Their powers were far-reaching, although, contrary to popular myth, this did not extend to summary execution. The sterling work that they did in keeping clogged roads open and directing traffic under intense shellfire was largely ignored by the rank and file, who regarded them as an unmitigated nuisance. One ex-soldier recounted the attitude of the men towards the MP:

A few were alright – they'd stick their heads into an *estaminet* and say, 'We'll be coming back in ten minutes,' which gave us a chance to leave, but others would burst in and lay about us with truncheons, no warning, nothing. We never trusted them, most were blokes who were no good for front line service, and a lot were bullies. When we were drinking with the Aussies it was different, though. I saw Aussies beat a group of Redcaps so badly that they were stretcher cases. They never bothered us if we had them with us.

COMBAT AND TACTICS

The tactics of the Great War in 1914 were based in part on the experience of colonial wars of the late 19th century, and the general feeling amongst the General Staff that any European war would be short and sharp, a notion challenged by the trench system that developed. Trenches meant stalemate, and the High Command tried the most obvious methods of overcoming them. In practical terms, this meant extended artillery bombardment to destroy wire and emplacements, which it conspicuously failed to do.

Despite the dangers, there was a familiarity about trench life that afforded the ordinary soldier a degree of comforting routine. All of this vanished once it became common knowledge that a 'big show' was in the offing. The illusion of security was soon shattered with the prospect of going 'over the top', as most experienced soldiers knew how slim their chances of survival could be. Probably the worst affected were those who had never before experienced battle, as their imaginations ran riot with the terrors of the unknown that lay ahead of them. It was the waiting beforehand that was the hardest thing to come to terms with, and it affected men in different ways. Some became quiet and withdrawn; others cracked jokes to cheer their chums up. A few had premonitions about their futures, taking a friend into confidence.

Having been told his battalion of the Manchester Regiment would be attacking the following morning, 19-year-old Private Will Wells could not sleep:

I crawled out of my dug-out and stood staring at the stars, thinking I may never see them again. We had a man in our company called Charlie, who I had become very friendly with. He'd been over since Loos, and was very experienced. Well, he came up to me and stood puffing on his pipe. He asked me if I was frightened, and I said yes. He told me about his first battle, and how he never once fired his rifle, and by the time he finished I was feeling better. He then said an odd thing, that he was sorry he hadn't got to know me earlier and it was a pity it was too late. Then he shook my hand and went.

At the appointed hour, officers would blow their whistles, and the men would file quietly forwards, using scaling ladders to negotiate the steep parapet, usually into a hurricane of retaliatory small-arms fire. Progress was slow, as the men were heavily laden: Private Jarman carried 250 rounds of ammunition, Mills bombs in a bandoleer, and a shovel, as well as webbing, rifle and bayonet. Once they were clear of the trench, the men theoretically would hold formation around their officers and keep extended line, whilst walking steadily towards the enemy. In practice, No Man's Land was an inferno of noise and smoke, with machine gun bullets, shellfire and screams. Few men could concentrate on the task in hand, and Will Wells's experience was to remain with him for the rest of his life:

Territorials of the Queen's Westminster Rifles, a unit of the London Regiment, practise the construction of trenches in an English wood. Digging and physical training took up a great deal of the volunteers' time as they waited for industry to supply the weapons and ammunition they needed. (Douglas Honychurch)

We got into No Man's Land, and I followed the first line into the smoke. Everything seemed unreal – the noise was so great that it just became a constant sound, and I could see men dropping, like puppets with no strings. I wondered why they didn't keep up. I didn't recognise it then as a sign they had been shot dead. I kept close to old Charlie, and soon we were up to the wire. We were told not to bunch up, but men did, which made them easier targets. A group of men were running along, trying to find a way through the wire, and just folded up as a machine gun caught them. Charlie jumped into a shellhole and I followed. When the fire slackened I asked him if we should go back, but he was dead, hit in the head by a bullet. At dusk I crawled back to our lines. It all seemed like a bad dream, but I didn't realise until next day how close I had been to dying.

Not all attacks were such dismal failures. It eventually became clear that frontal assaults on heavily defended positions were doomed to failure, and by 1917 a more flexible approach was being taken to fighting. For the battle of Messines, soldiers were taken to see scale models of the areas to be attacked, as well as being briefed on tactics and objectives. This was a far cry from previous years, and was appreciated by many rank and file. Harry Wood, by then a corporal, was impressed by the planning, and more so by the execution of it:

Before zero hour, we crawled into dead ground in front of our trenches and lay there. When the barrage started, we got up and were in the trenches before Jerry knew what was happening. Most were too dazed by the mines to put up a fight. We left our mopping-up party behind and followed the barrage over the next [trench] and took their second line with little trouble. I had the Lewis gun and got great satisfaction from shutting up a German machine gun post that had been bothering our flank. My officer told me that I'd get an award for it, but he was killed later, and I never did.

The worst bit was holding the trench and waiting for reinforcements. Jerry tried counter-attacking, but we beat them off. They got so close that I had to use my pistol when the Lewis was empty. I wasn't frightened at all then, but got a bit shaky when we were relieved. I was glad to come out alive.

Generally, men were too keyed up after battle to feel much except relief at their own survival. It was only after they were sent back to reserve lines or billets that their experiences began to prey on their minds. The loss of friends was particularly hard to bear, and small groups of silent men would be found wandering listlessly around, as Will Wells described:

After roll call, I went around to see if any men I knew had come out [alive]. There were almost no faces I recognised. I was really fed up and sat on my own. It seemed that the spirit of the battalion had gone with all the old faces, and I didn't think it would ever be the same. Six months later though, I was one of the 'old sweats', and I realised that you can't dwell on the past, you just keep going.

The lucky ones were those able to walk out after combat. For the others, it was a different story.

May 1918: a Vickers machine gun sited in a barn at Haverskerque. In the fluid fighting following the German offensive of March 1918, there was often no time to dig in. The nearest man has the shoulder title 'MGC' over 'I', indicating the 'Infantry' branch of the Machine Gun Corps. (IWM, Q6571)

CASUALTIES

Britain began the war with a small but relatively well-equipped medical service, and the system of aid posts, dressing stations, field hospitals and base hospitals served the army quite well at the outset. However, as the size of field armies increased, so did the numbers involved in battles, and the campaigns of 1915 such as Neuve Chapelle and Loos saw numbers of wounded arriving at the aid stations far beyond those contemplated in 1914. The system of dealing with casualties relied on a network of treatment centres – regimental aid posts behind the reserve trenches, casualty clearing stations behind them, field hospitals and base hospitals behind those.

The medical services had considerable experience of dealing with high-velocity gunshot wounds, based on earlier colonial campaigns. For the ordinary soldiers, exposure to the effects of such injuries was unsettling to say the least. Many men wrote home about the effects of 'explosive bullets' fired by the Germans: in fact the energy contained within a standard .303in bullet was awesome. At close range such a projectile would punch clean through a man's torso with little loss of power, creating exit wounds that were several inches across. Men hit in the head rarely survived, regardless of the range, as shock caused massive internal damage. Even slight wounds could be complex, as bullets often travelled along bones. One man struck in the right wrist by a bullet had it travel up his arm, deflect off his collarbone, and exit from the top of the opposite shoulder. Wounds from shells were invariably worse, with razor-sharp, jagged chunks of steel flying hundreds of yards, and lead shrapnel balls peppering the ground like giant shotgun blasts.

Lightly wounded men were expected to make their own way to aid posts, whilst the more serious cases waited to be collected by the stretcher-bearers, who did heroic work in trying to reach the wounded, despite being frustrated both by enemy fire and by the sheer numbers involved. In the first 24 days of the Somme battle, 136,000 men became casualties, 59,000 on the first day alone, overwhelming the medical service. Clarrie Jarman was one of them:

> We went over the top at Carnoy … I had a bad gunshot wound in my right leg and was lucky to fall into a deep shellhole. The ground was covered with lads in khaki, dead, dying and wounded, and was being spattered with shrapnel, high explosive and bullets. I lay where I had fallen all day – about 14 hours. Again, I was lucky as a lad from the RAMC happened to come my way looking for wounded … with the aid of a comrade they carried me back to the front line. After several hours I was placed on a stretcher and carried into the field dressing station, where my leg was dressed. Then I was sent to Amiens, but there were no beds, so I spent five days on the stretcher. I then went on a barge down the Somme River to Abbeville, where we got clean clothes before going by train to Boulogne. The hospital ships were full. At 3am on the 11th I arrived at Aberdeen.

By that time Clarrie's leg had been infected by gangrene and had to be amputated.

For an army that lived in the open, there were comparatively few minor ailments, such as colds. Fred Dixon commented that 'considering we were mainly volunteers, and not hardened to an outdoor life, we were all very healthy. If you got a cold it was gone in a couple of days.' More problematic were illnesses such as trench foot, cuts which invariably turned septic because of infection, and sheer exhaustion from lack of sleep.

Poor diet also resulted in boils and constipation, which was also, curiously, a common side effect of being under shellfire for any period of time. A form of trench fever also manifested itself sometimes, with flu-like symptoms. Most of these ailments were treated with a few days in a field hospital followed by 'light duty' for a week or so. Bad stomach problems were common, generally caused by drinking polluted water from shellholes. Water was always in short supply, and any source was welcome, the general assumption being that if boiled it would be all right. Private Will Wells, living in a trench near Delville Wood, wrote, 'all things considered I am fine. We have been taking our water from a shellhole behind, and were surprised to find that the boot sticking out of it was still attached to a German. We are using a new hole now, but I don't suppose it makes much difference.' The problem of 'trench foot' was a serious one, being a form of gangrene brought about by having constantly wet feet exacerbated by poor circulation. It was actually considered a crime to contract it, and an afflicted soldier could be punished. Various remedies were tried, including issuing whale oil, which was to be rubbed into the feet on a daily basis. The best solution was dry footwear, and removal of boots and puttees whenever possible, to relieve pressure on swollen feet and legs. In mud-clogged trenches, this was easier said than done, as Private Wells recalled: 'In Ypres, I never took my boots off for two weeks. When we came out of the line I had to cut my laces with a clasp knife, and when I got them [the boots] off the socks had rotted and my toes were black. I reported sick but I never lost any toes because the nurses were so good.' The problem eased with the more widespread issue of waders, and more stringent checks by medical officers, but was never entirely eradicated.

Another persistent problem was that of venereal disease, and medical officers could do little to prevent wholesale infection. Affected men were sent back to base hospital for treatment, but even placing notorious red light areas out of bounds could not stop the problem. On average 800 men a month were admitted to hospital with one or other form of the disease. Lectures on hygiene were given noting simple precautions that could be taken to reduce risk, most of which were met with a barrage of ribald comments, to the discomfort of the lecturer and amusement of the men.

A problem that the army took some time to come to terms with was shell shock. In the early days of the war victims were treated as cowards, and many were severely punished, even to the extent of being executed. However, as the frontiers of medical

knowledge moved forwards, so did the acceptance that the mental and physical trauma of war did cause mental instability, ranging from headaches and shaking to complete mental breakdown. Treating such cases was another matter, with therapy ranging from electric shocks to cold baths. Then, as now, recuperation tended to be very much dependent on the individual, with some men making a total recovery whilst others never did. George Wells was badly shell shocked and remained affected all his life, flinching uncontrollably at loud noises and suffering poor hearing and stuttering.

There was little that could be done for the dead except to give them a decent burial where time and circumstances permitted. Most regiments tried to ensure this was done where possible, and bodies were wrapped in groundsheets or blankets, then placed behind the parados to await removal to one of the small cemeteries that sprang up behind the lines. Burials were often attended by the dead man's comrades and presided over by the padre. Personal effects were gathered to be returned home, but useful items were usually shared out amongst friends. After Private Dawson was killed, his friend, Private Setchell, wrote a letter of condolence to the bereaved mother starting off, 'I am sorry about what happened as I was his friend. I have got his pocket knife'!

Thousands lay where they fell, to be buried later, or were hastily placed in shallow graves marked with a rifle and steel helmet, their sites lost in later fighting. Many were simply never found. Buried in dug-outs, or vaporized by high explosive, they merely became names added to the growing list of 'missing presumed killed'. The many monuments to the missing which dot the countryside in France and Flanders are mute testament to them.

Back from the battlefields of France and Belgium came the wounded, to be healed and, if possible, sent back out to the fighting. These convalescents posing with their nurses wear a mixture of service uniform and 'hospital blues' – a bright blue jacket and trousers, sometimes worn with a white shirt and red necktie. (Mike Chappell)

ON CAMPAIGN

There was a depressing similarity in the conduct of most of the major battles of the Great War. From the onset of trench warfare in 1915 to the final breakthrough in 1918, gains were measured in hundreds of yards and tens of thousands of casualties.

Although the battles of the Somme, which began in July 1916, are often taken as typical of combat on the Western Front, they were significant largely for the huge numbers of casualties and the amount of ordnance that they absorbed.

Arguably one could say the most important campaign was Cambrai, for although it did not achieve any lasting gain in terms of territory, it showed how trench warfare might be ended. The planning and operation of the Cambrai battle was witnessed by two brothers, George and William Wells, one in the RAMC, the other in the Manchester Regiment, who between them left behind an interesting record of the battle from the ordinary soldier's viewpoint.

The tactics of Cambrai were dictated by the staff of the Tank Corps, who had been begging for a chance to prove what tanks were capable of, given the right ground and sound planning. The concept of the battle was simple – a lightning attack along an extended front by tanks, with a creeping artillery barrage and the infantry in close support. There was to be no preliminary bombardment, always a giveaway of a forthcoming attack. The infantry involved included Private William Wells, who had already survived the slaughter of Passchendaele. Planning for Cambrai was, to him, something of a revelation:

One of the few photographs of the actual moment of attack; an officer of the 9th Battalion, the Cameronians (Scottish Rifles), leads the way out of a sap during the spring battles of 1917. (IWM, Q5100)

We knew that something big was up, as we had been withdrawn from the line and put into reserve. One day we were told by our officer that we were going to take part in a surprise attack. This was a revelation, I can tell you. We had never known anything about our objectives before, other than the place we climbed out of the trenches. We saw a big scale model of the line, and were told how the tanks would go in first. A lot of us were able to look into the tanks afterwards, and some of our officers had rides in them, which not many appreciated.

A major factor in the planning of the battle was that of surprise. There was to be no preliminary barrage, and 378 combat tanks would advance on a 6-mile front, working in groups of three and each carrying a fascine to fill the German trench, which was too wide to permit a tank to cross unaided. The infantry were to advance close behind, and as the tanks worked up and down the enemy lines they would rush the defenders with little opposition. Will Wells was naturally sceptical, having experienced the opposition from the Germans at Ypres despite being assured that the artillery would have destroyed the enemy trenches. 'I knew that Jerry was a tough fighter, and most of us reckoned it would be another Ypres. We didn't reckon much to the chances of the tanks.' On the night of 19 November 1917, he and his comrades were marched up to the front line near Flesquières, and issued with extra ammunition. He had been appointed runner, with instructions to stay close to his company commander. He promptly ditched most of his ammunition and grenades. 'If I was a runner, I reckoned the last thing I wanted was to carry an extra 10lb [4.5kg] of ammo.' They then settled down to wait for dawn.

In a front line aid post, George Wells had spent hours checking and double checking his medical supplies, stacking dozens of stretchers and hundreds of dressings. Having served since 1915, he was under no illusions what the following day would bring. 'When there was a big battle on, we simply couldn't stop to rest. I was used to being on my feet for two days without a break. I was used to the awful sights by then, and could tell quite quickly who was worth saving and who was not.'

At dawn on 20 November, the tanks started into No Man's Land as a deluge of shells crashed onto the German lines. As they lurched off into the early mist, the infantry rose stiffly, slightly fortified by an early issue of rum, and clambered over the parapet. For Private Wells, it proved an unusual experience: 'There was no retaliation from Jerry, and I kept thinking, "any minute, those guns will open up" but they didn't. They [the tanks] had simply crushed the wire flat. We just walked over it like it wasn't there, with almost no opposition.'

The first wave of British troops swept over the German front line, meeting only dazed German soldiers who soon surrendered. The British artillery barrage continued to move ahead of the advancing troops, forcing the defenders into cover until their attackers were on top of them. Opposition began to stiffen as return shellfire found targets with the crawling tanks, and German machine gun crews braved the shells to set up their guns. Private Wells found himself and his officer pinned down in the German second line:

We had lost contact with our company. I think a lot were still in the front trench. My officer pulled out a pad and scribbled a message, saying to me, 'Give this to the first tank you can find,' and off I went. It was quite clear by then, and I could see where the tanks were from the shells bursting around them. I got near one and realised it was burning so I made for another. I used my rifle butt to bang on the door and attract their attention. When a crewman stuck his head out I gave him the note, and ran back to the trench. I thought being near tanks was too unhealthy. When I got back my company had moved on, so I joined with another.

Meanwhile the battle moved ahead with incredible speed. In the space of 24 hours a salient 5 miles deep had been driven into the German lines across a 7-mile front. Initial casualties (1,500 men) were about one three-hundredth of what would normally have been expected for such gains. For George Wells in the aid post it was a puzzling time. 'Casualties started trickling back, but only in small numbers. They kept telling us how Jerry had upped sticks and left his trenches, but I didn't believe them. We kept saying that any moment the real works would begin, but it didn't.'

Unbeknown to him, his brother was in the thick of the fighting. Having pushed beyond the trenches into open country, his battalion was running short of ammunition and had dug in overnight. Meanwhile German retaliation had begun.

We could see a big wood away to our front, and the Jerries could see us. A couple of times one of their aircraft flew low over us, firing its machine guns. Then their artillery started up. We couldn't do much about it, but a while later it stopped suddenly, and we saw a mass of troops heading towards us. We let fly, and our Lewis guns stopped them, but after a bit we were told they were flanking us, so we started to fall back. On both sides of me, my chums were hit but we couldn't stop. One kept trying to crawl after us, and eventually I lost sight of him.

The success of the battle was to be short-lived, however. General Byng had insufficient reserves to support the advance, and German counter-attacks soon pushed the British line back. At the end of the day casualties and prisoners on each side were about equal, and no permanent gains had been made.

By then calls for stretcher-bearers ensured George Wells was fully occupied in the front line and beyond, collecting wounded, but it was to be his last battle:

On the second day we had an officer from the Tanks in, who was very worried about his crew, who he had left near their vehicle. He was badly wounded in the arm and hip, but insisted we went back with him to find them. Four of us followed him, and after some trouble found two of them in a shellhole. The tank was just twisted metal. I don't know how they survived, but we gave them morphine and dressed their wounds. As we were heading back I saw a flash, and then something blew me off my feet. That was the last I knew till I came to in base hospital.

Having survived a near direct hit from an artillery shell, Private Wells suffered from bad shell shock, which resulted in his being invalided out of the army in 1918.

If not an unqualified success, Cambrai, along with earlier 1917 battles, helped to pave the way for a more flexible form of warfare, doing away with wasteful preliminary bombardments (which mainly served to warn of impending attack) and relying on increased use of armoured units working in close cooperation with infantry and artillery.

The problem of supply had been addressed by the novel use of 98 supply tanks, hauling sledges full of ammunition, water and supplies, saving thousands of infantry man-hours. More importantly, it proved that the two greatest stumbling blocks – wire and trenches – could be overcome.

US Doughboy

Thomas A. Hoff

An old story illustrates the attitude of the doughboy in comparison to those of his comrades in arms. A sentry on duty in the inky dark of the night challenges an approaching figure:

> Halt! Who goes there?
> 'A soldier of the King.'
> Advance Englishman, to be recognized.
> Then another figure approaches.
> Halt! Who goes there?
> 'Soldat Français.'
> Advance Frenchman, to be recognized.
> And then yet another:
> Halt! Who goes there?
> 'Who the hell wants to know?'
> Advance American …

In 1917, the United States Army made a rapid change in its course of development. What had been a small professional force, functioning for the most part as a constabulary, blossomed into an army of continental European scale – a nation in arms, drawing manpower from all strata of society. It assumed a new role as well, for this army was intended to fight total war on foreign soil.

The average US soldier in World War I was a rifleman and a conscript as well. To understand the United States Army in the Great War, it is helpful to comprehend what the individual soldier underwent. With the exceptions of some aspects of training and actual combat, these experiences can be extrapolated to cover that of any member of a combat arms formation.

Conspicuous by their absence are the African-Americans who served during the war. Due to the racial prejudices of the time, they served in segregated regiments. This separation led to their operational integration into the French Army during the war. Black soldiers wore US uniforms, but with French helmets, equipment and weapons, and their tactical use was also in line with French theory. Their experience was therefore significantly different from that of white soldiers. Those black soldiers that remained attached to the American Expeditionary Force (AEF) often performed menial jobs for the Services of Supply. This led to their serving as labour at the ports where supplies were brought in and as grave diggers attached to Graves Registration units.

African-Americans were the only ethnic group so treated by the army. Besides a temporary experiment with ethnic companies assembled for training purposes, the army was well integrated. Whites, Hispanics, Asians and Native Americans all served side by side. The High Command even felt that the integration of Native Americans was a positive move, as white recruits would feel inspired to serve alongside members of 'warrior races'.

The level of importance attributed to the American entry into the war is somewhat controversial. Many Americans believe that the US Army won the war single-handedly, saving Europe on behalf of the Europeans. Conversely, the opposite opinion exists: that US involvement was insignificant, coming late in the war. The truth probably lies in between. When the war ended the doughboys were occupying a greater frontage than the British, although the British advanced much farther than the Americans during the great Allied offensives of 1918. While the Americans didn't 'win' the war, they played a crucial role in contributing to the Allied victory, in terms of finance and industry, morale and military involvement.

A lesser controversy is the origin of the word 'doughboy'. It was not the official word used to describe the US soldiers sent to France, but an informal term, much as the British soldiers were called 'Tommies' and the French 'Poilus'. The French, and to a lesser extent the other Allies, referred to the Americans as 'Sammies', after Uncle Sam. 'Sammy' does make an appearance in some of the popular songs of the day, but never seemed to catch on with the men themselves. The term doughboy, however, was one which was used by the soldiers. Prior to US commitment to the war, 'doughboy' was a term used to describe an infantryman; after the war it became a generic term for a US soldier, just as 'GI' covered a later generation. One traditional explanation for the phrase is a derogatory comment made by cavalrymen about the infantry: after marching in the dust of the South-West an infantryman would be covered with so much dirt and sweat that he resembled adobe, the common building material. 'Adobe' was in turn corrupted to doughboy. Another theory, not branch specific, was that the nickname came from the large buttons on the blouses worn by the troops, said to have resembled the lumps of fried dough called 'doughboys'.

Either way, the name evolved just as the US Army evolved in its size and ability. At the time of Pancho Villa's raid on Columbus, New Mexico, the army numbered only around 125,000 men, not counting the National Guard. During the course of the war 4,734,991 served, of whom 2 million went to France. It was a great expansion indeed.

The army was initially divided into three armies: the Regular Army, the National Guard and the National Army. This last force was to be composed of conscripts. However, due to the manpower needs of modern war the three were combined into one Army of the United States, with all divisions containing some conscripts.

CONSCRIPTION

Conscription was a very delicate subject in 1917; it had been implemented during the American Civil War amidst riots and bloodshed and had been extremely unpopular. It was reintroduced during World War I for several practical reasons. Conscription provided the army with a steady

Opposite:
Tours, France, 30 May 1918. The doughboy in regulation kit. (NARA)

'The Silk Stocking Regiment'
– 7th New York National Guard –
on 11 September 1917 en route
to training. The regiment was
renowned for recruiting from
the elite of New York City society.
(NARA)

flow of manpower and numbers that could be relied on, which in turn assisted the development of a training programme. Furthermore, the High Command of the army was dissatisfied with the way the volunteer system had worked during the Spanish–American War. By circumventing 'volunteerism' with conscription, the regular establishment thought they would have a better hold on the development of the army, and this would hopefully reduce political interference in the command structure. The weak link in this policy would be the National Guard, but with their eventual incorporation into a centralized army, that problem would pass as well. It should be noted that conscription did not prevent volunteering, but the volunteer would go into an existing Regular Army or National Guard unit. About 2 million did volunteer, the bulk volunteering for the navy.

Unlike the Civil War, conscription for World War I, known as Selective Service, was run by a civilian board instead of the military, and some 4,000 local draft boards went about choosing who would serve. They also made the decisions about deferments. A side effect was that African-Americans, due to poorer economic conditions and the attitudes of the draft boards, received fewer deferments and were conscripted in higher proportion than white Americans.

The draft had been introduced in May 1917. By registering on National Draft Day, 5 June 1917, men could avoid receiving the red postcard ordering them to do so. This date was for initial registration of men between the ages of 21 and 31; there would be additional enrolment dates as the war continued. Nearly 24 million draft cards were issued, and if the recipient was called upon by law enforcement or service personnel, he could produce it to prove that he was not a 'slacker', the term used to describe what a later generation would call draft-dodgers. It was a word that eventually described anyone who failed to support the war effort fully. The draft card could even be a lifesaver to a first-generation American with a German surname, as the occasional lynching was known to happen. Those who registered for the draft would be ordered to appear for a physical examination, and within a month could receive the fateful blue postcard, informing them that they had to be ready to report within 24 hours.

One of the first experiences of a new recruit in the army would be to take a rudimentary IQ test. This was one of many tests set up to determine who took which jobs in the military, with those adjudged the most deficient placed in labour units. One of the problems with the tests, and there were many, was the inherent bias. One test, eventually known as 'Army Alpha', was

CHRONOLOGY

4 August 1914	In response to the outbreak of war in Europe, President Wilson declares the United States' neutrality.
10 February 1915	The United States announces it will hold Germany solely responsible for the sinking of US ships by submarines.
7 May 1915	The *Lusitania* is sunk by a German U-boat off the coast of Ireland.
9 March 1916	Columbus, New Mexico is raided by Pancho Villa, a Mexican revolutionary, and 17 Americans are killed in the action.
15 March 1916	6,000 US troops under the command of John Pershing enter Mexico in an attempt to eliminate Pancho Villa. Additional troops are later committed and National Guard units mobilized and deployed to the border.
3 June 1916	The National Defense Act is enacted, which increases the manpower of both the Regular Army and the National Guard.
16 January 1917	The German Foreign Minister, Zimmerman, offers Mexico US territory in exchange for assistance in a war with the US. The telegram is intercepted by the British and released to the American public on 1 March 1917.
1 February 1917	Germany recommences unrestricted submarine warfare; two days later the US breaks off diplomatic relations.
6 April 1917	The United States declares war on Germany.
10 May 1917	General John Pershing is given command of the American Expeditionary Force.
18 May 1917	Conscription is authorized, as the Selective Service Act is passed.
26 May 1917	The first US troops arrive in France.
5 June 1917	National Draft Registration Day. Ten million young Americans enrol for selective service.
21 October 1917	Near Luneville, France, US troops enter the trenches.
7 December 1917	The United States declares war on Austria-Hungary.
27 May–5 June 1918	Battle of Château Thierry fought by 3d Division.
28–31 May 1918	Cantigny is taken by the 1st Division in the first US offensive.
6–25 June 1918	Battle of Belleau Wood fought by 2d Division.
4 July 1918	Four companies from the 131st and 132d regiments (33d Division) accompany the Australian 4th Division in an attack at Hamel.
18 July–6 Aug 1918	Second battle of the Marne. US 1st and 2d divisions, along with a French division, spearhead the assault at Soissons. US I and III corps involved in subsequent operations.
18 Aug–12 Oct 1918	US troops participate in the Amiens–Oise offensive.
12–16 Sept 1918	The St Mihiel offensive by US First Army and French II Colonial Corps.
26 Sept–11 Nov 1918	The Meuse–Argonne campaign.
11 November 1918	Armistice between Germany and the Allies.
15 March 1919	American Legion is founded in Paris.
1 September 1919	The last American combat division in France embarks for home.
3 January 1920	The last US troops in France leave.
25 August 1921	Peace treaty is signed between the United States and Germany.
24 January 1923	The last American occupational troops in Germany leave.

slanted towards literate, native, middle-class English speakers with urban experience. Many of the questions were multiple choice, and designed to test common sense. An example was: 'If plants were dying for a lack of rain, you should: water them, ask a florist's advice or put fertilizer on them'. Other questions were 'fill in the blank'. The problem with these was that only a specific word was considered correct. The test taker could be correct in concept, but still be graded as wrong. There was, however, a picture-only version of the test, Beta, that could be administered to the illiterate. Some 25 per cent of those inducted ended up taking the Beta version. As a result, recruits from rural areas, central Europeans and African-Americans tended to fare poorly. (Army Alpha was derived from the Stanford modification of the Binet test. This test, the Stanford-Binet, is still given to schoolchildren across the United States.)

Another series of examinations, the 'Trade Tests', were given to see if new recruits had any special skills or talents that the military could use. This mania for testing, natural in the progressive, scientifically minded society of the time, extended into the higher ranks as well. A test, based on one used to rate salesmen, was even administered to those wishing to be promoted to captain.

Conscripts made up 72 per cent of the army during World War I, and they were to be found in every division, be it Regular, National Guard or National Army. The balance of manpower came from the federalized units of the National Guard and the Regular Army. The United States had produced a new style of army for a new style of war.

Draftees on the way to Camp Upton, Long Island. The figure second from left is looking quite formidable, and reminds the reader that even Al Capone's brother was a doughboy. The number '145' probably signifies their draft number. (NARA)

Training: the Theory and the Reality

General Pershing had some very strong beliefs as to how the war should be fought which proved disastrous, all of which were the natural result of the recent experiences of the US Army. Based on lessons learned in combat against the Indians, the Spanish and the Filipinos, the official doctrine called for a war of fire and manoeuvre. It was also dogma that 'Fire + Maneuver = Offense'. Therefore what was needed to win the war in Europe was offensive action, which in turn meant a break from trench warfare. Open warfare was what Pershing wanted, and what his army was to be trained for.

The offensive attitude was catered for in the manuals used by the army for training. Two important books, *Infantry Drill Regulations* (1911) and *Field Service Regulations* (1914), both made the assumption that the rifleman was the decisive weapon, and that artillery and machine guns were merely there to help him get into within killing range. The continued use of these volumes ignored the massive changes to warfare that had occurred since the publication of *Field Service Regulations*. As a result, doctrine minimized the effectiveness of machine guns and did not address gas, aeroplanes or tanks, all of which were a battlefield reality for the combatants already engaged in Europe.

The regulations were also written with larger units in mind, because the pre-war organization for a division included three brigades of three regiments, giving an amazing 27 battalions to a division. It should be remembered that at this time most European divisions comprised nine to 12 battalions. The large US formation was quickly scaled down by the War Department, 15 battalions being pulled out, but American divisions were still massive compared to European formations.

The reorganization of July 1917 restructured more than the division; it also had consequences for the battalion, reorganizing it from four rifle companies to three, with an additional machine gun company. All of these changes caused consternation for the army, which saw the need for large combat formations that could maintain (as well as achieve) open warfare. The command staff of the army, to a degree still 'fighting' the Spanish–American War as opposed to the current conflict, felt that the division should be an independent entity capable of sustained operations, hence the need for more manpower. The July reorganization did reflect an understanding that too large a formation would be unwieldy and hard to command on a battlefield, yet there would be further changes.

In August 1917, the division was restructured again; it would retain this organization for the remainder of the war. The July organization of two brigades of two regiments was kept. However, every battalion had its fourth rifle company restored, and the regiment raised an additional company that became the machine gun element. Not only did this arrangement help to keep up the rifle strength, but the rifle companies also had their establishment raised from 103 to 256 officers and men, of which 216 were riflemen.

The company was subdivided into four platoons, each of which had four sections. Unlike in the army of World War II, these squads were not identical, but rather task-orientated. This organization catered to the principles of fire and manoeuvre. The first squad was comprised of 12 men designated as grenadiers; the second had nine men designated as rifle grenadiers. These men were equipped with a modified version of the French VB *tromblon* (a rifle grenade discharger). Many did not see these until they were deployed, and in some cases not until they had already been in combat in France. The third squad had 17 riflemen and functioned as the manoeuvre element along with the first squad. The fourth squad, 15 men with four Chauchat automatic rifles, provided a base of fire along with the rifle grenadiers.

Supporting all of these infantrymen was an array of heavier weaponry. The 'square' division, so called because of the four infantry regiments, was supported by three regiments of artillery. Two of these regiments, armed with 75mm guns, consisted of two battalions each. These were, in turn, broken down into three batteries of four guns. These 48 guns were the famous French '75'. Unlike a later war that saw the United States providing weaponry to her allies, 1917 found the future 'Arsenal of Democracy' unable to meet her own needs. The third regiment also had French guns, but these were 155mm howitzers. Organized into three battalions, each of two batteries, these 24 guns would greatly contribute to the firepower supporting the doughboys.

Machine gun supply was lavish, with guns purchased from France filling the void. The regiment controlled a heavy weapons company which operated six mortars and four 37mm guns, but the meat of the company was 16 heavy machine guns, much larger than the German machine gun company of six weapons, although comparable to the British machine gun corps companies held at brigade level. In addition to these regimental companies, every brigade had a battalion of three 16-gun companies, and at the divisional level there was an additional battalion of four companies. The divisional battalion was in theory motorized for quick deployment, but the vehicles proved a liability in the Argonne region. The machine guns were supposed to be US-manufactured Brownings, but due to supply difficulties the French Hotchkiss was often used. In total, an American division had an incredible 224 heavy machine guns on establishment. Compared to the 100 or so machine guns that a German division could theoretically deploy in 1918, it was a massive disparity in firepower.

A group of recruits prior to undergoing the psychological exam. They are dressed in only partial uniform; absent are items such as leggings and, in the case of the first recruit in the second rank and third from the right in the first, trousers. Instead the men are wearing overalls, typical of the agricultural workers of the time. (NARA)

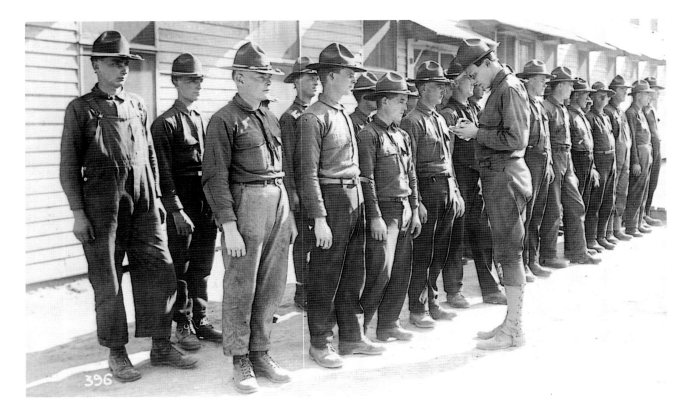

US Army organization supported the idea of 'open' or manoeuvre warfare, as was intended. As new material was developed to give some direction to training, it continued to emphasize open warfare. *The Infantry Drill Regulations* were reinforced in April 1917 with the *Manual for Non-commissioned Officers and Privates of Infantry of the Army of the United States, 1917*. While a step forward, this volume also failed to consider what was really happening on the Western Front. This ignorance was a problem until the War Department issued *War Department Directive No.656 Infantry Training*, which actually attempted to lay out a training course, suggesting a 16-week period. In addition to the skills of 'open' warfare, it took into account the art of trench warfare. Unfortunately, this book did not become doctrine; it was simply intended as guidance. The other drawback was that when Pershing read it he was taken aback at the emphasis laid on trench warfare skills: he thought it was bad enough that the British and French advisors were stressing these aspects. Ultimately, the US Army entered the war with a marked lack of direction in training.

Training was done mostly at unit level. Prior to the war, the policy was for a new recruit to undergo 12 months of training before being considered a combat soldier. The training involved six months of garrison training followed by six months of field instruction. The teachers were the NCOs of the unit, since after induction the recruit spent only a brief period in a depot being physically examined and receiving his uniform. For an army the size of the one that was intended for the Great War, such a system would clearly fail to produce troops in a timely manner, and the extensive garrison training proved to be unnecessary for the wartime army. The plan had been to build every division around a corps of 900 regulars who would provide the instruction, but in reality this was unfeasible. With the political need for the rapid deployment of troops to France, the Regular Army diverted considerable manpower into organizing the 1st and 2nd divisions, which nonetheless had a high proportion of conscripts.

The 40th Division at Camp Kearney, training for open warfare and giving a good view of the long pack. As the men are wearing so much early equipment and uniform items, this photo could easily be from the Mexican Expedition. (NARA)

Once the recruit had been inducted, he was assigned to a division. It was with this formation that he began to learn the basic arts of soldiering. While taking his aptitude tests, he learned the basics of close-order drill and the rudiments of military life. Classes were taught on the organization of the army, and the role the individual played in 'fighting the Kaiser'. Spare time would be put to good use in maintaining the buildings and grounds of the training facility. It was during this initial period that the recruit would slowly be equipped as a soldier. Due to initial shortages, it was not unusual for recruits to carry wooden 'dummy' guns while drilling, nor was it odd to see those on the extremes of the uniform sizing wear items of civilian clothing.

A good deal of time and effort were spent on the rifle range. Philosophically, this fitted in with Pershing's vision of mobile warfare: the desire was to create an army of marksmen, a skill still stressed in the US Army. In addition to becoming competent riflemen, recruits began to pick up the other tricks of the trade. Eventually, the training company would begin to teach the rudiments of fire and manoeuvre, as well as the use of cover and concealment. Alongside marksmanship, the application of the bayonet was taught. On occasion, all of these activities were done while wearing gasmasks.

Recruits were often transferred from their original formations. In late October 1917, for example, a draft of men, 5,600 in all, were transferred to the 33d Division, a National Guard formation from Illinois. This was not uncommon, the conscripts being used to bring regular and National Guard units up to full strength. Initially, the National Guard units relied on drafts from

An early lesson on trench mortars. The variance of clothing worn by the students is in direct contrast to the instructor who is in full uniform. The man standing second from the left has what appears to be a second shirt pulled over the first. The outer shirt is without breast pockets, but seems to have pockets at hip level. The man on the right of the group appears to be wearing the cotton drill trousers as opposed to the wool ones worn by his comrades. (NARA)

other National Guard units, such as when the 7th New York sent 350 men to beef up the 69th New York. Later, when going into federal service, the 7th New York received massive drafts from the 1st New York, and the entire organization was renumbered as the 107th US Infantry. Nor was it unusual to see large numbers of men transferred at a time.

Fortunately for all concerned, a good deal of the National Guard, some 110,000 men, had been active during the Pershing expedition into Mexico. While they were not involved in offensive operations, the Guard's duties along the Rio Grande had served as an excellent school for the soldier. This experience would give the guardsman the opportunity to do sustained service, living in camps and adjusting to military hygiene, communal eating and deprivation from family and normal life. The knowledge gained was beneficial after activation in 1917 and gave the army an expanded base of experienced manpower. It was not uncommon for units in France to value these 'Mexico men' as much as they valued a pre-war regular.

Experience did not translate into combat-ready formations. With the rapid expansion of the army, the aforementioned cannibalization of units was to prove detrimental. As divisions became combat worthy, men would be drafted out to fill the ranks of other units, dooming the division stripped to recommence aspects of training. Furthermore, the training received by many units was scanty and ill-organized, much being left to local commanders, as the army had not completely centralized training doctrine.

An additional problem was language. Roughly a quarter of the army during World War I was foreign-born. A sizeable proportion of these men had emigrated to the United States as adolescents or adults and as a result had poor, and in some cases no, command of the English language. For many of these men, the training programme was very demoralizing. Unable to understand the instructions, such men were used for menial purposes. Luckily the army was aware of this problem and took steps to correct it. A Foreign-speaking Soldier Subsection (FSS) was established to help train these men.

Chateau Thierry. Private G. W. Newbury of Company A, 9th Machine Gun Battalion of the 3d Division, with his Hotchkiss machine gun. The Americans made great use of French weapons during the war, not just artillery and tanks but smaller arms as well. Of particular interest is the overhead concealment over the weapon pit. (NARA)

The FSS organized its recruits in training companies that spoke the same language, jokingly referred to as 'foreign legions'. The men received instruction in their native tongue and also underwent 3 hours of English instruction a day. This was in addition to the 40 hours per week of military topics. It should be noted that these companies were for training purposes, not as final combat formations. The army did, however, deploy 'ethnic' platoons into 'American' companies once in France. The idea was that these men would integrate into 'mainstream' American culture through contact with their company, yet not be isolated as individuals. The military, influenced by the progressive movement, made great strides in the integration of various ethnic groups into a homogenous body. Catholic and Jewish chaplains became commonplace, and, while not as influential as the YMCA, both the Knights of Columbus – a Catholic organization – and the Jewish Welfare Board were given access to the men.

Throughout the United States, training camps were built, some hastily, to deal with the influx of manpower. When first arriving at the camps, the troops were classified as casuals. Not yet fully uniformed, they began to learn the rudiments of military life, and were also employed in maintenance jobs around the camp. While at these camps, the men were exposed to some of the realities of modern warfare. Many had their perceptions of war formed by hearing stories of the American Civil War, and for a considerable number the Spanish–American War was a childhood memory, complete with tales from older siblings and relatives. The war being fought in Europe was vastly different from these two conflicts, most notably in the dominance of technology. In an attempt to bring the nature of the 'new' way of war home, it was not unusual for recruits to be drilled in their gasmasks. These became a common item in the camps, and the men were often required to carry them everywhere. A gas 'drill' might even be called in the mess hall, where all present were required to put on their masks. Stateside training facilities also included sections of trenchworks, so that the recruits would start to understand the value of cover and the lethality of modern weapons. It should also be noted that the fatigue parties which built and maintained these works received some of the most accurate 'training' for the real war in France.

An additional advantage of the stateside camps was that they gave the army a chance to indoctrinate the new recruits politically. For many, particularly the foreign-born or the illiterate, the reasons for American participation were hazy. As part of the training course, classes were given in how the war affected life in the United States. Some of these were crude and served a propaganda purpose, but the instruction was deemed especially important after it was decided to accept recruits whose origins were in the German or Austro-Hungarian empires. The initial exclusion of these men was overturned when it was realized that many, particularly those of Czech or Polish background, were eager to fight against the 'oppressors' of their homelands. During the classes, citizenship and the importance of democracy were stressed. It was also an opportunity to present a set of moral standards that were deemed desirable. Many of the morals were clad in an aura of military necessity; for example, abstain from going to a brothel not because it is immoral, but because the risk of acquiring a sexually transmitted disease will impair your ability to be a soldier. Furthermore, the doughboy should consider the shame that he would feel if he became a casualty as a result of an STD, rather than from enemy action.

STDs became a real consideration once soldiers were overseas, due to the different attitude towards prostitution that existed in France. A cat and mouse game between soldiers patronizing these establishments and the Military Police became a frequent theme in the memoirs of the

Opposite:
The gasmasks were worn during all phases of training to acclimatize the troops to them. Sometimes this had a definite benefit for the wearer! Peeling onions for the 40th Division, Camp Kearney, California. (NARA)

Camouflage techniques …
the men oblivious to the reality of the Western Front. The framework that the men are behind supports a mirror angled slightly forward. This would reflect the ground before it, allowing the man pushing the mirror to advance unnoticed. (NARA)

soldiers. Stateside, things were done a little differently, with the inevitable rise of brothels near training camps being counteracted with 'prophylactic' stations. Those who did contract a disease were held to have done so willingly, and would, after court-martial, be given a punishment including confinement, labour and loss of wages.

The net result of much of the indoctrination was that the doughboy truly felt that he was fighting to make the world safe for democracy, a fight he shared with the soldiers from Britain, Belgium, Italy, Serbia, Romania and other countries from the Allied cause.

In theory, all troops would receive three months' training – not the four months suggested in *WDD No.656*, although foreign-speaking companies still got four months – and then be transported to France for an additional three months of training. In order to prepare the men for trench warfare, many camps created trench systems to be used in training exercises. Those who trained there considered the system constructed for the 27th Division Camp, Wadsworth, on the outskirts of Spartansburg, South Carolina, quite impressive. British and French officers also arrived in the United States to aid in the process. The foreign advisors and a good number of the American commanders understood the need for learning trench warfare – it was what the army was going to be committed to. General Pershing, on the other hand, favoured a school of open warfare and felt that more attention should be paid to field craft. As a result, the troops spent much time and effort on the rifle range, much to the bemusement of the visiting French. This is not to imply that grenades and other tools were ignored, but that the US Army exhibited a more conservative approach to training. Likewise, the men received instruction in close-order drill. This activity was continued in France, where units pulled out of the line and into 'rest' areas were regularly subjected to the drill ground.

UNIFORMS AND EQUIPMENT

It was customary for new recruits to be issued with bits and pieces of uniform, at first just a 'campaign hat' and a shirt. The hat, similar in shape to that worn by Canadian Mounties and drill instructors in the modern US Army, was of the same drab colour as the uniform. The shirt was a khaki drab pullover, with three buttons down the front and two breast pockets. Unlike the banded collar shirts that many European armies favoured, the American shirt had a stand and fall collar. As they were taking their Alpha and Trade tests, recruits typically wore this shirt along with their civilian trousers and shoes. Within a few days, they were issued the rest of their uniform. Cut from an olive drab wool, the trousers and jacket had a coarse feel to them, and areas such as the neck were lined with cotton. The jacket had a stand collar, which was adorned with two bronze circles, the one on the right bearing the letters 'US', the other a pair of crossed rifles. Some National Guard units originally had a state cipher in place of the 'US'. There were five bronze buttons, bearing the seal of the United States, which held the jacket closed. The trousers as originally specified in 1902 had a slight flare to them, but this was modified in 1917 to a closer cut. Suspenders could be worn, but the trousers were made with belt loops. Worn with this uniform were brown boots and a pair of canvas leggings. The leggings, cut from a khaki shade of material, were fastened with a cord. The cord was visible externally: at the top, at the bottom of the legging and, when worn, towards the front as an outward pointing '>'. Impractical for the realities of trench life, these leggings were soon replaced with puttees made from the same material as the uniforms themselves.

Cut in the same pattern, but out of a lightweight khaki duck material, was a uniform for wear in warmer climates. Many of the troops involved in Mexico wore this, often in shirtsleeve order, leaving the jacket behind. Some of these uniforms made their way to France, but the US soldiers who fought in the initial actions of the AEF in the summer of 1918 did so in the wool uniforms. The army also provided for cold weather with a greatcoat. Double breasted, it was adjustable by means of a belt in the back. It had two rows of four bronze buttons, similar to the ones on the uniform jacket. Unlike the uniform jacket, the greatcoat had a stand and fall collar. In addition, a brown leather jerkin, lined with green wool and closed with bone buttons, was approved; it was almost indistinguishable from the jerkin issued by the British Army. A shorter 'Mackinaw' style jacket and a peaked cap were also regulation for drivers and other personnel. Troops deployed to Siberia or northern Russia saw use of a variety of heavier coats, some acquired locally. Fur caps were also worn during these expeditions.

For rainy weather, two different options were available. A rubberized poncho was issued that was very similar to the ones used during the American Civil War, only in khaki instead of black, which could also be used as a shelter half. The poncho had certain limitations, particularly when soldiers had to don a gasmask quickly, and with this in mind the men were issued a raincoat made from treated canvas that was allegedly waterproof. The raincoat had an oversized collar and large buckles to keep it closed.

It was soon realized that, like the leggings, the campaign hat, sometimes referred to as a 'Montana' hat, was incompatible with trench warfare. An 'overseas' cap replaced it. A fore-and-aft style cap, it was issued in two different patterns. One had a higher point on the front and back, much like the French cap. The other was lower, with a slight crest to the centre. The cap was issued with the sides loose at the top; these would be stitched together by the soldier himself. The cap was

Camp Logan, Houston, Texas, 11 November 1917

Marcheville, 11 November 1918

Camp Logan, Houston, Texas, 11 November 1917

This is what an American doughboy would have looked like in 1917 (**1**), whether he was in training or already in France. He is carrying the 1903 Springfield (**1a**), the official rifle of the US Army at the start of World War I. His duffel bag (**1b**) was used for the storage and transport of his personal items. The doughboy's look would change radically over the next few months, the most notable disappearance being the campaign hat (**2**). The sleeveless vest (**3**) was not an actual item of army issue, but was made available through the YMCA. His collar is held closed by two hooks, and features two discs (**4**), the US to the right, the arm of service on the left. An early variant of the arm of service disc would have the unit number below and the state initials superimposed on the symbol, for example crossed rifles. His canteen (**5**) sits inside an aluminium cup, both fitting into the carrier. Two pairs of underpants were issued, the short pair (**6**) being for warm weather. The long pair (**7**) was popular even in warm weather due to the coarseness of the issue breeches. The back of the 1910 pack (**8**) shows the placement of the 'meat can' or mess tin pouch over the entrenching tool carrier. The cartridge belt (**9**) shows the detail of the

flaps as well as the arrangement of the grommets. These allowed equipment including the first aid pouch (**10**) to be arranged on the belt to the wearer's comfort. (Adam Hook © Osprey Publishing Ltd)

Marcheville, 11 November 1918

There were significant changes in the doughboy's uniform from 1917 to 1918 (**1**). The Americans quickly converted from the canvas legging to the puttee (**1a**) – a wrap of wool worn around the lower leg. The M1917 or 'Kelly' steel helmet (**2**) remained in service into the early days of World War II. The 1910 pack, shown in exploded view (**3**), (**4**), (**5**), would be festooned with what was needed in actual campaigning. The pick, shown disassembled as well as in its carrier (**3**), could be attached to the cartridge belt in the same manner as the bayonet. The entrenching tool and its carrier (**5**) were attached to the pack beneath the 'meat can' pouch. The 'campaign' or 'Montana' hat has been replaced by the overseas cap (**6**). Fighting on a chemical battlefield required a gasmask (**7**). Carried inside the bag is the filtering unit, contained within a yellow painted tin. The newly introduced 'Pershing boot' (**8**) withstood trench warfare much better than the earlier shoe. (Adam Hook © Osprey Publishing Ltd) often seen with a bronze 'US' disc on the front right side. The overseas cap had one great advantage over the campaign hat in that it could be easily folded down into a small size for storage while the helmet was worn.

For protection in the front lines, a steel helmet was worn. The US M1917 helmet was a copy of the helmet worn by British soldiers, with some minor differences in the liner and chin strap. The helmet was painted in a mixture of olive drab paint and sawdust, which resulted in a textured finish that cut the reflection of light off the metal.

It should be noted that while divisional insignia was approved during the war, it was not worn by the troops, and should be considered part of the Army of Occupation era, rather than of the war itself. It was not until the end of October 1918 that it was decided that a divisional patch, following the British model, should be worn on the left sleeve. Two weeks later the fighting had ended.

For infantrymen, the main piece of equipment was the cartridge belt. Made of khaki-coloured webbing, the belt had ten pouches, each capable of holding two five-round stripper clips. This gave the rifleman 100 rounds of ammunition immediately available. The belt was also equipped with eyelets, so that the bayonet and first aid pouch could be attached, although the bayonet was often carried on the side of the haversack. The canteen, or water bottle, carrier was connected to the belt in a similar fashion. Into this khaki fabric item was slipped the M1910 aluminium canteen, which nestled inside an aluminium cup. Two press tabs, similar to the tabs on each of the ammunition pouches, held the canteen in place. The canteen carrier was stencilled with the letters 'US'.

The belt was the central piece in the M1910 pattern web gear. Without it, the rest of the equipment could not be worn, as the haversack, not having shoulder straps, was equipped with front and rear suspenders that attached to the belt. The haversack was designed to be attached to a lower pack carrier to enable the infantryman to carry all of his equipment on a march. The entire combination was to be worn in a specific manner, which precluded carrying equipment that had not been visualized at the developmental stage. This system would prove to be a liability during actual combat conditions. There was a separate pouch to carry the mess tin/meat can, and the entrenching tool would connect to the back of the pack under this pouch. The entrenching tool carrier, designed to carry a T-handled shovel, could also be worn off the belt, and was also stencilled with the letters 'US'. After it was realized that a soldier would need to carry more than 100 rounds into action, cloth bandoliers carrying 50 rounds in five pockets of ten were made available. These came in both khaki and green. They were intended to be discarded as emptied, and were in fact issued with the ammunition already in them.

Inside the haversack itself would be carried, according to the regulations, the soldier's rations and his washing/shaving kit. Additional clothing was carried in the lower pack carrier, along with the poncho/shelter half, blankets and bivouac necessities. The M1905 bayonet and scabbard could be attached to the left side of the haversack, as could the M1917 pattern bayonet (this made it less of a nuisance while marching). The haversack and pack carrier were originally produced in a greenish shade of canvas, but this later changed to a khaki colour.

For those not issued a rifle, there was an alternative belt available for use. The 'pistol' belt was made of khaki webbing and fitted with the same grommets that the cartridge belt had. The grommets, set in groups of three, were spaced around the entire belt, allowing equipment to be hung off at various places. A very successful design, the belt continued in use with succeeding patterns of US field gear. The other item of equipment that became universally issued was one not visualized in the M1910 equipment design. This was the M1917 box respirator, which was carried in a khaki pouch on the user's chest. Based on the British design, the respirator and bag were supported by a khaki strap that went around the wearer's neck. The strap could be expanded to allow carrying on the hip. The bag also had a string attached to it that could be tied around the torso to prevent the gasmask from flopping about during movement. This piece of equipment was always worn facing inwards, so that when opened the top flap would be away from the soldier.

Company K, 111th Infantry, 28th Division. Three US divisions served alongside the British, the 33d eventually being returned to American operational control. The 28th and 30th, to ease logistics, were issued British weapons, and in some cases British uniforms with American buttons. The troops illustrated here have just been issued No.1 Mk III Lee-Enfields. (NARA)

WEAPONS

Initially, due to shortages of weapons, wooden rifles were issued to drill with, and use was made of dummy guns in bayonet training as well. The primary rifle of the army at this time was the 1903 Model Springfield. A .30 calibre weapon based on a Mauser action, it was a rifle that in various forms would have a service life into the 1950s. The integral box magazine held five rounds that were loaded with a stripper clip. The rifle was extremely accurate (its long service time reflected its value as a sniper's weapon), and with a turn-down bolt it was quick to rechamber and unlikely to get snagged on obstacles. The length was only about 43in (110cm) overall, so it was not an unwieldy weapon, like the 1898-pattern Mauser or the Steyr M95, for use in trench warfare. Furthermore, the rifle only weighed a little more than 8½lb (4kg), so it was not a heavy burden.

During the war, a modified version, the M1903 Mk I was developed. This rifle was compatible with the Pederson Device, which replaced the bolt of the original rifle, and functioned as a semi-automatic receiver. Top fed with .30 calibre pistol ammunition, it was envisioned that the device would give the doughboy overwhelming firepower. The Pederson Device was awkward to use, and was only issued late in the war and in limited numbers. It did, however, prove to be a step on the way for the US Army to develop semi-automatic weapons that led to the M1 Garand being introduced into service in 1936. For the American army, the main problem with the '03 was that at the outbreak of war there were only 600,000 in the inventory. The Springfield was partnered with the M1905 bayonet. Eighteen inches (46cm) long, it was carried in a scabbard made of brown leather and covered in khaki cloth. While extensive training was done with the bayonet, the men learning both French and British drill, it was seldom used in action.

As beloved as the '03 Springfield is in the American mythology of the war, it was not the primary service rifle for the doughboy in France. The British had been buying a Mauser-action rifle from the United States earlier in the war, known to the British as the No.3 Mk I or, as Americans refer to it, the P14 Enfield. A fine weapon in its own right, in British service it was overshadowed by the Short Magazine Lee-Enfield (SMLE). This was for a variety of reasons, including the P14's length at just under 4ft (1.2m), and its weight, 9$\frac{1}{2}$lb (4.3kg). Additionally, the magazine only held five rounds as opposed to the SMLE's ten. By these standards it was also inferior to the Springfield. The P14 had one major advantage as the United States entered the war. It was in production. Rechambered from .303 to .30-06, the rifle was taken into service by the US Army as the P17 Enfield. This rifle ended up equipping the bulk of the AEF, and was carried by such luminaries as Sergeant Alvin York. York was a conscripted conscientious objector who decided the war was a righteous cause. On 8 October 1918, as a corporal, he was part of a patrol in the Argonne that encountered a German machine gun unit. Eight of the 17 Americans became casualties, but York rallied up his men and took the German position, capturing 132 and killing up to 25 more. He received the Congressional Medal of Honor for his actions. (This award did lead to a minor controversy when a motion picture based on his life depicted him with a Springfield.) The M1917 Enfield bayonet was carried in the same scabbard as that of the Springfield.

Again, the African-Americans had a different experience. Just as they received French leather gear and gasmasks, so they were equipped with Berthier 07/15 rifles and bayonets (see p.68). The Berthier, a long, unwieldy weapon (51$\frac{1}{2}$in/131cm long) with a thin bayonet prone to snapping, also had a five-round magazine, although early versions only carried three rounds. This weapon reflected French reliance on the grenade and artillery, and was markedly inferior to the Springfields and Enfields carried by the AEF.

One last rifle merits discussion, even though it was not used in France. Just as Great Britain placed contracts to manufacture the P14 Enfield, the Tsarist government of Russia placed orders for the manufacture of the M1891 Mosin-Nagant rifle. Following the revolution, shipment ceased, and the Remington Company was left with an extensive inventory. When the decision was made to send American troops to Siberia as part of the expeditionary forces, they were equipped with these rifles. In .30 calibre and having a five-round magazine, they were similar to other rifles at the time, although longer than any other US-used rifle. The bayonet had a socket style of attachment, much like earlier muskets, and the blade resembled a spike. There was no special web gear introduced for use with this rifle as the standard equipment belt functioned perfectly.

Weapons and equipment.
(**1**) M1903 Springfield rifle;
(**2**) P17 Enfield rifle; (**3**) M1917
bayonet for the P17 and
Winchester 1897 shotgun;
(**4**) Pistol belt without any
attachments; (**5**) M1911
Colt semi-automatic pistol;
(**6**) M1917 Smith and Wesson
revolver; (**7**) Grenade vest;
(**8**) Cartridge belt. (Adam Hook
© Osprey Publishing Ltd)

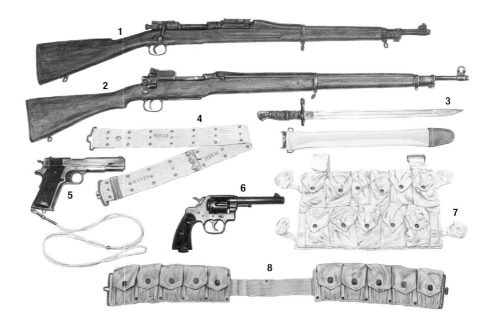

The training that the troops received reflected the realities of war as observed by the British. Emphasis was made on trench life, and on the use of hand grenades and supporting machine gun fire. This is not to imply that Pershing's desires were overlooked; individual marksmanship was still stressed, as was 'open' warfare. The troops were also instructed in British bayonet drill. The divisions that were placed with the French were getting the same types of instruction.

These training courses helped to compensate the men for the lack of access to weaponry in the US. In Europe, troops had access to actual trench mortars and light machine guns (LMGs) in order to better learn their functioning. Some weapons systems were still lacking, however. It was noted that originally rifle grenadiers were issued French rifles and discharger cups. A version for the Springfield and P17 Enfield was issued just in time for the 1st Division's attack on Cantigny.

Not only did the rifle grenadiers originally receive foreign weapons, but so did the automatic riflemen, and they kept theirs for the duration of the war. The French Chauchat (see pp.71–2) was issued as the standard LMG, despite the availability of better designs such as the Lewis gun. Weighing over 20lb (9kg), and armed with a 20-round magazine, the weapon had several major drawbacks. Some 19,000 of these awful weapons, chambered to accept the US .30-06 round, were ordered. Cheaply constructed, the weapon was prone to jamming and in some instances simply falling apart. The tendency to jam was aggravated by the half-moon-shaped magazine. With open sides, it allowed in dirt and grime that further exacerbated the Chauchat's malfunctions. It was not unusual for those issued with the Chauchat simply to discard it, acquire a rifle and cease to function as an auto-rifle squad. In the last weeks of the war, the Browning Automatic Rifle (BAR) was introduced, but most units suffered with the Chauchat (there was a post-war scandal over the contracts). The BAR, which saw service up into the Vietnam era, was well liked by the doughboys. A special version of the equipment belt, with pouches to hold the BAR magazines, was developed and issued. In place of an ammo pouch, a cup to hold the butt of the weapon while firing from the hip was installed on the far right side of the belt.

With the prolific American issuance of heavy machine guns, these weapons became a fundamental part of the tactics used even by small units. While a very small number of the 1895 Colt 'potato diggers' were sent over to France, the main American weapon used by the machine gun companies was the Browning M1917. Externally resembling the Vickers and Maxim guns, the Browning actually functioned differently, using what is known as a short-recoil system. Water-cooled, and fed from 250-round belts, it was a weapon that would see service in several wars. The other machine gun used in great numbers by the American Expeditionary Force was the French Hotchkiss Mle 1914 (see pp.70–1). Air-cooled and fed from 24- or 30-round strips (a longer strip of 249 rounds linked in three round groups was available, but unreliable), the Hotchkiss suffered from feeding mechanism problems and, due to the method of using strips, a low actual rate of fire. As a result of the low numbers of available Browning M1917s, the Hotchkiss was the most common machine gun used by the AEF. Due to the weight of these guns, machine gun companies were often supplied with carts to transport the guns and ammunition over distances. Pulled by mules, the machine gun companies acquired the nickname 'jackass batteries'. This use of animals to pull machine guns was not an American policy only, the Belgian Army being famous for its dog carts earlier in the war. Trench mortars were also used, these being of French or British design.

Just as the Chasseurs Alpins taught the Americans how to use grenades and other lessons of trench warfare, the Americans were quick to repay the debt by teaching French children how to use traditional American weapons. The American soldier had a reputation for getting along with the children of the local populace. (NARA)

Many US machine gun companies were armed with Hotchkiss guns, and US artillery was also of French design. Exceptions to this were the 27th and 30th divisions, which stayed with the British, and for supply purposes were equipped with British weaponry, and in some cases British uniforms with American buttons. For the rifleman, this meant being issued an Enfield – surprisingly not the P14, a .303 version of the same gun as the American-issued P17 Enfield (the Eddystone) with which US soldiers would have been familiar – but rather the SMLE.

The average American showed considerable skill in grenade-throwing, a skill commented on by their foreign advisors. There was a cultural reason for this – baseball was a favourite pastime of many American boys – although a baseball weighs somewhat less than the 22oz (624g) of a Mk II grenade.

US grenades were modelled after existing French and British models. The most common, and one that saw service up into the Vietnam

War, was the Mk II, aka 'the Pineapple'. The origin of this weapon was the Mills bomb (see p.106), as well as a French grenade known as the LeBlanc. Pulling out the pin that held back a striker armed the grenade, fused for 5 seconds. To keep the weapon safe after the pin was pulled, the doughboy would push down on a metal lever, or spoon. When the pressure on the spoon was released it would flip up, and the striker would hit a primer, igniting a fuse. The fuse in turn would cause a detonator of fulminate of mercury to explode. The resultant explosion would break apart the outer metal shell into fragments that could travel up to 80 feet (24m). Because of the blast radius the weapon was best used when the thrower had some cover to shelter behind.

The standard rifle grenade was the Viven-Bessières (VB). This was the same rifle grenade in use with the French Army (see p.70). The mechanics of the detonation sequence were similar to those of a hand grenade, only the fuse ignition was started by a bullet. Unlike some systems which used special 'grenade-launching' blanks, the VB used a standard rifle round, the bullet setting off the fuse as it passed through a tube which was in the centre of the grenade. The same gas that sent the bullet on its way propelled the grenade itself. Travelling nearly 200 yards (183m), and fired off the ground (never from the shoulder) at an angle of 45 degrees, the rifle grenade became an important part of the platoon commander's arsenal.

These were not the only grenades that the doughboy learned to handle. There was a French-designed thermite grenade, used to destroy captured or abandoned artillery when dropped down the barrel of the gun. The thermite charge would need to burn itself out, and the grenade would burn hot enough to 'weld' a breech mechanism shut. Other grenades were developed for other specific missions. An 'offensive' grenade, a charge in a cardboard tube, was developed. This caused an explosion with no fragmentation, the effect stunning those within the concussive zone. A gas hand grenade was also developed; it delivered a small amount of gas, and was to be used to clear pillboxes, cellars and the like.

At the other extreme were the variety of 'trench knives' and other 'nasties' acquired by the doughboys once in France. The M1917 trench knife consisted of a triangular blade set into a handle with a cross bar. The cross bar curved down like a hand guard linking up to the pommel. This bar was covered in jagged metal studs, being in effect a 'brass knuckle' of the type familiar to street brawlers of the time. Also popular were an assortment of 'trench-art' maces, clubs, daggers and other sundry unpleasantries. Considering the lack of bayonet fighting, one often wonders why the soldiers of World War I would equip themselves with, and in fact manufacture, these weapons: the psychological impact of being faced with a bayonet should not be underestimated. In the close confines of a trench, however, a rifle with an attached bayonet could be a liability. This is why many of the 1½ft-long (46cm) bayonets that started the war were ground down to a length of 10in (25cm) or 12in (30cm). The other consideration is that most patrol actions in No Man's Land were conducted in the dark. In night fighting, a muzzle flash would betray the firer's position, and this is one reason why there was a reliance on grenadiers, or bomb-throwers, on trench raids. This is not to imply that rifles were not carried on these excursions: they often were, and were used as well. But there always existed the possibility of close-up killing. This is also where pistols and revolvers fit in, although they too suffered from the drawback of muzzle flash.

Two handguns were issued by the army most often, both in .45 calibre. They were carried by officers and senior NCOs, as well as by machine gun crews and other speciality soldiers. Inevitably, they trickled down into the ranks and could be found in the possession of the occasional private or

Previous spread:
Jackass battery: machine gun company from the 18th Infantry on the move at Bonvillers, 30 May 1918. A US infantry division had a lavish complement of machine guns. For transportation mules were used to tow the guns and ammunition. (NARA)

corporal. The most famous of these guns is the M1911 Colt, a single-action semi-automatic. The M1911 and its derivatives spent seven decades as the sidearm of the US military, which speaks volumes for its performance. The weapon held seven rounds in a detachable box magazine, and for a single-action weapon was very safe, being equipped with both a grip safety and a lever safety. The main drawback the gun had was that it required a good amount of training in how to handle it and keep it clean. The revolver in service was the Smith and Wesson M1917, sometimes referred to as the 'Victory' model. Holding six rounds in a central cylinder, it used the same .45 calibre bullet as the Colt. However, unlike most revolver ammunition, the .45 is rimless. This resulted in the gun being loaded with three round 'clips'. These half-moon-shaped devices each held three cartridges in the chambers, as a kind of a sabot around the rear of the round. German pistols were coveted as souvenirs, in particular the '08 Luger, and were carried into action by those owning them.

One last weapon carried by the Americans deserves to be examined, as it caused some controversy during the war, yet ended up remaining, in different forms, in US military usage throughout the century. The shotgun was a sensible weapon for trench warfare, as it was very effective as a 'trench broom'. Naturally the German military was not as enthusiastic about American use of shotguns, and complaints were levelled that the weapon violated the rules of war. Of course, it should be noted that many other armies, including the British during the Malayan Emergency, have made extensive use of 'scatterguns'. The most common shotgun used by the army (and Marines) was the M12 Winchester, a further development of the M1897 used in the Philippines. A 12-gauge weapon using a pump action in combination with a tubular magazine, the Winchester could spray loads of .32 calibre pellets over an area with deadly speed. These guns were even equipped with a bayonet lug to take the 1917 Enfield bayonet, making 'the combat trombone' a truly formidable weapon. The main drawback to the shotgun was the shells. These were made of cardboard and were susceptible to damp. Given the muddy conditions on the Western Front, they were often reduced to a soggy mass that was useless for action. Brass-cased rounds were eventually developed, but did not see use before the end of the war.

MOBILITY

It was common for troops to be shipped over to France in requisitioned heavily modified ocean liners. Members of the 33d Division, for example, left Hoboken, New Jersey, on 10 May 1918 for a 13-day cruise to Brest. The enlisted men were confined to the lower decks and the officers had the upper berths. There were constant complaints about the quality of the food and the lack of decent drinking water. However, most of the two-week voyage was uneventful, largely thanks to the adoption of the convoy system and the addition of the US Navy to the war against the U-boats. Unfortunately influenza was starting to make inroads, and claimed the lives of some men on the trip.

The issue of transport was to cause serious headaches for the American High Command. There was never enough transportation available. In addition to the strain of shipping an entire army to Europe, the combined merchant marines were also bringing in food to the British and Italian civilian populations, a serious rival to the needs of the US Army. As a result of these other efforts, the British took a somewhat proprietary attitude towards the use of British shipping for the American effort. This manifested itself in the idea that US troops transported in British hulls should be at the disposal of the British Army, a policy which ran in direct contradiction to Pershing's desire for a unified American army in Europe.

After arriving in France, troops received additional training. Much of the training was focused on cooperation between infantry and artillery, as well as on how to function with tanks on the battlefield. This was done by British troops – while most US soldiers were taught by the French, the US 27th, 30th and 33d divisions all went into the British sector. The 33d was eventually withdrawn and returned to the control of II Corps, but the other two divisions fought alongside the British in the battles to break through the Hindenburg Line.

Movement from the ports – and it should be noted that some doughboys were shipped to Great Britain and from there to France – was usually by rail. As was common with other armies, the men were shipped in boxcars, the famous (or infamous) 'forty and eights'. This moniker arose from the markings on the side of the cars that they were for '40 hommes ou 8 chevaux' (40 men or 8 horses). The cramped conditions aboard the trains led one officer to comment that he had his 40 men on board, but if they tried to fit in some horses someone was going to get trampled. The French railroad officials closely monitored the number of troops who were transported this way, and a bill was submitted to the AEF for their fares. Railroads were also used to send the men from the training camps to the front lines, although it was not uncommon for the troops to be marched

6 April 1918. The 1st Battalion, 26th Infantry, head off to help stop the *Kaiserschlacht*, Maron, France. 'I've got my 40 men on board, but if you try to fit in eight horses, someone is going to get trampled …'. The French boxcars that the doughboys travelled on became one of the enduring memories of the war. (NARA)

these distances. Motor transport was supplied when available, usually to assist machine gun companies and other formations that had to move heavier equipment. This system broke down during the shift of troops from the St Mihiel to the Argonne fronts, resulting in some divisions having their infantry regiments arrive, and then having to wait some time before their supporting artillery and other services arrived.

The initial troops sent to France contained a high percentage of regulars, although it should be noted that they were not all regulars – the 1st Division contained a large number of raw troops transferred in at the last minute to bring up numbers. The majority of doughboys being trained in France had instructors from the Chasseurs Alpins, the 'Blue Devils'. The Americans quickly built a good relationship with the French, based in a large part on the consumption of alcohol. The Americans, receiving better pay than the French, often paid. This had an effect on the cost of liquor, which at the time of the Yanks' arrival was the equivalent of 70 cents for a quart of champagne or $1 for a fifth of cognac. As soon as US pay standards were figured out by the local merchants, champagne soared in price to $5 a quart and cognac went up to $10 a fifth. The situation was probably not helped by early arrivals paying for their alcohol in Mexican money and United Cigar coupons, taking advantage of the average Frenchman's limited knowledge of US currency!

INTO COMBAT

On 4 July 1918, four companies of the 33d Division supported an Australian attack on Hamel, in what proved to be a controversial action, not from the tactical but from the political perspective. The action was just the type of use of American troops that Pershing had feared, and finding out about it in advance he prohibited the use of the doughboys. General Sir John Monash, the Australian commander, realized that the withdrawal of US elements from the attack would tarnish relations between the troops of the two nations as well as interfere with the scheme of attack and insisted on using four companies instead of the original ten, pulled from the 131st and 132d regiments. The manner of their use fulfilled Pershing's worst nightmares. Rather than being used as a composite battalion, the companies were each attached to an Australian battalion. However, fresh, full-strength American companies were enormous when compared to their battle-depleted Australian counterparts. Rather than use the American companies as tactical groupings, each company was broken down into platoons. These platoons were then directly attached to Australian companies.

There is some evidence that the platoons themselves were broken down into squads and integrated into Australian platoons. This, of course, was the scenario that Pershing was trying to avoid at all costs – the dispersal of US fighting forces as replacements in Allied formations. The attack went extremely well. Despite Pershing's fears that the US troops would be mishandled, they acquitted themselves well. Australians themselves were complimenting the American participation. At the same time, though, the amateurish enthusiasm of the doughboys was commented on, it being obvious that the Yanks had much to learn about modern war. The important benefit was that US troops were seen by their allies to be taking a proactive part in the war. The debit column was outside of the perspective of the average fighting man – an enhanced distrust of the British commander Haig by Pershing.

While the troops shown here are actually from the United States Marine Corps, this image was repeated with all US troops arriving in France. Here French instructors teach the Yanks grenade-throwing technique. Of interest is the use of Adrian helmets by the students. (NARA)

The Hamel incident was not completely isolated, although future occasions would not be such a surprise to the American High Command. The two other divisions training with the British Expeditionary Force (BEF) would remain with the British for the balance of the war, taking part in the attacks that broke the Hindenburg Line. The 131st Regiment did their part in these offensives as well, jumping off on 8 August, the black day of the German Army. Under operational control of the British 58th Division, the prairie regiment would stay in the line until the 16th, taking several German positions but losing 750 men in the process. The 33d would return to American control, but would serve under French command in the future, as did several other American divisions. In this, the 33d was unique in having been controlled operationally by the Americans, the British and the French. It should also be noted that in these later operations the American formations acted as divisions; the troops were not broken down into small elements attached directly to foreign organizations. Elements of the 6th US Engineer Regiment had been used in March 1918 to help stop the German offensive, and no complaint was made due to the emergency situation and the fact that the troops were in the line of the German advance.

THE AMERICAN COMBAT EXPERIENCE

World War I battlefields have an unfortunate image in the collective memory of being a persistent meat-grinder devoid of any real leadership from above. While there is an element of truth in this, the reality is that by 1918 all the major players were sophisticated in a tactical sense. In fact, the criticism which is made of the Americans desiring 'open warfare' is slightly hypocritical. The development of stormtroop tactics, complicated artillery plans such as the rolling barrage and the use of technology (tanks, aeroplanes, chemical weapons) all point to the fact that serious thought was given to the problems of stalemated war and the desire to break free. Gone were the methods of 1914, and even those of 1916. No longer was a first day of the Somme likely. While heavy casualties were accepted, those being caused by faulty tactics were not. It was into this evolving form of warfare that the AEF entered.

While the Americans had accepted British and French training, the policy of 'open warfare' always lingered. As a result, the lessons of the war were not always digested, and the doughboys went into action imbued with the spirit of 1914. The problem with the American desire for open warfare was aggravated by the backward state of the army in 1917. The army was neither physically nor materially ready for war. Efforts were made to adapt quickly to the new reality of war, but, ironically, these were undermined by a certain belief that the American army was already mentally equipped for modern war. This is not to imply that nothing had been learned. The army made use of the latest in French artillery techniques, and ample use was made of machine gun support (in fact, the Americans in their tables of organization provided more machine guns at the divisional level than any other combatant). The heavy issuance of automatic weapons extended to the platoon level. This can be illustrated by the fact that in the 1st Division the average night patrol in No Man's Land was of 20 men armed with pistols, knives and hand grenades, along with two automatic riflemen.

In the attack on Hamel, and subsequent offensive operations, the troops would have lightened their burden. Greatcoats, blankets and any excess equipment were usually dumped together, and two men from each company were left to guard it. There were several good reasons for this, one being the physical condition of the men. Ration parties often had difficulty getting food to the line during periods of intense fighting, and as Captain Evarts of the 18th Infantry pointed out in his memoirs,

Many American units moved into the line in the winter of 1918. Here a doughboy from the 101st Infantry, 26th Division, formerly the 5th, 6th, and 9th Massachusetts National Guard, takes aim at the Germans, January 1918. (NARA)

attempting to march at double time in full gear on one meal a day was difficult at best. A very common theme in the memoirs and diaries of soldiers is the breakdown of supply services in getting food, which was moved up at night, to the troops in combat. In one 1st Division soldier's journal, every page out of the first 17 makes reference to such incidents. Food, when it did arrive, was often what the troops called 'slumgullion', a type of stew made with poor quality beef, referred to as 'monkey meat' (or '*singe*', by the French), and whatever else was lying about. After several days of living on hardtack, it was appreciated none the less. One veteran, quoted in Berry's *Make the Kaiser Dance*, recalled finally getting cold steaks brought up by the mess sergeant after five days without getting rations. He had brought up enough for the entire unit, but due to casualties everyone got double rations.

One anecdote, as related in Evarts' *Cantigny: A Corner of the War*, revolved around the fact that the ration parties had been blown up by artillery fire, resulting in an additional 14 hours of hunger. A sergeant, looking into No Man's Land, observes a line of 20 dead Moroccans, killed weeks before by machine gun fire. The NCO then crawls out 200 yards (183m) to the corpses, searches six and recovers two cans of corned beef that he brings back to his section. While this seems extreme, the fight against hunger was a day-to-day battle, and not one fought by the Americans alone.

In addition to problems with food and supply, being in the combat zone had other risks. Lingering gas was a problem faced by many troops, and arsenic poisoning acquired in the bottom of shellholes was known to occur (arsenic poisoning came as a by-product of the explosives burned in detonations). Mustard gas, which would eat into flesh like lye, particularly in damp or moist areas, was known to destroy the testicles of those who took shelter in holes where the gas lingered. Being a persistent gas, this could be for some time. It should be noted that mustard gas injury often had a long-term effect for returning doughboys. Many wounds were so disfiguring, particularly those from chemical agents, that many American cities in 1919 and into the 1920s passed laws

167th Infantry, 42d Division, bring Pershing's dream of open warfare to life at St Bonat on the Meuse, 15 September 1918. (NARA)

about being seen in public, lest women and children be frightened. The disfigured veteran was required to be hooded or masked. If not, he faced criminal prosecution for 'Being Ugly on the Public Way', which is how the law was titled in Chicago.

To a certain degree, the doughboy would have enacted Pershing's desire for 'open warfare'. A great deal of the time that US forces were in the line, they were involved in various offensives. While much of the fighting can be seen as an attempt to break out of trench warfare, it takes on the flavour of a transition to open warfare. As the fighting progressed through the Argonne forest, the extent of fortifications dug by the Americans fell off. It was not unusual to have front line trenches that were only 4ft (1.2m) deep. Furthermore, it should not be assumed that the trench lines were all connected. Often a battalion would find its companies holding supporting but separate trenches. This could even happen within the company, becoming more frequent with the expansion into the German lines. Barbed wire was to be strung five strands tall, but due to shortages it was often less.

The 132d Infantry in a front line trench towards Alexandre, Meuse, 17 September 1918. Note that the position is both narrow and fairly shallow. Some accounts of the fighting mention that front line trenches were often only 4ft (1.2m) deep at this stage of the war. (NARA)

The trenches themselves were no guarantee of safety from enemy fire. Many of the sectors occupied by the Americans had trenches cut out of chalk. Chalk being very hard, shell splinters would often ricochet off the walls and cause mayhem down the line as chunks of chalk were added to the shrapnel. Due to the difficulty of digging in these conditions, 4ft deep was sometimes rare for trenches, and orders were issued that for a trench to be placed on a map it had to be deeper than 2ft (0.6m). It should always be remembered that World War I took on the form of trench warfare for a very definite reason: the killing power of modern weaponry. Dominated by artillery and machine gun fire, the common infantryman had very little in the way of personal protection. The trenches bogged the war down and led to great bloodbaths as both sides looked to break through, but on a daily basis they provided protection for the fighting man. As the Americans lost the ability to dig in, so they lost significant protection.

The reduction in defensive works had much to do with the terrain. The Argonne is heavily wooded and quite hilly. This landscape would curtail the laying out of defences to the extent that was seen in more open areas like Flanders. Fields of vision were greatly restricted and the ability to direct artillery fire diminished. Command and control would also be hampered, and much of the fighting would be hard to direct at any level higher than the company. The restricted terrain had other malevolent side effects as well. Unlike open areas, a high-explosive shell exploding in the woods would shower its target not only with metal, but also with splinters of wood gouged out of the trees. These could prove as fatal as shell fragments. Luckily, the quality of German shells was

The band of the 132d Infantry, Germonville, Meuse, 15 September 1918. A band may seem an incongruity in a combat zone during the modern era, but they did provide morale behind the lines. (NARA)

not always high. According to Captain Evarts, a quarter of all German 77mm rounds fired at his company were duds; the problem was that the '155mm shells were always good!' Evarts also related that an attempt to move forward to relieve another company during the Soissons offensive led to 50 per cent casualties in just 100 yards (91m) of movement over open ground. Quite clearly, even with a certain amount of 'duds', artillery dominated the battlefield.

After Hamel, the 33d Division was moved from the British sector. The men were shipped to the area of Verdun, relieving French troops on Hill 304 and in the Cumières-le-Mort-Homme sector. As this sector passed from French to American control, the 33d became part of the US III Corps. Having seen combat experience, the men of the 33d were now cast into a teaching role, helping to acclimatize the US 4th Division to the front lines. Not part of the St Mihiel operation, the division prepared itself for its role in the Meuse–Argonne offensive.

The plan called for III Corps to advance along the left bank of the Meuse, and to push on towards two objectives. Forming up during an artillery barrage on the night of the 25th, the 66th Brigade, which contained the 131st and the 132d, prepared to go over the top. The sector of the Hindenburg Line that they were to attack had seen off many assaults earlier in the war, and was considered to be well fortified. In addition to the German fortifications, the terrain was cut by a series of ridges, which were for the most part solid. The problem was the depressions in between; these areas were marshy in nature. Additional hazards were the Forges brook and the closed terrain of the Bois de Forge, occupied by German troops. Troops would have to traverse difficult terrain that featured obstructed lines of vision, complicating their ability to locate their objectives. Furthermore, in an era where much of a commander's ability to control his troops depended on being seen, it limited an infantryman's ability to respond to his officers and NCOs. One way to counteract these problems was to keep closer together, but this ran the risk of higher casualties from artillery fire and automatic weapons.

Under cover of the artillery bombardment, the 108th Engineer Battalion prepared approaches over the water obstacle to assist the attack. The assault that morning jumped off at 5.30am, partially concealed by a heavy fog, and the 66th Brigade advanced toward the German positions. It took nearly an hour to cross the brook and re-form, and then, supported by a rolling barrage, the attack recommenced. The brigade, and in particular the 132d, were in an important position for the entire battle plan. Being at the right of the US line north of the Meuse River, they were the door-hinge on which the American front was swinging. With this important task, the 132d could not afford to be delayed. Taking fire from the village of Forges itself, a company was detailed to capture the town quickly. Fighting in a built-up area led to many of the same difficulties as fighting in woods.

The town itself was in a fairly destroyed state, as was common with most formerly inhabited places along the line. This gave the German defenders a certain advantage, as they had some cellars and the remains of other buildings on which to anchor their defence. These localities could be connected with trenches to provide an integrated system. Furthermore, the ruins of the town could be used for concealment, and the broken nature of the area would disrupt any attackers. As had been shown in earlier fighting in towns such as Fleury near Verdun, these 'strongholds' could become deathtraps. The time needed to reduce these positions could also be disruptive to the battle plans devised by the High Command.

To take Forges, the company broke down into smaller groups, the platoons becoming reliant on their sections as fighting teams. In a like manner, the 132d's sister regiment was setting about

MPs bringing in German prisoners, Mesnil-St Firmin, 28 May 1918. Note the two different ways of wearing the box respirator bag, the man on the left of the photograph having his at the ready position. (NARA)

removing the threat of German machine gun positions in the Bois de Forges. While the village could be defined as a built-up position, the training for 'open warfare' was now to come into practice. To storm the German positions, the Americans fell back on the principle of 'Fire + Maneuver = Offense'. As defensive positions were identified, the automatic rifle and rifle grenadier sections would lay down suppressive fire. This was designed to prevent the Germans from responding to the assault teams. Hopefully, the fire would force them to remain in shelter, and away from a firing position, or at least disrupt their ability to shoot accurately at the attacking squads. While this was taking place, the 'bomber section' and the riflemen, with bayonets attached, would move to a position close to the defenders, and preferably sheltered from them. Once they were close enough, the bombers would throw grenades into the objective, and the riflemen would quickly follow up before any survivors could recover. If any of the defenders fled, the riflemen would be in a position to pick them off. Once the position was captured, the automatic riflemen and the rifle grenadiers would move forward and the cycle would begin anew.

Often, if the objective were a village or other fortified area more advanced than the usual entrenchments, specialized assault engineers would accompany the troops. In American operations, these men were often French. Equipped with flame-throwers and explosive charges, they could help the infantrymen quickly overcome hardened defences. French tanks often supported US troops until the American army had developed a strong enough armour force. At Cantigny, in May 1918, both French engineers and Schneider tanks accompanied the 1st Division. Eventually, the

Americans developed their own armour corps to assist in these operations. While having some British heavy tanks, most of the American armour consisted of Renault FT-17s.

The defenders would, of course, try to make the attackers' job as difficult as possible. Fighting positions would not be isolated, but rather be sited so as to support each other with interlocking fire. This put an additional burden on the US fire element, in that they would have to suppress several locations to protect the manoeuvre element. Depending on the terrain, the squads might be broken down further, so as to provide more direct support for the assault. Luckily for the US troops, the attack on the 26th went swiftly and the town was cleared with a minimum of loss. Prisoners were taken, and the company had to hustle to catch up to the rest of the battalion and the main assault on the woods. The US troops kept up at a rapid pace, and within 4 hours the entire brigade had achieved the assigned objectives, with a penetration of 4 miles into the German positions. By the standards of 1914–17, this was a significant advance. Moreover, the casualties had been extremely light, again by the standards of the day. Only 36 men out of a total of 241 casualties were dead. The defenders had suffered heavily in comparison, relinquishing over 1,400 prisoners in addition to their casualties. Twenty-six artillery pieces and roughly 100 machine guns were captured as well. It was fortunate that the Germans were in a state of collapse. During an earlier attack at St Mihiel, one officer reported the Germans walking out with their hands up, crying 'Kinder' to signify that they were older men with children at home in the hope of not being shot out of hand (Berry, *Make the Kaiser Dance*).

After being brought up through the communication trench, the men of Company M, 102d Infantry, enjoy, or at least eat, the food out of the bacon can. (NARA)

All things considered, it was a fantastic success for the 132d. This is not to imply that the attack had been easy. In the broken terrain, communication would have been difficult, and an infantryman would feel isolated from his squadmates. With the overwhelming noise of artillery fire and the constant rattle of machine gun fire, voice contact would be difficult. In woods and gullies, with the impairments of gas and smoke, visual relay of orders would suffer as well.

On a grander level, the plan for the capture of the Bois de Forges was to follow the principles of pinning fire and manoeuvre. Rather than attack directly into the German defences in the forest, it was planned to use the two regiments of the brigade to encircle the woods, and then attack from an unexpected direction. To keep the defenders in place, the supporting artillery often fired on areas that would not be attacked in an effort to mislead the Germans, and, more importantly, prevent them from shifting troops to meet the real hazard. The attack itself was distinct from many similar operations. The two regiments attacked in a standard formation, two battalions forward and one in reserve. What was odd was the frontage over which the regiments attacked. The 132d had a frontage of nearly 2,000 yards (1.8km). Given manoeuvre room between the assault battalions, each was covering a frontage of 800 yards (731m). By the standards of World War I tactics, that was an incredible frontage more appropriate for a regiment than a battalion.

After this assault, the focus of the attack shifted away from the 33d Division, and the troops had the time to consolidate their positions and prepare new defences. The divisional artillery were not given a rest, as they were added to the fire plan of other formations, but the infantry would not attack again until mid-October. This pause was not a rest period. The division held its place in the line, and was subjected to all sorts of 'hate mail', or harassing fire, from the Germans, usually in the form of heavy artillery bombardments on different trench sectors. Patrol actions, both for security and to gather intelligence about the opposition, continued. Such actions could be dangerous, adding to a growing casualty list even in quiet sectors. Invariably sent out at night, patrols would head off to determine the condition of German wire entanglements and assess the strength of the enemy line. Often the Germans would be doing the same, and the two parties would stumble across each other in No Man's Land. These patrols could be quite large in size, up to a platoon of 40 or so men. On occasion, a trench raid would be organized that would involve up to a battalion. The object of these would be to occupy temporarily part of the German line, take prisoners and gather intelligence.

As has been shown with all the warriors on the Western Front, life in the trenches was never 'restful'. In addition to patrols, there would be fatigue parties to rebuild damaged sections of trench and parties to bring forward the supplies: sandbags, barbed wire, 'pig tails' (the iron rods that the barbed wire attached to) and other tools. Other details would include bringing up rations, and bringing out the wounded and the dead. Even on quiet days, casualties would be incurred from artillery and snipers. When a unit was pulled out of the line, the time was used to repair equipment, acclimatize new equipment, absorb replacements for the men lost and train for the next offensive.

Then, on 9 October, the push against the Germans began anew. For this 'stunt', a term referring to an attack or raid, there was a change. Instead of attacking as part of the US III Corps, the 33d Division found themselves under French control as part of the French XVII Corps. The Prairie Division was unusual in this – they were the only formation to serve under the command of the Americans, the British and the French. As part of this French attack, the mission was to drive across the Meuse and on to Highway 64. The offensive ran until 13 October, and then dug in on new defensive positions and was relieved by French Colonial troops.

HEALTH AND DAILY LIFE

Artillery was dreadful under any circumstances. The primary killer of the war, artillery bombardment disrupted communications and movement as well. The psychological strain of being under prolonged shelling was debilitating. 'Shell shock', sometimes referred to as 'neurasthenia', became a recognized problem during the war. A mental breakdown brought about by the stress of living and fighting in the trenches, it was originally thought to derive from the anxiety of being under bombardment with no way to retaliate and no control of one's surroundings. Later, the condition was understood to be broadly based, a cumulative effect of the various stresses of life in the front lines. Treatment of this phenomenon varied from country to country, but early in the war could be brutal, sometimes including execution for cowardice. By the time the United States entered the war, shell shock was better understood, and psychologists in all the warring countries were examining the condition. The US Army was very forward thinking in this regard, and psychologists were included in the medical staff deployed to France. This inclusion is not as surprising as it may seem, as the early 20th century was a time of great social reform with progressivism penetrating all strata of American society, including the military. That the army, already inclined towards a more 'modern' outlook of the world, should continue this trend is only natural.

Doughboys were not shy about frequenting taverns and brothels in France, and venereal disease became a problem. This had been anticipated, and the men inducted into the military had been

The 'cootie' truck. Clothing would be put into the chambers and heated and fumigated in an effort to kill the seam squirrels, i.e. 'cooties' or lice. (NARA)

given a battery of lectures on the dangers of sexually transmitted disease. The matter was taken so seriously that the informational pamphlets given out were translated into different languages, so that soldiers who had been born in Poland, Russia, Italy or several other countries could have the material in their native tongue.

As was inevitable considering the AEF attitude towards prostitutes, treatment of those with venereal diseases was designed to be as painful and unpleasant as possible. In light of the fact that Pershing himself had twice contracted gonorrhoea while stationed in the Philippines, his attitude does appear a little hypocritical. Of course, it can also be argued that as a result of his experience he was aware of how disruptive the disease could be. Sexually transmitted diseases did in fact become a considerable problem within some units of the US Army at the time. It became even more notorious among the Americans in the expeditionary forces serving in Russia. A US contingent began arriving at Archangel in September 1918; within six months of service they had accumulated 129 incidents of gonorrhoea and 54 of syphilis.

Treating the wounded on the battlefield was fraught with difficulties. Infantrymen often participated in the removal of casualties, as the number of stretcher-bearers was never adequate for the task. When a man was wounded, it was not always possible to recover him immediately due to the demands of the fighting. This was part of the rationale of having each man carry a first aid kit on his belt – if he was able to, he could dress his own wound. If unable, with a little luck a nearby comrade would be available to do immediate first aid. Ideally a medic would attend to the wounded man, but they could be in short supply during battle. When the time came to evacuate the wounded, teams of stretcher-bearers would carry them out. The ideal ratio was to have four bearers per casualty, but this was not always practicable. Trying to manoeuvre a wounded man down a communication trench could be awkward with only two bearers. The fatigue factor would be very high, and relief for the bearers would often mean coercing infantrymen into helping.

The casualty evacuation route would be as follows: first the injured soldier was brought to an aid station, at either the battalion or regimental level. He may have been carried in by stretcher or his friends, or walked on his own two feet. From the aid station, he would be taken to a dressing station. This is where the wounded man would be loaded into an ambulance and driven to a field hospital. A division had four of these hospitals, but only two were brought forward and used at a time. By standing down two of these facilities they would be prepared to move forward if needed, and in a condition to deal with any changes on the front.

While at the field hospital, triage would be performed, as well as any additional immediate aid needed. At this point, where a patient would go next depended on his wound. There were separate hospitals established for the treatment of gas casualties, and a special ambulance was even devised for these men. Nearly a third of the casualties treated in US hospitals were gas casualties. Wherever possible, field hospitals were situated along rail lines, so that further evacuation could be done by railroad. This was usually the case as France had an established rail network, and US railway engineer companies were aggressively repairing the lines and refurbishing the rolling stock. The trains that would transport the wounded from the field hospitals were not equipped with the 'forty and eights' but were dedicated medical trains staffed and run by the Sanitary Corps.

The base hospitals were planned to be 500-bed facilities, although they would often have up to 1,000 beds. The AEF High Command desired enough hospital space for 15 per cent of the troops deployed to France. The rapid expansion of the army had caused a crisis for the

Medical Corps, and much of the manpower needed to staff these hospitals was obtained by taking the American Red Cross into the military wholesale. Doctors received reserve commissions; the nurses went into the Army Nurse Corps; and the balance of the personnel went into the Regular Army.

Following the Armistice, the army did not immediately return to the United States, much to the disappointment of many. The army, slowly following the retreating Germans up to the Rhine, began to take over occupational duties. Many units were hit hard by influenza, the pandemic killing more people around the world than the war had. The influenza, or 'La Grippe' as it was often known, was a particularly efficient killer. Death on the same day as becoming symptomatic was not uncommon. Due to the strain on the medical establishment, room in military hospitals was quickly used up, and some of the afflicted stayed with civilian families. For some families, the patient became a proxy for a lost son. Of course, fraternization, even in this manner, was forbidden, but carried on openly nonetheless.

Treatment was for the symptoms, not the cause. The victim manifested mahogany-coloured splotches over the cheekbones, which quickly spread across the face. The lungs rapidly filled with liquid, as the 'flu' was a type of pneumonia, and the patient could die. Although the disease was not always fatal, some 20 per cent of the world's population suffered from the flu in 1918–19, including 25 per cent of the American population. The US Army had 43,000 flu fatalities during

A special surgical ambulance designed by a French officer, Second Lieutenant Julian A. Gehrung, for use by the Red Cross of the Allied armies. It was equipped for the treatment of gas victims, or for those suffering from eye, ear, nose or throat troubles. (NARA)

this period, the hospital at Camp Devens, Massachusetts, reporting over 100 a day during the height of the epidemic.

Those who recovered remained with their company. In April 1919, the 33d Division began to redeploy to the United States, sailing from the same port where they had arrived, Brest. Prior to their departure from Europe, a new group arose among the soldiers – the American Legion. Inspired by Teddy Roosevelt, the organization was to become a political powerhouse during the 1920s. The group, ostensibly for all those who had served, became a bastion of white, middle-class values. Those suspected of having ties to radical labour or bolshevist leanings were excluded. This in particular affected those who served in Siberia, many of whom were considered tainted by the experience. The American Legion was to take umbrage with groups such as the International Workers of the World, also known as the 'wobblies', conscientious objectors and anyone deemed a slacker. With this attitude, the Legion played a role in the 'Red Scare' of 1924.

DOUGHBOYS AND THE YMCA

The YMCA, or Young Men's Christian Association, had an unusual role during the Great War. A development of the 'progressive' movement in the United States, the 'Y' offered its services to the government during the war. This in itself is not strange: the Catholic Knights of Columbus and the

St Nazaire, a sight seen by hundreds of thousands of American eyes. The gentlemen holding up the sign, despite the uniforms, are probably not military personnel but rather 'Y-Men' from the YMCA, an organization that eventually earned the loathing of many doughboys. (NARA)

Jewish Relief Board did the same, and were employed in helping to acclimatize Catholic and Jewish soldiers into the military. The YMCA did much the same type of work, providing library and other services to the men in the training camps. The role for the 'Y' did, however, expand greatly beyond that of the other organizations.

The YMCA went to France in great numbers, establishing offices in most US Army facilities. These were often in the nature of welcome centres, such as that found in St Nazaire. Due to their ubiquity, the 'Y' became a pseudo-branch of the military. The federal government gave them the concession to provide cigarettes and other sundries to the troops, much in the way of a 19th-century sutler. This led to a certain amount of resentment from the troops. One of the items they provided was a pea-green sleeveless sweater, which was approved to be part of the uniform.

The hostility stemmed from the sale of items to the ranks. Objects such as cigarettes were viewed as staples, not luxuries, and the men objected to paying for them. As many of the cigarettes had been

The Toulon sector on 22 March 1918. A 'Y' man serves hot chocolate. The trench construction is very French, an impression reinforced by the *poilu* standing by the entrance to the dug-out. (NARA)

donated, there was just cause for the resentment. The image of the 'Y' man – close to the front but out of danger, selling cigarettes and hot chocolate to the wounded – became a negative stereotype. In post-war literature, such as John Dos Passos' *Three Soldiers*, the 'Y' man becomes the embodiment of corruption. Veterans often spoke with hostility about the YMCA, particularly when compared to the American Red Cross, which did give away cigarettes and other items to the men.

A further cause of resentment was the fact that many 'Y' men were seen as slackers. They were in France and they were in a variation of official army uniform, but they were not seen as taking all the risks that the men did. Coupled with the 'mercenary' behaviour, the YMCA staff were often viewed as slackers of the most noxious type. As a result, the soldiers often took out their frustration in the YMCA's direction. It would not be out of place if one night, while out of the line, some doughboys broke into the YMCA's wagon or hut and made off with a lot of the cigarettes. Their NCOs and junior officers, who shared their attitude, would be likely to look the other way.

In mitigation, it should be pointed out that the 'Y' did provide free stationery for the soldiers to use to write home. A US Army manual on the management of soldiers stressed that writing home regularly was an important part of the life of the troops. At a YMCA hall, not only could men write to their relatives, but also help would be given to illiterate soldiers so that they could stay in communication with their families.

To give an example of the extent of YMCA influence, by the end of the war there was even a 'Y' hall in Fort Douaumont, Verdun. It should be noted that the YMCA, following the lead of the US Army, had separate, and usually inferior, facilities for black soldiers. In addition to these functions, the YMCA also helped provide entertainment to the doughboys, much as the United Service Organizations (USO) would for their sons in another war. Elsie Janis, one of the more popular performers of the day, who had made her name in musical comedy, was sponsored by the YMCA on a tour of the front.

In marked contrast to the relationship with the YMCA was that between the average doughboy and the Salvation Army. Where the 'Y' man was often seen as a slacker, lurking in the rear and taking the doughboys' money while spewing hypocritical 'moral' advice, the Salvation Army made a different impression. Stateside, their activities were in line with other organizations. They maintained a presence in training camps and provided 'comfort' services. The Salvationists would also go to the homes of soldiers serving overseas and make sure their families' needs were being met. This in itself earned them a great deal of good will. The positive attitude among the servicemen was reinforced by Salvation Army activity in France. While having nowhere near the numbers deployed by the YMCA, the Salvation Army became an important symbol to the average soldier. Far from staying in the rear, they brought their mission into the front lines, and it was not unheard of for the 'lassies' to give doughnuts and coffee to doughboys within range of the German guns. Out of the line, the canteens run by the Salvation Army seemed devoid of the hypocrisy so often found in other similar establishments. This difference was often commented upon in letters home from the men in the trenches.

And of the doughnuts? It was decided to serve them in France as they were easy to make under difficult conditions, and were not something that had been done before. The Salvation Army had decided that to make the troops as comfortable as possible fresh baked goods would be served, and the doughnut was very suitable. It became such a strong image with the AEF that it had wartime associations well into the succeeding decades.

British troops attack 'over the top' with fixed bayonets, 1916.
(Stephen Bull)

PART II:

TRENCH WARFARE

THE EARLY YEARS OF WAR

Dr Stephen Bull

THE ARMIES IN 1914

From the end of the first decade of the 20th century, arms races, imperial ambitions, complex international alliances, Balkan wars, France's wish for revenge for the humiliations of 1870–71, and – perhaps most importantly – Germany's claim for a 'place in the sun', all conspired to make a major European conflict seem inevitable. History seemed to suggest that such a war might be bloody, but mercifully brief. It was generally accepted that non-European conflicts, such as the American Civil War or the Boer War, were unlikely models for a future European war. For this eventuality there were other precedents, such as the Franco–Prussian War of 1870–71, which had lasted barely six months: or the 'Brothers' War' of 1866, in which Prussia had defeated Austria in a mere seven weeks. In the face of this threat of a short campaign, most powers – with the possible exception of Britain, protected by her navy and her natural moat – seemed to accept that only preparation for swift and aggressive land warfare on a massive scale could bring security.

NUMBERS

How many fighting men a nation could field, and how quickly they could mobilize, were vital factors in 1914. France, with a roughly static population of 39 million, had a standing army of about 700,000: this could immediately be increased to 1,150,000. Reserves and Territorials would bring the total to 4,200,000; but to maintain such a high proportion of her manpower under arms for anything but a short period would be difficult. The Germans had 840,000 troops before the war, but a larger population and swift mobilization over good rail links could put more than 5,000,000 into the field, with scope for some further increase. Austria-Hungary's pre-war strength was only 415,000, but could be much expanded – though she was hampered not only by the polyglot nature of her army, but by the enmity of her smaller Serb neighbour and her uncertain relations with Italy. By contrast with Austria, Russia's potential strength was almost limitless, yet her peacetime army numbered 1,300,000, and the time she was expected to need before she could bring her 'steamroller' into action was of critical concern to the planners. Britain had never fielded a mass army, and her immediate contribution would be less significant than that of Belgium; the fighting strength of the British Expeditionary Force in August 1914 would be less than 90,000 men. In a longer war it would remain to be seen whether her industry, financial resources and empire could be translated into an armed strength comparable with that of the Continental powers.

The armies of Europe were acknowledged for their diverse national characters and strengths: the Austrians, for their super-heavy Skoda siege artillery; the French, for their dash; the Russians, for their numbers and doggedness; the British, for their discipline and steadiness and their skilled musketry. Yet there were many underlying similarities in structure and purpose. The fighting component of all the European armies was divided into artillery, infantry and cavalry, and though there were differences in detail and quality, the main technological developments and tactical doctrines were common to all.

Artillery was universally divided into field and heavy – the latter also termed 'foot' or 'siege' artillery. 'Quick firers', capable of rapid accurate fire, equipped the field batteries. The model for many modern field pieces was the M1897 French 75mm, which used 'fixed' ammunition in a brass case, and had hydraulic buffers to absorb recoil. Each French field battery was led by a lieutenant and comprised four such guns. Each gun was part of a section with its own ammunition wagon, six gunners, six drivers, a corporal, and a sergeant in charge. As Gunner Paul Lintier put it, each section 'lived the same life ... a microcosm, with its own friendships, antipathies, and habits'. The French fighting *batterie de tir* was supported by its *échelon de combat,* which contained the support wagons, stores, and mobile forge.

The field guns of most armies fired shells of less than 10kg (22lb) weight, predominantly over open sights – i.e. by direct, observed fire – in immediate support of troops in battle. Metal gun shields provided some protection for the crews against small-arms fire. The medium and heavy artillery was intended primarily for siege work, and was comparatively ponderous, but provided a possible antidote to field fortification. Despite this, few armies possessed heavy guns and howitzers for delivering indirect fire in any quantity. Some of the best were the various types of German 15cm schwere Feld-Haubitze, the 1913 model of which was capable of 9,000m

Opposite:
German infantryman, *c.* 1915, in full marching order. (Stephen Bull)

Greatcoated French infantry firing the 8mm Lebel from behind a stone breastwork in training. They wear no knapsacks, but retain the M1892 musette or haversack, and the M1877 litre-capacity water canteen of characteristic two-spout shape. During 1915 the two-litre model designed for African campaigning would become general issue on the Western Front; in the new world of trench fighting troops were often cut off from supplies of drinking water. (Stephen Bull)

British recruits for Kitchener's New Armies at Aldershot in 1914, wearing re-issued full dress uniforms without badges and carrying Long Lee-Enfield rifles. Many men who volunteered at the outbreak of war would not be committed to action until 1915 or 1916. Training and equipment took time, and some British politicians hoped that the drastic step of commitment to all-out war could be avoided. (Stephen Bull)

(5.5 miles) range. The Germans had the highest proportion of guns, with more than six pieces per thousand infantry – marginally higher than the French and Russians, and roughly double the concentration fielded by their Austrian allies.

The cavalry was no longer contemplated as a battle-winning weapon, but was widely and correctly assumed to have an important role in reconnaissance, in skirmish actions, in pursuit of a beaten enemy, and as a tool to exploit gaps and breakthroughs in the enemy line. Cavalry were universally trained in the dismounted use of rifles and carbines; even so, the British manual of 1907 accurately stated that the firearm had not replaced the 'magnetism of the charge' and the 'terror of cold steel'. Sabres were still carried by most cavalry, and lances by many; German mounted troops were issued with them whatever their precise designation, leading their enemies to assume that 'Ulans' were present at almost every engagement early in the war. Perhaps those who maintained the greatest faith in horses were the Russians, with their relatively ill-developed rail infrastructure. Just prior to the war more than 10 per cent of the fighting troops of the Russian Army were mounted, and the mobilized strength of the Cossacks alone was 939 squadrons – almost 140,000 men.

Yet it was the infantry that was the most numerous arm and was expected to decide the issue of battle. German *Field Regulations* described the infantry's significance:

> In tandem with artillery its fire will batter the enemy. It alone breaks his last resistance. It carries the brunt of combat and makes the greatest sacrifices. Consequently it garners the greatest glory. Infantry must nurture its intrinsic drive to attack aggressively. Its actions must be dominated by one thought: forward against the enemy, cost what it may!

Accordingly, though many nations also fielded large formations of cavalry, the infantry division was the building block of armies. General officers directed the movements of divisions and brigades, which were composed of regiments and battalions. Divisions were commonly of a dozen or more battalions, with a total strength of between 8,000 and 16,000 rifles. Typical regular divisional organizations of 1914 included:

Austria-Hungary:	12–16 battalions, in two brigades (12,000–16,000 rifles)
Belgium:	18 battalions, in three brigades (c. 18,000 rifles)
Britain:	12 battalions, in three brigades (c. 12,000 rifles)
France:	12 battalions, in two brigades (c. 12,000 rifles)
Germany:	12 or 13 battalions, in two brigades (c. 12,000 rifles)
Russia:	16 battalions, in two brigades (c. 16,000 rifles)
Serbia:	16 battalions, in four regiments (c. 16,500 rifles)
Turkey:	10 battalions, in three regiments (c. 8,000 rifles)

Most nations divided battalions into four companies, an exception being the Turks with three companies per battalion. Though there were smaller subdivisions, useful for administration and training, the company, with a full strength of roughly 250 men, was the smallest unit expected to have any tactical significance.

The individual infantryman was the pawn of the battlefield, whose perceived value was to carry his rifle over long distances, to react reliably and predictably to orders from his officers, to shoot and, if necessary, to close with the enemy to decide the outcome with butt and bayonet. The British *Infantry Training* manual of 1914 stated that the objective of training was to make the soldier better 'mentally and physically' than his adversary – the essentials being to develop 'soldierly spirit', a trained body, and facility with 'rifle, bayonet, and spade'. Drill in close order was used to produce cohesion, discipline and obedience to orders.

Perhaps the biggest single difference between the armies was in their method of recruitment. On the Continent conscripted armies, composed of a sizeable percentage of all men in a certain age group, had been the norm for many years. Under the French system (see pp.54–9), as modified in 1913, a man became liable for service in the year following his 19th birthday, and his military responsibilities could continue for at least 21 years thereafter. Three years were spent full time with the active army, whereafter he passed into the Reserve. Although he could then return to a civil occupation, 40 days' training a year was required. After 11 years he would pass from the Reserve to the Territorial Army, with which he would spend a further seven years with a reduced liability of nine days' training per year. In theory, when war came reserves would take their place in the line with the regulars, while territorials were employed in home garrisons. It was also possible for unmarried men to join the active army voluntarily for four or five years under the *devancement d'appel*; and re-engagements of five, ten or 15 years were available to officers and NCOs. The German system (see pp.29–30) was somewhat similar in that conscripts from the active army passed into the Reserve after two or three years; thence to the Landwehr; and finally into the Landsturm.

It was Britain that provided the most radical contrast, with a fully professional regular army recruited by voluntary enlistment, and no conscription until 1916 (see pp.92–6). General von Moltke called the British Army 'that perfect thing apart', but it was a perfection in miniature, overwhelmed by the demands of mass warfare. Ex-regulars provided a small pool of reservists, and a second line force was provided by the part-time 'Territorial Force', which had been reorganized in 1908. However, massive expansion from 1914 was only achieved by accepting a huge wave of citizen volunteers at the outbreak of war, and marshalling them into 'Kitchener' Service Battalions of the New Armies. These would be neither fully equipped nor trained for many months. The British system was cheap in peacetime, but provided only a very small, if highly trained, force in wartime. The Continental system of conscription, though more expensive, offered the benefit of widespread military experience throughout the population, and relatively easy mass mobilization.

TACTICS

The initiative in battle was believed to lie with the attacker, and though schemes varied in detail most nations concurred that successful actions consisted of a series of phases including an advance to contact, firefight and conclusive finish, most likely involving the deployment of a strategic reserve and a charge to take the enemy position. Essential to overcoming enemy firepower was the soldiers' high morale and strong offensive spirit. The German *Drill Regulations* of 1906 and *Field Service Regulations* of 1908 outlined an ideal plan in which the infantry manoeuvred in columns until within about 1,000m (1090yd) of the enemy. Relatively close formation would allow personal voice command by the company commanders and NCOs. With the enemy position under direct observation, the artillery attached to the German brigade would open fire. If the shelling shook the enemy sufficiently the columns could continue to advance; if the enemy remained steady, the attackers would deploy into loose linear formations of smaller units, and bring the enemy under effective fire from about 500m (550yd). A reserve would be prepared for the final attack on a flank or weak point. Once superiority of fire had been achieved the German force could close with the bayonet.

The French were even more aggressively disposed, having come to the conclusion that their defeat in 1870 was at least in part attributable to lack of offensive spirit. It was also thought that since the attack gave an advantage, and since French forces might be outnumbered, repeated and vigorous assaults were imperative. Similarly, Russian regulations of 1912 held that 'offensive action is the best method of obtaining our object; only thus can

The use of stereoscopic binoculars at an observation post of the Prussian Guard heavy artillery. Each German battery had a six-horse 'observation wagon', and the seven-man battery commander's staff included observers and telephonists for the relay of data. 'Observed' fire was the norm in 1914: 'predicted' or map fire techniques were in their infancy, but developed rapidly after 1914. (Stephen Bull)

we seize the initiative and force the enemy to do what we wish'. The Russian battalion was supposed to deploy into lines from column at about 2,500m (1.5 miles) from the enemy, with each battalion advancing on a front of about 1,200m (1,300yd). At about 800m (875yd) the firefight would commence, perhaps aided by a unit firing in from a flank. When within 50m (55yd) of the enemy the infantry could charge home, either with the firing line itself, or with a reserve brought up specifically for the purpose.

In the British synthesis it was envisaged that a commander would use part of his force to engage and wear down the enemy, until the 'general reserve' could strike the decisive blow. Fire was important but it was only the means to the end of making 'the advance to close quarters possible'. The forward troops were to advance 'by rushes' if checked by fire, with either the whole line going on as a body or 'by portions of it alternately'. Bugles were to sound the charge as the assault was made. Battalions were to retain 'local reserves' as required. Infantry advances were to be supported by rapid fire from the artillery, though coordination was acknowledged to be tricky, and best managed through a variety of means of communication including liaison officers, signals and runners. Similarly, it was admitted that scope for changes of plan during an action was limited, and battalion commanders were enjoined to give clear orders with definite objectives from the outset.

The British company commander was instructed to 'make full use of his horse' in communicating with both nearby companies and his battalion commander. The company would form the firing line, its immediate supports, and possibly provide a 'few scouts' to 'feel the way' for the advance. Platoon commanders were to supervise their men directly, and section commanders to control the fire of their men. As in the German system, British troops were expected to close with the adversary once superiority of fire had been gained, and the impulse to the final advance was often expected to come from the firing line itself:

> The fact that superiority of fire has been obtained will usually be first observed from the firing line; it will be known by the enemy's weakening of fire, and perhaps by the movement of individuals or groups of men from the enemy's position towards the rear. The impulse for the assault must therefore often come from the firing line … On rarer occasions the commander of the attacking force may be in a position to decide that the time has come to force a decision, and may throw in reinforcements from the rear …

INFANTRY WEAPONS IN 1914

RIFLE AND BAYONET

All the major powers used bolt-action rifles, capable of firing ten or more rounds per minute. The majority used pointed, jacketed bullets with smokeless propellants, and were sighted to about 2,000m (1.2 miles) – though unless large bodies of men shot at large targets, few casualties were likely to be caused at such distances. According to British definitions, 'close range' was anything up to 600 yards (550m); 'effective range' was from 600 to 1,400 yards (550 to 1,280m); 'long range', from 1,400 to 2,000 yards (1,280 to 1,830m); and 'distant' from 2,000 to 2,800 yards (1,830 to 2,560m). Though nearly all riflemen were capable of generating murderous fire at close ranges, the diverse weapons and levels of skill of the combatants did cause variations in effectiveness. British regulars were arguably the best all-rounders, professional soldiers who were taught 'volume' fire, rapid fire, snap shooting and fire from cover as well as simple accuracy. Their efficiency was aided by the 0.303in Short Magazine Lee-Enfield (see p.105), a weapon developed as a universal arm for infantry and cavalry in the wake of the Boer War. Its useful features included a handy length, a bolt that could be manipulated without taking the gun away from the aiming eye, and a ten-round magazine that could be swiftly loaded from five-round chargers from the top. Fifteen rounds a minute was a perfectly feasible rate of fire; speed trials at Hythe actually reached 28 rounds under ideal conditions.

The Germans were well served by their 7.92mm Gewehr 98 Mauser rifle (see p.20), which had a particularly robust action and good accuracy, though it was somewhat long for confined spaces, and had only a five-round magazine. It was reasonably fast, and the most skilled soldiers achieved up to 12 rounds per minute, despite a long bolt pull; one British test at Hythe achieved 14 rounds per minute. Other Mauser-action rifles were used by Belgium (which used a slightly outdated 1889 model), Serbia and Turkey. Austria-Hungary, Italy and Romania all had Mannlicher rifles, which were effective enough, though perhaps marginally hampered by a five-round clip loading system. Given the advanced rifle technology of France in the later 19th century it is perhaps strange that she should have entered the war still using the 8mm M1886 Lebel (see p.67–8); this was good at the time of its introduction, but its eight-round tubular magazine under the barrel, loaded with single rounds, was outdated by 1914. The Lebel was supplemented by more modern Berthier rifles by 1916, but these suffered from a ludicrously small three-round magazine; capacity was later increased to five rounds.

The Russian rifle – officially termed the '*3 lineyaya vintovka obr 1891*' or M1891 'three line' rifle, in reference to an obsolete measurement of calibre – was also known as the Mosin-Nagant after its Belgian and Russian design team. Shorter variants of this 7.62mm weapon were also produced for the cavalry. All featured a five-round box magazine, and most a long, slender socket bayonet which terminated in a screwdriver point. All the powers suffered from rifle shortages as the armies burgeoned: the British trained on obsolete models and imported from America, before committing their New Armies to action; the Germans took some old models to war, but made up their deficiencies by captures from the Russians and hugely increased production. The Russians were perhaps the most unfortunate, attempting to unlock the country's vast human resources with inadequately developed industry and distribution. Approximately 4,500,000 Russian rifles were on hand at the outbreak of war, but recruitment and losses in action made it impossible for the Tula arsenal to keep up with demand. Austrian captures and a motley range of imports were seen in widespread use.

All rifles developed considerable power, most being able to cut through a half-inch (1.3cm) steel plate at very close range, or a house brick at 200 yards (183m). The human frame was considerably less resistant, but the precise result of a bullet strike was difficult to predict. At moderate range a direct hit could produce a neat hole, little blood and a swift death. Close ranges or tumbling ricochets were a different story: the medical journals recorded exit wounds 5 inches (12.7cm) across, and there were instances of men with shattered heads and spilt brains who took hours to die. Frenchman Marc Bloch recalled facing some 'superb marksmen' who hit three of his company in the head:

When a bullet hits the skull at a certain angle, it explodes. That was the way L died. I went to bring him back. Half his face hung like a shutter whose hinges no longer held, and one could see the almost empty cranial box. I covered the horrible wound with my handkerchief … I knew that L had died without suffering; it was less terrible to see his poor head than, later, to find the photograph of his small sons in his wallet.

Yet there were also many lucky escapes. Bloch himself was hit in the arm by a round that had 'the decency to exit immediately, merely burning my skin'. Corporal John Lucy of the 2nd Battalion, Royal Irish Rifles, recorded a man called Muldoon, hit in the head on the Aisne in 1914, who 'slid grinning' to the ground, only to rise again later covered in blood: 'He got back safe, with a peculiar wound, not at all fatal, for the bullet had hit him near the top of the head, and had passed under his scalp and out at the back, without injuring his skull. The curious behaviour of some bullets, as in this case, puzzled us then and afterwards.' On the other side of the line, near Dixmuide, German Ulrich Timm, a former theology student, reported being hit by a bullet that threw him to the ground. He survived; close examination determined that the shot had passed through both legs, a bundle of field postcards and some books.

For all but a few specialists bayonets were a universal feature of the soldier's equipment in 1914. It was commonly assumed that the longest blades were the best, giving maximum 'reach' in bayonet fighting. The slender blade of the original Seitengewehr 98, issued with the German M1898 rifle, was 52cm (20^1/$_2$in) long; and though the M1905 bayonet most commonly seen during the war was 37cm (14^1/$_2$in) in the blade, it was a broad and intimidating weapon. Pioneers received a version with a saw-back blade for cutting purposes; later in the war these saw-backs were abandoned or ground smooth, since there was a fear that they contravened the Geneva Convention and might lead to men captured carrying them being shot out of hand.

German MG08 Machine Gun Team, Infanterie-Regiment Nr.85, Spring 1915. The MG08 was a typical and effective water-cooled Maxim design, fed with 7.92mm ammunition from 250-round fabric belts. With a total weight of around 50kg (110lb), it was generally transported behind the lines in machine gun company carts. In the front lines tactical movement could be achieved either by unclamping the gun from its 'sledge' mount, or by pivoting the latter's legs to allow it to be carried stretcher-fashion, as here. (Adam Hook © Osprey Publishing Ltd)

The British carried the M1907 'sword' bayonet with the SMLE, with a blade 43cm (17in) in length. *Infantry Training* certainly took its use seriously:

A bayonet charge will normally be delivered in lines, possibly many deep, against a defending force also in lines, over rough ground ... Single combat will therefore be the exception, while fighting in the mass will be the rule ... In a bayonet fight the impetus of the charging line gives it moral and physical advantages over the stationary line. Infantry on the defensive should, therefore, always be ready to meet a bayonet charge with a counter-charge, if their fire fails to stop the assailant.

Such counter-charges were not, however, to be launched prematurely, since a charging enemy actually offered a very vulnerable target to the defenders' fire as he moved in the open, unable to take aimed shots during the rush forward. British trainees were taught not only to rush at dummies, but to parry, jab with the rifle butt and trip the enemy to the ground. Dummy 'fencing muskets' with telescopic collapsing bayonets were sometimes used for realistic one-to-one training.

MACHINE GUNS

Hiram Maxim had designed his famous machine gun in the 1880s, but though it had seen employment in colonial and Far Eastern contexts, it was essentially untried as a battlefield weapon in a major European war. Maxim had referred to one of his early models as a 'World Standard', and though there were differences in detail and nomenclature, his boast was not far wrong in 1914. By this time Germany, Britain, Russia, Bulgaria, Romania, Serbia, Turkey and the United States were all using weapons based on the heavy but devastatingly efficient Maxim gun. Typical, and perhaps most important, of these Maxim weapons was the German MG08 (see pp.23–4). This gun, developed from an earlier 1901 model, was a belt-fed, water-cooled, fully automatic weapon based

0.303in Maxim machine gun, Somerset Light Infantry, *c.* 1914. Britain had purchased small numbers of the machine guns designed by Hiram S. Maxim as early as 1887, and on the eve of the Great War the scale of issue was two guns per infantry battalion. Heavy, too few in number, and at first unimaginatively employed, British Maxims were progressively replaced by the more modern Vickers gun which had been approved in 1912. (Stephen Bull)

on the Maxim 'toggle lock' system. After cocking and firing the first shot the mechanism would continue to operate as long as the trigger was pressed. Fed from 250-round belts, its cyclic rate was about 400 rounds a minute, though it was more economical and less prone to overheating when fired in shorter bursts. Its basic mount was the Schlitten or 'sledge', a steady, versatile but heavy platform. Carried on the march in carts, the gun and mount could be moved like a stretcher on the battlefield, dragged or dismounted and carried over the shoulders. The main nations not having Maxim system guns were France and Austria. The former used the air-cooled Hotchkiss, fed with rigid metal strips; though marginally lighter, this was not as efficient as the MG08 in sustained fire. The Austrians used the Schwarzlose, a robust water-cooled weapon with a relatively short barrel, but somewhat similar performance to the Maxim's.

In defence the various models of machine gun were potentially murderous, especially when dug in and arranged to fire over preregistered, enfilading 'beaten zones'. However, machine guns were available in relatively small numbers in 1914, largely because of financial concerns: the British and several other nations allowed only two per infantry battalion, while the Germans provided a company of six per three-battalion regiment. The Germans had marginally more machine guns proportionately, since each Jäger 'light infantry' battalion also had a machine gun company. Tactics for the aggressive use of machine guns were as yet poorly developed. They were carried forward with advancing troops, but their weight and relative tactical immobility made them less effective in this role.

As British instructions pointed out, the main advantages of the machine gun in 1914 were its high volume of concentrated fire (thought to equal that of about 30 riflemen), its small frontage and relative ease of concealment. At various ranges, 'beaten zones' could be created from 50 to 150 yards (46 to 137m) in depth. Conversely, the machine gun was 'defenceless when on the move', used large amounts of ammunition, and was prone to temporary stoppages. For these reasons the machine gun could be regarded as a 'powerful auxiliary to infantry', a weapon of opportunity suitable for surprise effect, or as a mobile reserve of fire to be moved up by wagon.

Under the British system machine guns provided close supporting fire for an attack and were then to be moved up rapidly once the ground was won by the infantry. The machine gun section was accounted part of the battalion headquarters, and though the entire personnel of the section were trained to fire the gun, a crew of two usually fired it in action. The gun was carried to the desired position in two parts, barrel and tripod, and re-assembled on the command 'Mount gun'. On the command 'Load' the starter tag of an ammunition belt was put into the breech mechanism, which was cocked to load the first round. The 'Number One' took his position behind the spade grips, the 'Number Two' by the belt box. Weapons were usually used to give 'rapid fire' in a series of 30- to 50-round bursts on concentrated areas; or 'traversing fire', in which five- or ten-shot bursts were distributed along linear target areas.

THE BATTLES OF THE FRONTIERS

The now-infamous Schlieffen Plan – the basics of which had been drawn up by Field Marshal Count Schlieffen, the German Chief of Staff, long before the outbreak of war – was arguably the best that Imperial Germany could have adopted in the event of a general conflict. Yet Schlieffen's plan was born of desperation and helped to usher in the very disaster that it was intended to avoid: all-out war on two fronts.

On the diplomatic map, Germany was encircled by Britain, France and Russia; her only dependable friend was Austria. Against such a background, it appeared that the only way in which a war could be won was by a massive pre-emptive strike against one of Germany's principal antagonists. Russia was a vast and unpredictable battlefield; with her primitive infrastructure she also seemed likely to be slow to mobilize. France appeared to offer the greatest threat, as the best able to mobilize quickly. It was therefore against France that Germany would throw the bulk of her force: seven armies, committed to a vast concentric wheeling movement or 'right hook' from the north-east, which would ignore Belgian neutrality to push west and then south around Paris, repeating the glories of 1870. The daring part was the risk of leaving just one German army – the Eighth – facing Russia in the East.

Following the assassination of Archduke Franz Ferdinand at Sarajevo, Austria went to war with Serbia on 28 July 1914. As Russia was mobilizing Germany followed suit, declaring war on Russia on 1 August. With the Schlieffen Plan now dictating her actions, Germany also declared war on France, the first of her troops entering Belgium on 4 August; and this violation of neutrality was the trigger that brought Britain into the war on the side of her French ally.

Germany had amassed about 1,500,000 men on the Western Front. The three armies under generals von Kluck, von Bülow and von Hausen on the northern flank were committed to the

The Kaiser and his generals. Note at right von Hindenburg, Ludendorff and François, victors of Tannenberg; and at left, von Falkenhayn, von Kluck and Crown Prince Wilhelm. (Stephen Bull)

longest swing through Belgium, with the intention of encircling Paris. Yet 'plucky little Belgium', which had been expected to collapse without a fight, manned her forts at Liège and Namur. Six German brigades under General von Emmich were deployed to crush resistance at Liège, but the result was unexpected. One Belgian officer described the carnage: 'They made no effort at deploying but came on line after line, almost shoulder to shoulder, until, as we shot them down, the fallen were heaped on top of each other in an awful barricade of dead and wounded that threatened to mask our guns.' On the afternoon of 6 August, General Ludendorff's 14th Brigade managed to penetrate between the ring of forts, but none were taken. The Germans were forced to bring up their 42cm Krupp siege guns; only on 16 August did the last of the forts fall, the wounded Belgian General Leman having bought valuable time for the Allies. (It has been conclusively proved that the reported widespread German atrocities in Belgium – once dismissed as propaganda – did indeed take place, apparently prompted in part by frustration over these delays and casualties.)

While the Schlieffen Plan made much slower progress than expected, French offensive operations, as outlined in 'Plan 17', were soon to degenerate into farce. Mesmerized by the lost province of Alsace, France concentrated her efforts in an attack by her Third, Fourth and Fifth armies eastwards from Verdun. Beginning the advance on 7 August, the French entered Mulhouse the next day; but on the 10th, after fierce fighting, the town was lost again. The offensive soon ground to a halt.

In the north, the 'revolving door' now swung decisively, as the German First and Second armies smashed into the little British Expeditionary Force at Mons on 23 August. As one 16-year-old eyewitness reported, the Germans walked into a wall of fire:

> The rifles blazed, but the Germans still came on. They were getting nearer and nearer and for the first time I began to feel rather anxious … They weren't an indeterminate mass any more – you could actually pick out details, see them as individual men … Ten rounds rapid! And the chaps opened up – and the Germans just fell down like logs. I've never seen anything like it.

Despite the losses on both sides, weight of numbers was soon pushing the BEF back into the now famous retreat from Mons.

According to Marshal Joffre's memoir of the Marne fighting, he had decided as early as 25 August that the French First and Second Armies would remain in Lorraine while the centre and left pivoted back on Verdun, with Third, Fourth, Ninth and Fifth armies and the BEF fighting to halt the German advance. Behind the British a further French army, the Sixth, would be assembled to cover Paris and, if possible, to manoeuvre to outflank the enemy. In an extraordinary twist, General von Kluck now took an apparent opportunity to strike to the left of the French Fifth Army, but this led to his army wheeling south short of Paris rather than encircling it as had been intended. On 2 September orders from General von Moltke confirmed this direction, envisioning that the main body of the French armies would thus be cut off from Paris. By 5 September the battle had been joined along a frontage of over 100 miles. That day Joffre issued his injunction that 'every effort must be made to drive back the enemy. A soldier who can no longer advance must guard the territory held, no matter what the cost. He must be killed in his tracks rather than fall back.'

'Campaign in Belgium and Russia 1914' – studio portrait of German veterans of the first campaigns, winter 1914. The NCO at left displays the *Schützenschnur* or marksman's lanyard, and a recently awarded Iron Cross 2nd Class from a buttonhole. Since he is not wearing his pack, a 'bread bag' (haversack) strap is rigged to help support his belt equipment. The lance corporal (note collar button) at right carries a 98AZ short carbine as issued to communication troops, cyclists and independent machine gun units as well as the cavalry. (Stephen Bull)

In the experience of French artilleryman Paul Lintier, this was often exactly the result. Distant battle sounded like 'rollers on a pebbly shore', but when a shell hit close the experience was very different:

A faint noise of wings, an unfolding of some silky material. It grew and swelled into a buzzing of hornets ... and then something indescribable – the very air became sonorous, became one great throb, and the throbbing was communicated to our flesh, our nerves, the very marrow of our bones ... I was a beast, terrified of death ... Crash! The thunderbolt seemed to have fallen at my very feet. The shrapnel bullets whizzed through the air in a great blast of wind.

Soon it was impossible to tell one sound from another. Firing back with the 75mm would be experienced as a vibration of the skull, and a taste, rather than a discernible noise. Battering attacks with artillery and rifle over open sights would cost a total of over 100,000 lives.

The German forces started with at least a local superiority of numbers, but the shifting of the French had tilted the balance until they were actually slightly outnumbered. To make matters worse, Russia had mobilized far more quickly than had been expected and, even as battle was joined on the Marne, vital German reserves had to be sent eastwards rather than to the West. Though General von Prittwitz's failure at Gumbinnen would be more than redressed at Tannenburg by General von Hindenburg by the end of August, this would be too late to allow any last minute changes of disposition in favour of the Western Front.

Employing every means of transport then invented, including the legendary Paris taxi-cabs, the French Sixth Army were now in a position to threaten the enemy's flank. The German advance was halted, and there was no plan to cover such an eventuality. On 9 September attacks were called off and General von Moltke ordered a retreat to the Aisne. Crown Prince Wilhelm blamed von Moltke squarely for the disaster: 'Military genius was conspicuously absent ... The battle was conducted in a wholly mechanical and conventional manner. The resultant trench warfare was the natural outcome of an exhaustion brought about by a failure on both sides to develop a decisive strategy.' The battle of the Marne was followed by the so-called 'Race to the Sea' which was actually, as Joffre observed, a series of attempts by the German and Allied armies to outflank each other to the north until they came right up against the coast. With the Germans in possession of Ostend, dry land eventually ran out; the war had nowhere to go.

THE FIRST TRENCHES

Trench systems came into existence for good practical and tactical reasons. The idea of all field works was to protect and hide troops, and the particular conditions that emerged during the latter part of 1914 made trenches a necessity rather than an option. Killing power had developed exponentially. In 1814 a soldier in battle would have been lucky to achieve three musket shots per minute to an effective range of about 100m (110yd); in 1914 the bolt-action rifle made ten aimed rounds per minute at 500m (547yd) perfectly practical. Taking into the equation the areas swept, as well as speed and accuracy, this suggests that each infantryman was now capable of generating ten times the volume of fire of his Napoleonic predecessor. Similar calculations applied to the artillery. In 1814 field guns could not usually be fired more than once a minute; they generally used solid shot, and few were of much effect beyond 1km. By 1914 'quick firer' breech-loading field

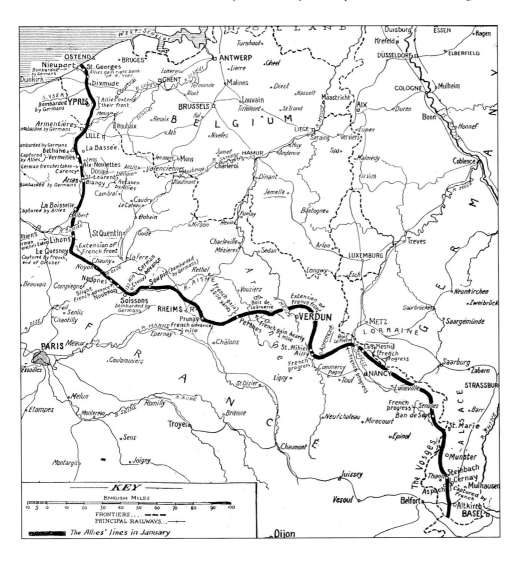

The Western Front, January 1915.
(Stephen Bull)

185

Ein Gruss aus dem
Schützengraben, 'a greeting from
the fire trenches': a postcard sent
back to the family Meyer from the
Western Front by a member of
10th Reserve Division, April 1915
(note the non-regulation socks
with laced ankle boots). Above the
fire step is partial revetting with
brushwood; by 1916 this was the
recommended method, although
trenches on the Eastern Front
made more extensive use of
timber. (Stephen Bull)

Bei den Armierungs-Soldaten! Der fertige Schützengraben

guns were routinely throwing air-bursting shrapnel rounds, more than ten times a minute, out to more than 5km (3 miles).

At the same time the numbers of men and weapons had vastly increased. The German Army had seen the greatest expansion, being ten times the size of the Prussian Army of the Napoleonic period; but all armies had grown several-fold. In 1814 armies could cross large areas like Spain or central Europe and in the process evade or outmanoeuvre each other. By 1914, rapid movements were channelled by timetable through a relatively crowded Europe, along rail tracks, while telegraphs, telephones and balloons gave warning of their approach. Moreover, on the Western Front at least, the forces of the Entente and the Central Powers were too finely balanced to admit of immediate victory. The Germans had greater numbers than the French, but any initial advantage was offset by the two-front war, the resistance of the Belgians, and the small but steadily increasing contribution of the British.

The alternatives in late 1914 were stark: dig in and accept heavy casualties, or stay on the surface indefinitely and be annihilated. As a Canadian writer would put it within a few months of the actual events, 'They had to hide in the mud of the trenches to escape German bullets. It was a choice of mud or death.'

Though it was still presumed that winning would mean attacking, not just defending, there were precedents for temporary and localized field entrenchments, as had been used in the Russo–Turkish and Russo–Japanese wars. The British *Manual of Field Engineering* explained the purpose of field fortifications:

By Field Fortification is implied all those measures which may be taken for the defence of positions intended to be only temporarily held. Works of this kind are executed either in the face of the enemy, or in the immediate anticipation of his approach … Field Fortification presupposes a defensive attitude, and, though recourse to it may under certain circumstances be desirable, it must always be regarded as a means to an end, and not an end in itself … The principal aim of field fortification is to enable the soldier to use his weapons with the greatest effect, the second to protect him against the adversary's fire. By thus reducing losses and increasing the power of resistance in any part of the theatre of operations or field of battle, more troops will be available to swell the force destined for decisive action there or elsewhere.

The conundrum of the Great War was that there were so many men, with such effective weapons, so evenly balanced, that there was no 'elsewhere'. It has been suggested that the trenches were to become a 'live and let live' system, and in quiet sectors, where exchanges of fire tended to become ritualized, this was sometimes the case. Yet the war was only ever static in a geographic sense: there was a constant tactical, technological and industrial evolution whereby the trench deadlock would eventually be broken. The war would develop so quickly that a man wounded in 1914 and returning to the front in 1916 would have had difficulty understanding that it was the same war. It was also the case, as General von Falkenhayn would later remark, that as one side developed a weapon to break the defence, the other gained time to employ the latest defensive methods.

DIGGING IN

The infantry were universally supplied with entrenching tools to provide their own cover. Typical of many was the French *pelle-bêche*, a short-handled shovel that hung from the belt in a leather carrier. This was supplemented with the small *pioche* or pick, bills, saws and hand axes, allowing a company to break ground and deal with small trees and foliage as well as dig in. A new *pelle-pioche* had been introduced in 1909, a dual purpose two-piece demountable pick head and handle that was used by a proportion of troops at the outbreak of war. By 1916, a French infantry company was provided with 48 *pelle-bêches*, 56 *pelle-pioches*, 30 short M1916 spades, 32 picks, 8 hand axes,

British troops demonstrate the ideal trench-digging method, with traverses marked out with pegs, and sods laid to cover the parapet. (Stephen Bull)

12 bills, 16 wire cutters and a folding saw. Long-handled spades and other tools were carried with the baggage and engineers, or provided when specifically required. Short-handled, blunt-ended shovels similar to the *pelle-bêche* were carried by the Germans, Russians, Belgians and Austrians, while the US Army M1910 and cavalry M1912 implements featured a pointed blade.

The British 'implement, intrenching, Pattern 1908' was a dual-purpose tool with separate helve and head which, though not the most efficient digging instrument, was pretty versatile. It saw use not only as pick and shovel, but as a general purpose hook, and was even regarded by some as improvised protection when the metal head was suspended against the user's body in its webbing carrier. Just how useful digging tools were only really became apparent when they were left behind, as Lieutenant Hall of the 20th Hussars discovered after crossing the Marne – he spent much of one night 'digging a trench with the aid of a broken plate, mess tins, knives and forks'. Some of his men used their bayonets, others begged spades from civilians.

Improvised cover could be dug fairly quickly, and to give temporary protection for a prone rifleman a scrape 30cm (12in) deep was just adequate. Edmund Dane's estimate was that a good job could be made within the hour. British troops were taught to work 'lying down, and to commence at the rear of the selected position. Hard soil is more easily broken up by this method and a hollow for the disengaged arm is gradually provided, which helps to keep the digger under cover.' Marc Bloch, serving with the French 272e Régiment d'Infanterie (RI), saw the Germans use exactly the same method in 1914, burrowing away to create what appeared to be a 'yellowish ramp', leaving only their hands exposed from time to time as they threw earth from their implements. Such scrapes could save a man's life, but were uncomfortable and vulnerable to shrapnel.

Some advantage could be expected from natural features such as rises or hedge banks and bulletproof objects such as rails or bags of earth, but as E. J. Solano observed in his *Field Entrenchments; Spadework for Riflemen* in 1914, care had to be taken lest items be scattered 'by the impact of bullets and become a source of danger'. French instructions encouraged the use of piles of stones provided that they were at least 30cm (12in) in thickness, and covered with earth to prevent fragments flying. Fallen tree trunks were similarly useful, but again were best combined with earth, and fired around rather than over.

Kneeling cover could be made by linking individual scrapes together, but was better done on pre-planned lines, using reliefs of troops in a systematic manner. According to the manual, a 3ft (1m) fire trench of adequate dimension to cover its diggers could be created in 100 minutes. A standing fire trench would require upwards of 5 hours, and was likely to require two shifts or a rest period during construction. Sandbags and barbed wire were in very limited supply in 1914, and brushwood, sacks, sods and timber revetments were all used. At least one account records soldiers' packs being filled with earth to give cover. The destruction of crops, and the laying of planks studded with nails and caltraps, both opened up the field of fire and impeded the enemy advance. Soon the battlefield would show little sign of life above the surface: as the Canadian historian would put it, the nearer you came to the front line, 'the more difficult you find it to set eyes on men'.

French manuals placed particular emphasis on the making of fascines and gabions from natural materials. Yet their trenches soon acquired a reputation for slovenliness and poor construction; Robert Graves even observed that bodies were actually buried in the floor of the trenches, thereby making them shallower as the casualties mounted. Some of this was fair criticism, but the rather temporary French attitude to trench construction was in part born of unwillingness to admit a permanent enemy presence on their territory, and a natural preference for the offensive. It was also the case that in terms of producing the materials required for thoroughly professional field works, the French were worse placed than their allies. A higher proportion of their workforce had already been called up, and the length of their front line was much greater. In late 1914 Marc Bloch was complaining not only that his countrymen were lax in digging, but that building materials were as yet entirely lacking. Ordinary wire of the type used to hang door bells and train lines was being strung in place of barbed wire.

Text book trench lines were sited, as the British *Notes on Field Defences* put it, to give the maximum field of fire while denying the enemy a clear view of the position. The best form for the excavations themselves was 'deep, narrow and with low command. The rifle, when resting on the parapet, must sweep the ground immediately in front … strong traverses should be provided every four yards or so to localise the effect of high explosive shell falling into the trench, and also give protection against enfilade fire.' Such was the ideal, but at times this was impossible. In Flanders in particular the water table was so near the surface that any deep excavation filled with water. Sometimes the only solution was to build 'trenches' upward rather than digging down; parapets were built up above the existing ground level using sandbags and timbers. These were known as 'command' or 'box' trenches; but many units preferred to dig down, stand in water and risk trench foot, since box trenches took huge labour to construct and were painfully obvious features in the landscape. At Houplines in the winter of 1914, Frank Richards of the Royal Welsh Fusiliers would describe how hand pumps would be worked day and night in a vain attempt to clear knee-deep water. Bailing with buckets drew enemy fire – one man so engaged had his thumb shot off.

German soldiers trench-digging in the Argonne, 1915. Trench layouts were governed by topography and available materials as well as the official manuals. Although German trenches generally had a well-earned reputation for thoroughness, so far this example is revetted only with a few flimsy brushwood hurdles. (IWM, Q45584)

British trench system, winter 1914–15, from the official manual. There are two lines, the 'fire trench' and the 'cover trench', linked by 'communication' trenches. Both fire and cover trenches have alternating bays (12ft–15ft long) and traverses (6ft–8ft long, 3ft–6ft front to back). The cover trench is characterized by a series of dug-outs with overhead cover (bottom right), and is shown as 2ft wide at the bottom. (Stephen Bull)

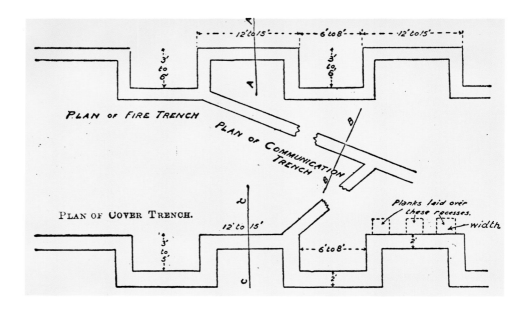

PLAN OF FIRE TRENCH

PLAN OF COMMUNICATION TRENCH

PLAN OF COVER TRENCH.

Planks laid over these recesses.

width

OVERHEAD COVER

This was rudimentary at first. The pre-war British *Manual of Field Engineering* was of the opinion that it would most likely take too long to construct, and that in any case materials would 'often not be available'. Even so, it predicted that as aviation and shells improved, such cover would become more important. To this end, it was recommended that protection against shrapnel and grenades be provided using 9in–12in (23cm–30cm) of earth supported on boards or corrugated iron. Similarly, it warned that splinterproof shelters should not weaken the parapet, curtail the numbers of rifles available for defence nor be difficult to get out of quickly. 'Numerous and simple' shelters were declared preferable to a few elaborate ones. In practice many men scraped out individual cubbyholes under the parapet – the Germans called these 'Siegfried' shelters, and the British, 'funk holes'. They aroused a mixed response from officialdom, since they might collapse and trap the occupants, and tended to leave odd arms and legs sprawling out into the trench to be stumbled over during the constant traffic of men to and fro.

In an incident at Ypres in November 1914 Brigadier-General Gleichen recorded being covered in dirt by exploding shells, and then a dug-out collapsed and broke the legs of two officers of the West Yorkshires. Three Cheshires were buried alive and not rescued, and a dozen others killed or wounded, the result not only of flimsy overhead cover but of the high water table and shallow trenches. The French sergeant Marc Bloch recalled that in September 1914 his first experience of overhead cover was shelters clumsily made out of branches, skimpy constructions which did not even keep out the rain. Afraid to lie down in the water which had turned the trenches 'into brooks' and wearing only the issue uniform, he spent one entire night standing up, feeling as though he was 'naked in an icy bath'.

Fire trenches could be given overhead cover, and good examples appear in the manuals of various nations; however, unless the roof was propped and loopholes provided, the defensive function was seriously undermined. Though in vogue in several sectors, particularly in 1915, this system of

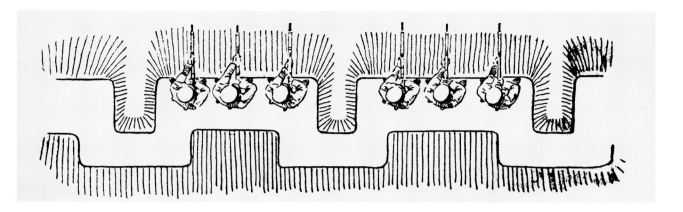

The 'modern fire trench' with bays between traverses, from Edmund Dane's book *Trench Warfare*, 1915. (Stephen Bull)

overhead protection was never common. Looking back at such early efforts, Lieutenant Edmund Blunden, 'Field Works Officer' of 11th Battalion, Royal Sussex Regiment, thought them flimsy to the point of quaintness.

While sheltering the individual soldier received scant attention, it was acknowledged that machine guns, dressing stations, observation posts and artillery all required particular forms of cover. In the British instance covered dressing stations were supposed to be provided in the rear of the trench line, including provision for a board table 6½ft (2m) long for the patient. Machine guns similarly were better covered over, provided it did not make them more obvious. Machine gun pits were best made with an arc to the front and a shallower section on which the tripod mount could rest.

DEEP COVER AND MULTIPLE POSITIONS

The first trenches were seen as protection for front line units *in situ*, rather than as semi-permanent defensive features in their own right. The result was a shallow position with a single line of trenches, or a double line if a support trench was included. (Note that in this text the terms 'deep' and 'shallow' are normally used in the sense of the horizontal arrangement of lines of defence, i.e. more or less extensive from the front to the rear of the trench system.) Moreover, at this stage of the war, attempts were usually made to accommodate whole units in the front line simultaneously. Trenches therefore tended to be crowded and tactically inflexible: the line was either held or lost. Early German instructions, as General Erich von Falkenhayn recalled, stated that 'the line apportioned to the troops for defence was to be maintained at all costs, and if lost was to be retaken'. It was also widely believed that if troops were given any possibility of 'interpretation' in their orders the likely effect would be surrenders or voluntary retirements. Yet with time came the realization that deeper defences and less dense manning had signal advantages. Shells caused fewer casualties, reserve lines gave firm bases from which to launch counter-attacks, and multiple lines of field works absorbed the power of an attack, which could be shot at from many directions.

The degree to which trench planning and construction developed in the first 18 months of war is perhaps best illustrated by the German practice, as outlined in the *Manual of Position Warfare, Part 1*, on '*Stellungsbau*' or the construction of field positions, 1916. This explicitly stated that it was now 'a ruling principle that ground to be held must be fortified in such a way that an obstinate defence by sectors is obtained, and to such a depth that the loss of or withdrawal from parts of the position does not endanger it as a whole'. Trench systems were to consist of several continuous but not parallel lines 150m–200m (164yd–219yd) apart. Moreover, the first defensive position was to be backed with another, between 2 and 5km (1.2 and 3.1 miles) in the rear, so that both zones could not be attacked simultaneously. Both areas, and parts of the intervening ground, were to be studded with strongpoints, blockhouses and 'holding points'. Machine gun positions were held to form the 'framework of all infantry fighting lines', and arranged so as to enfilade the ground between zones. Relatively few guns were to be kept in the very front line, and those were to increase their power by mobility.

Mere 'splinterproof' cover was now dismissed as a liability which had a tendency to fall and block trenches. The German system now aimed to provide in the front line 'shellproof' shelters capable of withstanding 'continuous' shelling from guns of up to 150mm calibre, and at selected spots 'bombproofs' capable of taking bombardment from 200mm guns and occasional hits from even heavier pieces. Concrete and reinforced concrete had now begun to make their appearance in shelter construction; not only were they strong, but they had the added advantage that even a relatively shallow dug-out could provide protection; these shallow dug-outs were less likely to flood, and quicker to evacuate.

For the trench parapets themselves the German ideal was now sods or brushwood anchored with pickets. This was a strong and cheap arrangement, and had the advantage that it was unlikely to obstruct the trench if blown in; sandbags were seen as suitable for quick work. Flint, stone and brick were regarded as objectionable since they fragmented dangerously when hit. Though narrow trenches were admitted to give the best protection, German theory now suggested that they should

French fire trench, 1915; troops aim through loopholes in the parapet while standing on an elaborately made wooden fire step. A deeper cover walkway passes behind the step, with a drainage channel running alongside. (Stephen Bull)

be relatively deep and broad, with the sides not absolutely vertical. Little revetting was therefore required and men could move quickly along them.

MANNING THE TRENCHES

Though Allied trenches often lacked the apparent permanence of the enemy fortresses, they too offered significant evidence of change. Most nations tried to get men out of the line from time to time, and French accounts speak of a week-on, week-off system in some sectors within a few months of the outbreak of war. The British were soon able to adopt a highly organized policy of rotation in which each brigade put only two of its battalions in the front line, with others further back in 'support' and 'reserve'. Even in the two lead battalions only half the available manpower was actually stationed in the front line trench. Unless a 'big show' was in progress, only a very small proportion of the troops were actually in range of the enemy rifles, though more might fall prey to artillery. Systems of rotation entailed much stumbling back and forth by night along cramped communication trenches, burdened with heavy equipment, and a good deal of frustrating paperwork as 'trench stores' were accounted for and handed over; but they improved morale considerably, and allowed training and rest.

E. B. North, the Brigade Major of 124th Brigade, went so far as to have *Trench Standing Orders* printed up, bound in card covers and distributed along with the 'official' War Office publications. These standing orders specified that company and platoon officers of relieving units would visit their new sector, gain information and sign receipts. Machine gunners, bombers, snipers and signallers would arrive a day early, taking up their posts in daylight so as to be familiarized and in position before the rest of the trench garrison. The rest of the men would march up under cover of darkness, extinguishing lights and cigarettes at an agreed point, then would make contact with the units on either flank, and exchange posts with the men being relieved at the fire step. Within 24 hours the new company commanders were expected to have submitted a thorough report detailing, amongst

Trench smashed by shellfire, Argonne front – probably in the French lines. Wicker gabions have been torn up and the sandbagged walls have collapsed. (Stephen Bull)

other matters, fields of fire, distances to enemy posts, state of the wire, reserves of ammunition and gas precautions. Nineteen categories of materials were designated 'trench stores' and had to be accounted for. Daily returns were expected at brigade headquarters on weather, casualties, intelligence and stores required, the first of these to be completed at 5.15am, the last at 9pm; the response of some harassed company officers to these bureaucratic demands may be imagined.

Along with a highly organized routine, British planners became particularly keen not only on positions in depth, but on prefabricated dug-out frames made behind the lines and so-called 'elephant shelters'. These were arcs of corrugated iron, sunk into the ground and covered with different layers of materials including concrete, wooden sleepers and soil to create a quick and easy-to-build shellproof shelter. The French adopted a similar device which translated approximately as a 'cover of arched iron', but they also made widespread use of bunkers constructed of logs. Though there was sometimes difficulty in getting compliance in practice the French *Manual of Field Fortification* warned that an infantryman had to be good not only with a rifle but with a spade, and that it was up to commanders to exercise 'unrelaxing care' to ensure that field works were not only completed but kept in good repair. It was also accepted that positions could now be held not only by bodies of men in lines, but by strongpoints in depth. Garrisons did not have to occupy every sector of a trench system simultaneously but could be so arranged as to 'economise on personnel' by using flanking fire.

THE 'SHELL SCANDALS'

As soon as the trench lines were dug it became apparent that the existing ways of waging war were inadequate. Trenches had no flanks, and conferred an almost insuperable advantage on the defender. Alarming French calculations of January 1915 suggested that a rifle-armed trench garrison, with a clear field of fire, would need to be assaulted by 12 times their number to ensure that a roughly equal number of attackers actually reached the enemy trench. Even if successful, such a suicidal attack would cost the attackers 11 times the casualties of the defenders. If machine guns were involved it was postulated that the attackers would suffer 14 casualties for every defender, and would probably not reach the trench at all.

The immediate consequence was a scramble to procure weapons that could deal with trenches: shells and heavier guns for the artillery, grenades for the infantry. As a bemused Major-General Rawlinson put it in December 1914, 'this trench warfare in which we are now engaged is causing a demand for all sorts of things which are not recognised by regulation'. Failures in pre-war planning led to most countries promptly suffering a 'shell scandal' – an inability to meet the needs of their guns for ammunition. This was perhaps best documented in Britain, and most catastrophic in Russia. One British diplomat, touring the Eastern Front by bicycle, was moved to reflect the current Russian opinion that the war had become one of 'men against metal'. At Gumbinnen it has been calculated that the Russian guns were being supplied with 244 rounds per day, but firing them at a rate of 440. In September 1914 the Russian High Command predicted that it would now require 1,500,000 shells per month, but within weeks this estimate had been revised upwards to 3,500,000. In the first part of 1915 only 500,000 shells a month were actually delivered, and at critical moments Russian batteries would fall silent. The Germans managed to produce the better part of 4,000,000 rounds a month, but this was still less than the requirement, and in any case something like three-quarters of their ammunition was destined for the Western Front.

The artillery problem was further complicated by the fact that shrapnel was inefficient against trenches; only the few rounds that burst immediately above them would shower the heads of the defenders. What was really needed was bigger high explosive shells, with fuses that burst on or around ground level to blow out sections of trench, causing earthquakes which shattered dug-outs and blast which concussed and tore the defenders like an iron hand. Such shells and such guns needed technologies, materials, and labour forces that most countries were ill equipped to provide. Even in Britain, nine out of every ten rounds manufactured were shrapnel shells, and the vast majority of projectiles produced were for light field guns and 4.5in howitzers. Heavy high explosive shells were conspicuous by their absence: for the 9.2in howitzer, total production for 1914 would be just 200 rounds. Rushed production by an inexperienced industry also led to such dangerous fiascos as the 'fuse, graze, No.100', an impact-detonated shell fuse lacking proper safety devices or any external indication of its arming status, which led to a rash of premature detonations in the gun breech with serious loss of life.

The shell scandal would help bring down the British government and led to the formation in late 1915 of a Ministry of Munitions under David Lloyd George; but there was no instant panacea. The experience of Lieutenant-Colonel D. H. Drake-Brockman of the Garhwal Rifles at

The manufacture of 'jam tin' bombs as depicted in *Illustrated War News*, April 1915. (Stephen Bull)

Aubers Ridge in 1915 was probably typical: 'If one telephoned up to the gunner officer for a little ammunition to be expended on some bomb gun or *Minenwerfer* that was annoying us, the reply generally received was "Sorry, but I have used my allowance!" This was, at that time, 18 rounds daily per battery.' It was, as BEF commander Sir John French complained to the Secretary of State for War, Lord Kitchener, so inadequate as to render successful offensive operations 'quite out of the question'.

For the Germans, balancing the demands of munitions production with keeping the maximum number of troops in action was partly achieved in September 1914, when General von Falkenhayn, the Minister of War, also became Chief of the General Staff. Yet the Germans were later frustrated by lack of raw materials, since metals like tungsten, copper and chromium, and materials like cotton and silk had all been mainly imported before the war and were now subject to blockade.

NEW WEAPONS

HAND GRENADES

The situation regarding grenades was just as bad. Before the war the grenade had almost universally been seen as a 'siege' weapon, unlikely to be of much use in a war of rapid manoeuvre. At the outbreak of war Britain had only one type of hand grenade, available in very limited numbers and used only by the Royal Engineers. This was the expensive, long-handled, impact-detonating 'Grenade, Hand, Mark I' which had been introduced in 1908. Expansion of supply to meet demand would be a Herculean task, first faced by Colonel Sir Louis Jackson as part of 'Fortification and Works', later as part of 'Engineer Munitions Branch', and finally as Trench Warfare Department of the new Ministry of Munitions. At the outset the French were little better off, with their antiquated ball grenades; and even the Germans, who had given more thought to the matter, had only a few hundred thousand grenades. These were mainly the impact-detonated 'discus' bomb, and the M1913 black powder ball or Kügel grenade with a friction-ignited time fuse.

The gross inadequacy of grenade provision was all too apparent. In late 1914 Sir John French estimated demand for hand grenades at 4,000 per week; deliveries ran at only 70 per week in November, rising to a slightly more respectable 2,500 by the second week in December. Meanwhile demand was spiralling out of control, with 10,000 bombs a week demanded in the first week of 1915. Within six months estimated demand would be 2,000 bombs a day, with a projected requirement of anything up to 50,000 per day when Britain's New Armies took the offensive in the field. Under such conditions, and with a lead time of months required to design decent bombs for mass production and establish proper factories, improvisation was the keynote. 'Emergency' supplies of bombs were

The grenade designed by the Belgian Captain Leon Roland, which inspired the British Mills bomb. Only a court case would sort out the issues of ownership of the ideas involved. (Musée Royal de l'Armée, Brussels)

therefore rapidly obtained from two major sources: conversion of existing home factory production lines of other goods to produce very simple types of temporarily expedient bombs, and the ingenuity of the troops themselves. Other nations came to much the same conclusions.

So it was that in and behind the front line trenches the troops took to producing 'jam tin' and 'racket' bombs. The 'jam tin', a particular favourite with the British, consisted of a tin filled with dynamite or gun cotton packed round with scrap metal or stones. From the top of the tin projected a length of Bickfords fuse connecting to the detonator. As the official publication *Notes From the Front* explained, it was crucial that 'very careful' experiments be conducted to establish the correct length of fuse. It was generally calculated that each inch of fuse would give a 1.25 second delay. The grenadier lit the fuse manually and hurled the bomb, hoping that the time fuse had been correctly cut to explode neither so quickly that it blew him up, nor so slowly that the enemy had time to pick it up and throw it back. The fuse could be lit with matches, but the uncertainty of ignition and difficulty of manipulating matches and bomb meant that men tended either to work in pairs, or to keep a glowing pipe or cigarette in their mouths.

Naturally enough, the exact design of the 'jam tin' varied with the materials available. Fighting at Gallipoli, Lieutenant-Colonel M. E. Hancock of the Northamptonshire Regiment favoured a fairly heavy bomb made by the Royal Engineers, with an 8 to 10 second fuse lit by cigarette, which was 'bowled' out of the trench to a distance of about 30 yards (27m). The Turks replied with similar but lighter devices with thinner cases. Some of these failed to explode, so Hancock and his men gathered them up at night to throw back later. Major G. E. Horridge of the Lancashire Fusiliers was provided with 'jam tins' with wooden lids and 'friction igniters', which in theory were set alight by rubbing against a rough surface. At Le Pantin in the winter of 1914 men of 2nd Battalion, the Black Watch, made bombs under the instruction of an artillery officer which consisted of gun cotton packed in tobacco tins. The Australians sometimes used a slightly more sophisticated factory-made variation with a percussion-ignited time fuse, which they dubbed the 'Welsh Berry'. Just how petrifying a duel with such bombs could be is underlined by the account of Lieutenant P. Neame of the Royal Engineers, who was called upon to stem an enemy bombing attack near Neuve Chapelle:

> I ran forward and asked what was going on. The first answer was from the Germans, for a black object the size of a cricket ball came sailing through the air, landed in the trench behind us and burst with a terrific bang and the whine of whirling bits of metal. The sergeant told me that he was the bombing sergeant of the West Yorks and that the two men with him were all that was left of his bombing squad, the rest having been killed or wounded. He said that the German bombs out-ranged our own, that our bombs were 'duds' and he could not get them lighted.
>
> We were interrupted by a fusilade of bombs this time coming from two directions, some of which landed in the trench and some on the parapet; one of the men with us was wounded … I realised then what it meant to be caught like a rat in a trap … I stood up on the fire step … and threw my first bomb.

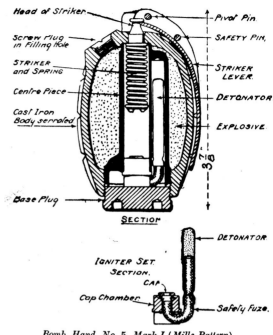

Bomb, Hand, No. 5, Mark I (Mills Pattern).
Scale ¾.
PLATE I.

Sectional diagram of No.5 Mills grenade, first ordered in April/May 1915. This classic segmented cast-iron fragmentation grenade, which soldiered on with few changes for half a century, weighed just under 1½lb (0.7kg). The base plug was unscrewed and the igniter set inserted only when the bomb reached the troops. The spring-loaded striker was retained by an external lever and safety pin. When the pin was removed the lever could be held down in the closed hand; released when the grenade was thrown, it allowed the striker to ignite a time fuse set for various delays between 4 and 7 seconds. (Stephen Bull)

It hit the parapet near where I could see the Germans and exploded with a roar. Our bombs, though heavy to throw were very violent and destructive … As I stepped down a rifle bullet cracked past close to my head and a fraction of a second later there was a stutter of a machine gun … While I crouched a German bomb came over, fell right in the crowded trench just behind me and burst with a frightful crash, killing and wounding many of our men … A bomb inflicts terrible wounds. I never saw anything worse in the succeeding years of war.

A rather more elegant emergency bomb was brought into use by Major Basil Condon Battye of 21st Field Company Royal Engineers, who had small cast-iron cylinders manufactured at

British 'Bomb Catapults', 1915

On the left, two Tommies from the 7th Battalion, the Royal Sussex Regiment, prepare to loose a No.9 grenade from a Leach bomb-thrower. The Leach consisted of a wooden Y-shaped frame (sometimes with the triangular bracing plate shown here, sometimes without); the rubber ropes for the sling were pulled taut by a windlass system, with a wire cable running along the top and bottom of the wooden beam and engaging the sling with a hook. The corporal is about to use an entrenching tool helve to strike the hook's release trigger, while the private positions and lights the grenades. On the right is a West spring gun. The iron catapult was bolted down to base boards, which were piled with sandbags to prevent it moving while it was cocked, by forcing the throwing arm back and down against the tension of the powerful spring 'battery' by means of a long dog-leg setting lever – this usually took the weight of three men to achieve. The setting lever was then removed, and replaced by a straight firing lever engaged with a bolt on the left side plate; downwards pressure released the mechanism. (Adam Hook © Osprey Publishing Ltd)

Béthune. Like the soldier-made 'jam tins', these 'Battye' or 'Béthune' grenades were fitted with a safety fuse and a detonator, but usually ignited by a Nobel fuse lighter, which the soldier could initiate by banging down a cap. Safety was slightly improved by separating bombs and detonators in transit.

At its most basic the 'racket' bomb consisted of explosive attached to a wooden handle shaped roughly like a hairbrush, again lit by means of a length of fuse. In the version recommended to British troops in *Notes From the Front*, a slab of gun cotton was wrapped in a sacking covering which also contained metal fragments, and the whole was wired to a wooden handle about 50cm (19in) long. Though most nationalities used racket bombs they were most

British snipers, 1915–16
The centre figure represents an officer of the early 'freelance' period when British sniping was conducted on an individual basis, largely by officers with pre-war game hunting experience who provided their own weapons. He is armed with a sporting rifle. From early 1916, British First and Second armies set up scout-sniper schools, and battalion sniper sections were established. The Irish Guardsmen (left) has improvised a camouflage hood from a sandbag and vegetation. His weapon is a selected example of the standard 0.303in SMLE, fitted with pre-war 2x power Lattey optical sights. The sniper on the right wears a camouflage canvas robe and matching hood and mittens. He carries an SMLE rifle fitted with a Periscopic Prism Company 2x power telescopic sight off-set to the left of the receiver. (Adam Hook © Osprey Publishing Ltd)

popular with the French, who referred to them as *pétards raquette*. They produced a number of types, from simple sticks of dynamite wired to wooden paddles, to examples in which the explosive was contained in a metal pipe or provided with a separate method of ignition. The final French version made use of factory-produced components and a percussion lighting device, and was known as the F2, M1915. The Australians also made use of the racket bomb, though they tended to refer to it as either a 'cricket bat' or 'brush back' bomb. An 'emergency' pattern racket bomb was also made in Britain; this No.12 grenade featured a percussion ignition system and an iron fragmentation plate.

Rifle Grenades

Though rifle-projected grenades had been invented by Englishman Frederick Marten Hale before the war, he had been unable to arouse much interest at the War Office. Indeed, only the Germans had shown very much enthusiasm, with the result that the Allies were on the receiving end of their 1913 and 1914 model rodded rifle bombs. Britain was therefore forced to start almost from scratch, at first ordering small supplies of the 'J' or 'Commercial Pattern' rifle bomb which Hale's Cotton Powder Company was making for export to Brazil. Later, and not entirely successfully, they attempted to place contracts elsewhere.

The basic method of use was similar for all rodded rifle bombs. The rod was slipped into the muzzle of the rifle, and a special blank cartridge was loaded into the chamber. Any safety pin was removed from the bomb, and the trigger squeezed. The pressure created by the explosion of the cartridge hurled the bomb into the air, hopefully to explode on impact in the enemy lines.

Lack of accuracy and heavy recoil were significant problems. The Germans soon introduced properly made steel launching stands with shock-absorbing springs, which could be adjusted for range; the British used wooden stands, made either by Royal Engineers workshops or locally by the troops. In either case the mobility of the rifle grenadier was sacrificed. When used without a stand it was recommended that the rifle be held with the trigger guard upwards and the toe of the butt resting on the ground, so as to minimize the damage to both soldier and weapon.

Trench Mortars and Bomb-Throwers

These weapons and devices threw bigger missiles and helped to bridge the ranges not covered by hand-thrown bombs or artillery proper. Again, the Germans had taken the initiative, and study of the sieges of the Russo–Japanese War had influenced them to design and introduce two types of trench mortar. The heavy 25cm (9.8in) smooth-bore Ehrhardt model *Minenwerfer* had equipped pioneer siege trains from 1911 (see pp.26–7), and at the outbreak of war they had about 190 available. Yet despite this early lead, production of German trench mortars was never sufficient to keep pace with demand, so obsolete and stop-gap models were commonly seen. A frequently encountered type of the early years was the Lanz, a small, crude 91mm smooth-bore capable of throwing a 4kg (8.8lb) bomb about 300m (330yd). In the medieval-looking Albrecht mortar a wooden tube was wound with wire for short-range, low-velocity projection. Locally improvised 'earth mortars' fired 24kg (53lb) projectiles relatively short distances from tubes sunk into the ground. There was even a spring-powered *Wurfmaschine* for mechanically propelling hand grenades, which could throw the discus bomb about 200m (220yd).

The Allied response was even more patchy: not until October 1914 did Sir John French ask for the supply of 'some special form of artillery' capable of dealing with trenches at close range, with the result that no 'official' trench mortar was delivered from Britain until December 1914, and even then the model supplied was declared unsuitable. So it was that until at least the summer of 1915 the British were dependent on a motley selection of experimental and improvised weapons. These included a few shells bored out to form crude bomb projectors; alarming weapons locally fabricated from iron water pipes; and 'pipe guns' which were dug into the ground to throw 4lb (1.8kg) tin pots.

Another, and ultimately rather less successful, line of development was the 'bomb engine'. On the face of it such weapons had the advantages that they were quiet and required less complex technology, but they were limited by their size, range and the weight of their missiles. Some were simply catapults improvised by the troops themselves; some, like Dawson's 'Spring Arm Projector' and Pellet's 'Propellor' bomb-thrower, were granted patents. Only two such devices were accorded official issue status and manufactured in large numbers. The first of these was the Y-shaped overgrown schoolboy's catapult designed by C. P. Leach and supplied by Gamages, the London department store. Capable of flinging a 2lb (1kg) projectile 200 yards (183m), each Leach catapult cost £6 17s 6d. First orders were placed in March 1915, and, by 3 October, 152 had been delivered, the official scale of issue being 20 per division. Thereafter, it was intended to replace the Leach with a French-designed *Sauterelle* projector.

The other British catapult to see widespread use was Captain West's 'Spring Gun', a heavy metal contraption with a bank of 24 springs, a throwing arm and a cocking lever. This could be carried around like a stretcher by two or four men. A test conducted by the author, with the kind cooperation of the Imperial War Museum at Duxford, Cambridgeshire, showed that even more than 70 years later, and set at three-quarters of its full power, the West was capable of throwing a Mills bomb 150 yards (137m); during this test the bomb remained in the air for 5.2 seconds. Guy Chapman, who actually used the West in 1915, was less impressed, observing that anyone unlucky enough to stand in front of its 'whirling arm' was likely to be decapitated. Production of the West and other British catapults was officially halted in the spring of 1916.

Arguably the first really successful British trench mortar, combining power and range with adequate production and supply, was the '2in Trench Howitzer', popularly known as the 'toffee apple' or 'plum pudding' bomb-thrower due to its spherical, rodded 60lb (27.2kg) projectile (see pp.108–9). The weapon itself comprised a relatively small elevating barrel on a heavy wooden bed, fired using a converted rifle mechanism and a lanyard. Capable of a range of about 500 yards (460m), the 'toffee apple' made a considerable impact, blowing revetments high into the air, collapsing dug-outs, and hurling steel splinters as far back as the British lines. Ernst Junger, of Fusilier-Regiment Nr.73 Prinz Albrecht von Preussen, described them as treacherous and 'personally malignant'. By the time of the Somme offensive in 1916 about 800 had been manufactured.

The French experience offered many parallels. Short of mortars in 1914, they had quickly resorted to 19th-century museum pieces and a device known as the *Taupia*. This consisted of a modified shell casing mounted on a wooden block, throwing relatively small bombs a short distance; alarmingly, it was often ignited using a glowing cigarette. They also employed a variety of

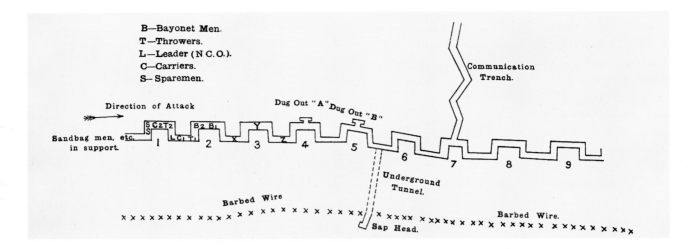

B—Bayonet Men.
T—Throwers.
L—Leader (N C.O.).
C—Carriers.
S—Sparemen.

Direction of Attack

Sandbag men, etc.
in support.

Communication
Trench.

Dug Out "A"   Dug Out "B"

Underground
Tunnel.

Barbed Wire

Barbed Wire.

Sap Head.

British bombing tactics, from *The Training and Employment of Grenadiers*, autumn 1915. This shows how a trench might be cleared by a grenadier party, with the enemy being 'rolled up' rather than attacked frontally. The party is led by two 'bayonet men', followed by a 'thrower' and 'carrier', and then by the NCO. A second thrower/carrier team follows him, followed by two 'spare men', and then by a support party with sandbags, etc. for building quick barricades across the end of the cleared section of trench. (Stephen Bull)

mechanical bomb-throwers, which used both sprung arms and catapult-style slings for their motive power. One example illustrated in the *Times History of the War* was very similar to the Leach; another used parts of a bicycle to cock the mechanism.

Later the French approach became more professional and a number of more conventional designs were produced on a much larger scale. These included a Dumézil model with a 58mm barrel, over which was fitted the tail of a much larger finned 'aerial torpedo'; and a super-heavy 240mm weapon designed by the Société de Construction de Batignolles, and capable of hurling a 100kg (220lb) bomb about 1,100 metres (1,200yd). Due to its weight the mortar could be dismounted into three pieces and trundled about the battlefield in two-wheeled, steel-framed hand barrows. The French heavy mortar received a British patent in July 1915, and in 1916 was adopted by the British and Empire armies as the 9.45in (the 'flying pig').

Another French innovation was the Brandt-designed 'pneumatique' mortar, in which the propellant was compressed gas from a cylinder. The barrel was mounted on a small metal tripod; the M1915 barrel weighed about 22kg (48½lb) and the tripod a further 16kg (35lbs) without the cylinder, and was capable of lobbing a 950g (2lb) shell out to about 400 metres (440yd). For short periods the Brandt could produce impressive showers of shells, at a rate of anything up to 18 rounds a minute. It also had the advantage of being relatively quiet. The German compressed gas 105mm and 150mm mortars fabricated by Ehrhardt & Sehmer at Saarbrücken, which were used on a limited scale, are widely believed to have been copies of the French device.

New Combat Tactics

Finding new systems of combat and tactics would prove even more difficult than the provision of new war materials. It was made less than an exact science both by the fact that the enemy was also developing new methods, and by the realization that new weapons required new patterns of human organization. Yet almost as soon as weapons became available, tactics were evolved for their use.

In the face of horrendous casualties the German infantry, already under instruction to advance only in more open formations less vulnerable to artillery, were soon experimenting with other methods to reduce losses. One of the first was to launch attacks at dusk or under cover of mist. Another involved using the metal shields from machine guns as improvised cover. This was less than a total success since the metal plates were heavy to carry, slowed the advance, and protected the soldier from only one direction.

In December 1914, the Garde Schützen were experimenting with assaults by companies rather than battalions, which attempted to break into the enemy line at selected points under cover of darkness and then move down the trenches from either end. At about the same time British troops were reporting particularly galling engagements in which the enemy were pushing forward just a few machine guns and snipers to enfilading positions, and attempting to clear trenches by weight of fire, without launching a conventional attack. Sometimes they would open rapid fire, forcing the defenders down below their parapets, and then advance. By January 1915, the Germans were using grenade-throwers drawn from pioneer battalions to front attacks against enemy trench lines. A month later a German assault party made an attack advancing along disused communication trenches without 'going over the top' at all.

One promising line of German enquiry was the attachment of field guns to attacking infantry to deal with machine guns and strongpoints, but the ordinary 7.7cm was found too heavy to manhandle over rough terrain. The firm of Krupp therefore designed a new 3.7cm *Sturmkannone* for the purpose. As mentioned previously (see p.12), in March 1915 the High Command ordered the formation of a *Sturmabteilung* or 'assault detachment' for testing the new guns with assault pioneers. Their proposed tactics included an advance by the pioneers following a conventional bombardment, the manhandling forward of the *Sturmkannone*, and then a full-scale attack by both pioneers and infantry under cover of fire from the light guns. The results were mixed, but did show, even at this early stage, a commitment to experiment on the part of the German leadership.

British theory was not far behind. Before 1914 was out, the first little volume of *Notes From the Front,* compiled by the General Staff, was warning about the avoidance of close formations when artillery and machine guns threatened. Enemy machine guns were admitted to be 'the very devil and magnificently handled', though German rifle fire was not thought equal to the British. Infantry acknowledged that its dispositions were likely to be dictated by exposure to enemy artillery; and a remarkably percipient note by one general officer suggested to his colleagues that 'an advance should

Following a mine explosion, bombardment and gas shelling, five officers and 50 men of Reserve-Infanterie-Regiment Nr.110 launched a raid on the trenches of the Royal Irish Rifles at La Boiselle on 11 April 1916. In the ensuing mêlée 29 British were captured and a greater number claimed killed; the raiders had only one man wounded. Depicted here are three of the raiders: a junior officer (foreground); private (left) and NCO (back). (Adam Hook © Osprey Publishing Ltd)

not be made on rigid lines, but with clouds of skirmishers – 5 or 6 yards apart – thrown forward according to the ground and available cover'.

A few months later, the second part of *Notes From the Front* warned of the danger of rigid formations:

> small columns in what are known as 'artillery formations' should never be adhered to when there is a possibility of their coming under close or medium range fire of infantry or machine guns. Troops have suffered severely from insufficient extension and the adoption of rigid lines, and also from pushing forward in close formations without taking the proper military precautions. Loose elastic formations adapted to the ground with 8 or 10 paces interval are the least vulnerable.

Notes on Attack and Defence, published in early 1915, recommended both that attacking parties should always be equipped with bombs, and that an organized plan should be prepared 'for keeping the occupants of captured trenches supplied with these missiles'. By May 1915, General Headquarters had published a composition for a 'Trench Storming Party' which was to consist of 14 or more men led by an NCO. The personnel were to have four distinct functions, respectively:

Men of the 2nd Battalion, Argyll and Sutherland Highlanders, in the trenches at Bois Grenier, 1915. The foreground men hold both No.2 or 'Mexican' type long-handled stick grenades, and No.8 or No.9 'double cylinder emergency pattern' or 'jam tin' bombs. Note the assorted headgear and lack of badges. On the brushwood-revetted trench wall hang sets of 1908 pattern webbing and a goatskin winter jerkin. At left, note a 'funk hole' dug into the parapet and curtained with a groundsheet. (IWM, Q48958)

grenadiers, grenade-carriers, 'bayonet men' to cover the party and winkle out the opposition, and 'sandbag men' who followed up, blocking side entrances and forming a final barricade at the furthest point of the advance into the enemy trench system.

By the latter part of 1915, it was accepted that new weaponry had fundamentally changed the method of combat. As the British *Training and Employment of Grenadiers* put it that October: 'The nature of operations in the present campaign has developed the employment of rifle and hand grenades to such an extent that the grenade has become one of the principal weapons of trench warfare.' Accordingly it was recommended that not only should every infantryman receive grenade training, but that every platoon should include an NCO and eight men selected from the 'very best, bravest and steadiest' to act as a ready pool of grenadiers, who could act with the platoon or separately.

At roughly the same time, the Germans were thinking in terms of the use of the *Handgranatentrupp*, a six- to eight-strong party of grenadiers. In the attack, these would lead the way down the trench, bombing and advancing by bounds, rushing each traverse, until they achieved their objectives. In defence, the party would either drive the enemy out immediately or form 'blocks' in the trench. The lead grenadiers would carry no rifles, but pistols, trench knives and bombs. The squad leader would be similarly armed, or if carrying a rifle would advance immediately behind the two lead men ready to fire over them. Strongpoints required that a couple of members of the team take up positions firing on the loopholes of the objective, while the remainder worked around it, prior to rushing the enemy with bombs.

REPRESENTATIVE ENGAGEMENT: 2ND BN, LANCASHIRE FUSILIERS, 7–9 JULY 1915

A good example of how things could work out in practice is provided by the defence of captured enemy trenches south of Pilckem by the 2nd Battalion, Lancashire Fusiliers, from 7 to 9 July 1915. The sector had been taken by the Rifle Brigade and Somersets, and now the narrow trenches were 'reorganised to a certain extent' with some parapets reversed, and fresh sandbags thrown up, though they were much battered and many of the dug-outs 'smashed in':

The night of 6–7th was fairly quiet, with the exception of enemy bombing parties coming down the three saps. These were kept back by our bombers, who, throughout the time we spent in these extremely unhealthy trenches, acted with the greatest gallantry and devotion to duty. At 11.30am on the 8th the enemy commenced shelling very heavily with 5.9 inch. At about 12 noon a shell landed on the Headquarters dug-out on the canal bank, wounding Colonel Griffin, Captain Spooner, Lieutenant Appleby and Lieutenant Charleston (the machine gun officer), who died a day or two later. A Royal Field Artillery observation officer, who had arrived only a few moments before, was also wounded by the same shell. A box of hand grenades was set on fire at the same time, and Captain Spooner, although wounded … threw them into the canal, thereby averting a very much worse disaster.

This heavy shelling continued until 3pm, practically every dug-out in the trenches and on the canal bank having been blown in before this hour. At 3pm, immediately preceding their infantry attack, the enemy developed an intense shrapnel bombardment of our lines – a perfect tornado of light shrapnel and 'Whistling Willies' mainly aimed at the supports and reserve, and lasting about 20 minutes … Our artillery had an exceedingly good observation post, and kept opening fire and driving back attacks, which our infantry were unable to see from their trenches. All attacks were beaten back. On one occasion the enemy rushed a sap by the hedge, but a party was promptly sent up from 'C' Company, and the trench was regained. It was, however, untenable, as our own artillery were firing into it …

Their attack having failed, the enemy recommenced shelling with 5.9 inch, and continued without intermission during the night and during the whole of the 8th except when they launched infantry attacks … During these bombardments many were killed, wounded and buried, and the trenches in many places blown absolutely flat. Machine guns were turned onto the gaps which became almost impossible … Lieutenant G. C. Martin, in command of No.14 Platoon, 'D' Company, against whose portion of the line the infantry attacks had been principally directed, dug himself in about ten yards in front of his trenches, which had practically all been blown in, thus avoiding to a certain extent the effects of the heavy shelling, the shells going over the new trenches and bursting in the trench previously occupied.

One of the main features of the action was the bombing. From the beginning to the end it was one continuous bomb fight down one sap, and there was also more intermittent fighting down the other two saps. At the end of this sap there was no protection, as it was too exposed … In the centre of the sap a barricade was constructed of sand bags built up across the trench. The enemy was on one side of this and our men on the other … The Germans were 10 to 15 yards off the barricade. The casualties in this sap were mainly from sniping.

During a period of little more than 48 hours of defensive action, 2nd Lancashire Fusiliers threw 8,000 grenades, and lost 93 men killed or died of wounds, 13 men missing, and 274 wounded. During their ten-week tour of duty, casualties amounted to 50 officers and 2,300 rank and file, or more than double the initial strength of the battalion.

1915: an Overview

Despite rapid advances in weaponry and small unit tactics, no offensive on the Western Front was rewarded with anything but the most trivial of gains throughout 1915. The French winter attacks in Artois were dogged by bad weather and lack of artillery, and beat fruitlessly against Vimy Ridge. The Champagne offensive which continued until 17 March resulted in massive French casualties in exchange for a few insignificant villages. In the Vosges, the Chasseurs Alpins duelled with German Jägers for the tactically useful height of the Hartmannsweilerkopf, which they eventually secured, but without any breakthrough. This was all rationalized as a 'nibbling' strategy; but to the enemy at least it seemed likely that France would eventually be defeated by such victories.

British efforts were no more successful. Sir John French's resources were as yet comparatively modest, and in view of the 'Easterners' commitment of what new British forces were available to Gallipoli, Mesopotamia, Egypt and elsewhere, his attacks were hardly likely to be conclusive. Neuve Chapelle in March 1915 demonstrated that good preparation and a short bombardment could get troops into the enemy trenches; but it was not clear how they were to get beyond them without either a way to get artillery swiftly across the battlefield, or communications that could deliver information that was not already long out of date.

Renewed Allied offensives during May at Vimy, Festubert and Aubers Ridge, and in June at St Mihiel, could claim no more than the most localized impact. In the autumn a more coordinated effort, with the French again attacking on the Champagne and the British at Loos, generated more casualties and acrimony, which would lead to the replacement of Sir John French with General Sir Douglas Haig in December. While the year was essentially a catalogue of failure, it should not be assumed that all attacks were the same, still less that no one was giving consideration to new ways to break the deadlock.

Allied Gasmasks, 1915–16
The Barley mask (**1**), May 1915, was a pad respirator. The bottle contains 'hypo' solution for re-soaking the pads. The Hypo helmet (**2**), summer 1915, was made of impregnated flannel and fitted with a small mica window. The hood gave about 3 hours' protection. The Harrison's 'tower' or 'large box' respirator (**3**), June 1916, featured a face piece linked by a tube to a separate filter box carried in a haversack. (**4**) depicts a French P2 mask, October 1915. Already obsolete by this date, French pad respirators were upgraded by the issue of extra colour-coded pads impregnated with different chemicals. The snout-shaped French M2 mask (**5**), October 1915, was a multi-layered cloth bag with integral isinglass eye pieces. The Russian Koumant-Zelinski respirator (**6**), 1916, made advanced use of rubber technology, having a full head piece which fitted tightly round the face. (Adam Hook © Osprey Publishing Ltd)

The 'small box' respirator gave protection to the wearer's eyes and lungs; here it is worn by an officer of a cavalry regiment – note the breathing tube running from the 'face piece' (mask) to the 'small box' filter canister contained in the haversack on his chest. Note also the crude respirator protecting the nostrils of his horse. (Mike Chappell)

In this context, the document that has undoubtedly attracted most attention is Captain André Laffargue's influential *Attack in The Present Phase of War*, based on his experiences at Neuville St Vaast in May 1915. This suggested that infantry should attack in waves supported by their own light machine guns and mobile artillery, overwhelming or bypassing the enemy. Most critically, he argued that defences in depth could not be 'nibbled' away, since an enemy would take advantage of the time to reinforce or dig more lines. Bitter though it might be, trench systems had to be 'swallowed in a single gulp'.

Versions of Laffargue's appreciation were later circulated not only by the French, but by the British, the Americans and even the Germans. Yet Laffargue's critique was only one of many, and certainly not the first. As early as April 1915 the Germans had prepared a detailed memorandum which analysed the latest French attacking methods. Among other things it criticized the French for reliance on artillery, failure to use counter-battery fire, and the narrowness of the frontages assaulted. It offered the advice that the attacking companies should be in from four to six lines, that assault troops should go lightly equipped using grenades, and that reserves should be 'brought up as far forward as possible', having infantry gun teams with them. Delay was to be avoided at all costs, otherwise 'we shall find ourselves in a cul-de-sac in far more unfavourable circumstances than we started'.

Both this paper and others, which detailed the latest thinking on defensive positions, were captured by the British and widely circulated. It was very clear that both sides learned from each other, often within a few weeks of an event. Furthermore, the beginnings of 'big pushes', hurricane bombardments, infiltration and mixed combat groups were apparent even by mid-1915. The problems would lie in integrating these disparate ideas, training and equipping the troops and using them for a worthwhile strategic result.

NEW WEAPONS: POISON GAS

Though there had already been small experiments in the use of gas, the first major discharge was made from the cylinders of Pionier-Regiment Nr.35 near Ypres on the morning of 22 April 1915. Entirely unprepared, the French Colonial troops in the path of the cloud of choking yellowish-green chlorine broke and fled 'like a flock of sheep'. Serious inhalations of chlorine had hideous effects, destroying the alveoli of the lungs, and drowning men in the liquid that their own damaged bodies created. It was the ability of the Canadians to create a new front behind the existing line and the lack of German reserves to follow up the success that prevented a disaster.

The Germans' use of this new weapon seems to have been regarded as an atrocity – 'frightfulness', in the usage of the day – by even tough-minded front line eyewitnesses. Company Sergeant Major E. A. Shephard of the 1st Dorsets, whose battalion suffered badly at Hill 60 on 1 May, linked the gas attacks in his diary with the loss of women and children aboard the torpedoed *Lusitania*, and wrote that 'the Dorset Regiment's motto now is, "No Prisoners"' – but he also urged immediate British retaliation in kind.

Over the next few weeks, while German gas attacks continued, the Allies struggled to find effective counter-measures, beginning with handkerchiefs soaked in water or urine, and 30,000 cotton wool pads made up as a result of a *Daily Mail* appeal. Yet gas was no wonder weapon: it was dependent upon the right weather, ideally a gentle breeze blowing towards the enemy; upon the ability to get cylinders into the front line; and upon the ability to protect one's own men

A German assault squad from Fusilier-Regiment Nr.40 Karl Anton von Hohenzollern. They wear *Pickelhaube* helmets without spikes in accordance with regulations of late 1915, and are fully equipped for bombing their way along trenches before setting up a blocking position. Stick grenades, ammunition bandoliers, spades, planks and empty sandbags are carried. The soldier in the centre carries the *Infanterie-Schutzschild*, or 1916 type metal loophole plate. (Stephen Bull)

from its effects. Moreover, as the war progressed it was proved to be surprisingly non-lethal: while more than a third of men hit by shell splinters and bullets were killed, fewer than one in 20 of gas casualties died. Indeed, official figures showed that though the British Army suffered nearly 13,000 gas casualties in 1915, there were only 307 fatalities. During 1916, just 1,123 were killed by gas out of a total of well over 100,000 fatalities to all causes: furthermore, though there were those who were permanently disabled, 93 per cent of all gas casualties returned to duty, most of them within a few weeks.

Like so many other facets of trench warfare, the use of poison gas would become a technological, tactical and industrial struggle in which both sides strove month by month to stay one step ahead of the enemy. The race was both offensive and defensive. Within a month the British had begun to produce their own chlorine; within two months they had decided on the formation of 'Special Companies' of Royal Engineers for the release of gas, and were conducting experiments at Runcorn, Cheshire. In the summer both sides were working on new gases, with the French producing phosgene on a small scale in Calais by August 1915, though the Germans were first to use it that winter. Phosgene proved more powerful than chlorine, and was relatively difficult to detect.

In the meantime, British and German scientists were experimenting with artillery shells that could deliver gas. Though both shells and cylinders would ultimately be widely used, in the short term the theorists came to opposite conclusions as to their respective merits: the British believed that shells were inefficient in delivering the necessary concentrations; the Germans, that shells were more useful than cylinders, for both their surprise value and their ability to hit specified targets.

There was also marked divergence on the defensive side. By 8 May 1915, the British were graduating from impregnated pads to flannel 'helmets', which were pulled right over the head and tucked under the uniform collar to close the open end of the hood (see pp.101–4). The first of these was the 'Hypo' helmet developed by Captain Cluny Macpherson, a medical officer to the Newfoundland Regiment. The modified Phenate-Hexamine model, with two eye pieces rather than a single window, improved chemical impregnation and an exhalation valve for the mouth, was known as the 'PH' or 'tube' helmet. Captain F. C. Hitchcock of the Leinsters received his in July 1915; though a great improvement over gauze and pads, it was sticky and messy due to the impregnating solution. A few months later, Captain J. C. Dunn described how the 2nd Battalion, Royal Welsh Fusiliers, went into action at Loos wearing their 'awful' gas helmets rolled up on the head, pulling them down only at the last moment, mainly to protect themselves against British gas, which was blowing back in their faces.

French gasmasks showed similar stages of development. Impregnated pads secured around the head with cloth loops, which had been in use from soon after the first use of gas, were followed by experiments with a hood design. By August 1915, the French Army was using an impregnated fabric design which covered the face, but not the top of the head, and was fitted by means of metal strips and tapes. Though this was improved to produce the M2 mask in April 1916, French troops were still poorly protected (see pp.66–7).

Following the variously impregnated pads, which were of only limited use, the Germans came to a more complex solution. This was a rubberized fabric mask with eye pieces, and a separate cylindrical screw-fit filter which could be changed once its filling had become ineffective. The mask came in three sizes and was carried in a grey cloth bag. Yet even as the new German mask entered full-scale production in September 1915, the firm of Boots of Nottingham was cooperating with the British Ministry of Munitions in the development of a new generation of 'box' respirators. In these the masks were attached by pipes to separate and still more effective filters.

FLAME-THROWERS

The use of flame as a weapon of war had a history dating back to ancient times, but the problem of the early 20th century was to harness it in a practical form and develop suitable tactics for the battlefield. As mentioned in Part I, as early as 1910 German inventor Richard Fiedler had patented a double cylinder backpack device with a flexible hose for delivering squirts of flame under the power of compressed gas. A form of this was adopted by the War Ministry as the *Kleif* (short for *Klein* – 'small' – *Flammenwerfer*) in 1912. In January 1915 a flame-thrower detachment for active service was formed under the leadership of Captain Reddemann, a Leipzig fire officer in civilian life who had collaborated with Fiedler's experiments before the war.

The *Flammenwerfer* detachment first saw action against the French at Malancourt in February 1915, when pioneers with light flame-throwers advanced across a particularly narrow stretch of No Man's Land which had already been scorched by fixed *Gross* – 'large' – flame-throwers. As a result of this successful experiment the detachment was enlarged to a full battalion, designated the 3rd Guard Pioneers. However, the Allies were now alerted to the problem, and actually managed to capture at least one equipment by March 1915. Later *Flammenwerfertruppen* were attached to the *Sturmbataillone*.

This MGC Vickers team in early 1916 use the Mk IVB tripod mount, but a small 'emergency' mount is also stowed folded under the barrel jacket. Both men have Phenate-Hexamine ('tube') gas helmets tucked down inside their collars, with two eye pieces and a rubber exhalation valve for the mouth. The firer wears a padded waistcoat with rope 'stops' at the shoulders, to help bear the weight of the gun or tripod in transit. (Stephen Bull)

Flame-thrower attacks were terrifying both to receive and deliver, as the 2nd Leinsters discovered when subjected to 'liquid fire' at Hooge on 31 July 1915. Captain F. C. Hitchcock recorded the following:

> The defenders of this sector had lost few men from actual burns, but the demoralising element was very great. We were instructed to aim at those who carried the flame spraying device, who made a good target. It was reported that a Hun who had his cargo of frightfulness hit by a bullet blew up with a colossal burst. Counter-measures against an attack were with rapid fire and machine gun fire. As the flames shot forward they created a smoke screen, so we realised we would have to fire 'into the brown'.

As a response to the German *Flammenwerfer* the British and French rapidly commenced programmes of their own. Devices were quickly put forward to the military by the American inventor Joseph Menchen and the French Hersent company. A practical-looking 'portable flame projector' was patented in London by W. A. Hall. In December 1915, British captains Vincent and Hay actually produced a 'knapsack' flame-thrower capable of about 35 yards' (30m) range, which was demonstrated experimentally at Wembley. Yet the Allied powers were slow to be convinced of the practicality of man pack models, and concentrated instead on larger installations and light mortars for projecting canisters of flaming fuel.

By the end of 1915, the German General Staff had issued detailed instructions for tactics to be used with flame projectors. Essentially flame weapons were seen as offensive, although the small models could be used against counter-attacks. The six-company 3rd Guard Pioneer Battalion now had 20 or more large flame-throwers, and 18 man pack weapons per company. Prior to attacks, the large projectors were to be built into positions where the German front came within about 30 yards of the enemy line, with each projector covering a front of about 55 yards (50m). A flame company was thus capable of mounting an attack over a frontage of 1,100 to 1,640 yards (1,005 to 1,500m).

The assault party, which was to include both pioneers and infantry, was ideally to be rested prior to the attack. It consisted of the assault party proper with bombers, engineers for the demolition of obstacles and small flame-throwers; a consolidating party; a group for the construction of new communication trenches to the captured zone; and a carrying party to take forward barbed wire, grenades, sandbags and ammunition. Special stores like short ladders, loophole plates, concentrated charges and signal pistol ammunition were similarly to be stockpiled in advance. Assault troops were to wear 'assault order', without packs but including greatcoat, shelter quarter, water bottle, four days' rations, rifle and bayonet with at least 200 rounds and two hand grenades. 'Consolidating' men were similarly equipped but carried their rifles slung without bayonet, and carried a loophole plate, 50 sandbags and a heavy entrenching tool.

The flame attack was prefaced by the explosion of charges to create gaps in the obstacle zone, and wire-cutting. Following a signal the large projectors were then ignited, spraying the enemy line for no more than a minute before the troops attacked boldly, as described in the General Staff document:

> The assaulting troops must be instructed that they have nothing to fear from the flames and smoke, nor need they fear that they may themselves be caught by the fire jet, as this is cut off simply by

turning a tap prior to their advance. They must understand that they can advance immediately after the cessation of the spray without danger, as small bursts of flame on the ground … will burn out at once, and a little fire on the ground is at once extinguished when trodden upon. It is most important to impress upon the troops that the assault is much facilitated by the use of the flame projector, as after a flame attack the enemy fires very little or not at all …

The assault is made immediately after the flame attack. The assaulting party charges, followed closely by the consolidating party. The small flame projectors allotted to the assaulting party attack any machine guns that are still in action, blockhouses that are still being defended, etc., with short spurts of fire … It is of the highest importance to drive out the enemy simultaneously to a considerable distance on either flank by means of bombing and flame projector detachments, and to construct sandbag barricades at these points.

VERDUN

The end of 1915 marked a nadir in Allied fortunes. The Russians had been pushed back across their western province of Poland, and Franco–British efforts on the Western Front had been thwarted. The Gallipoli adventure had proved to be just another bloody blind alley; and unrestricted submarine warfare now appeared to offer Germany an escape from blockade and encirclement. While the Allies planned great efforts for 1916, involving both Britain and Italy on an increasing scale, the initiative lay with Germany. The German High Command faced serious strategic choices.

An indefinite defensive posture was at best unproductive, and one in which the 'balance of numbers' might still lead to slow strangulation. Attack on the Eastern Front appeared pointless, since Russia's offensive power was now blunted and internal strife seemed likely to keep her weak, while 'advancing on Moscow takes us nowhere'. Yet, as General Erich von Falkenhayn, Chief of the General Staff, observed, 'Within our reach behind the French sector of the Western Front there are objectives for the retention of which the French General Staff would be compelled to throw in every man they have. If they do so the forces of France will bleed to death … '. Thus was born the plan, codename *Gericht*, for attack at Verdun: a salient strongpoint in the front surrounded by forts, symbolic of French national pride and resistance. Secrecy was paramount, and every precaution was taken to distract attention from the vital *Schwerpunkt*. Diversionary actions were begun at wide intervals elsewhere along the front – at Maisons de Champagne and Neuville in January 1916; at Ste Marie à Py, Tahure, Obersept, Vimy and Souchez in February.

Von Falkenhayn assumed, correctly, that the assault on one of France's most important fortresses would result in retaliation elsewhere, and his initial dispositions included reserves left in other sectors to deal with such responses. He was, however, incorrect in thinking that the Allies would be able to mount major operations immediately – and totally in error if he thought that these events would revive a war of movement, as he is said to have opined to General von Kuhl. He was also unrealistic in his chauvinistic assumption that the French would suffer five casualties for every two German.

Though only nine fresh divisions were allotted to the first onslaught at Verdun, planning was thorough, and it was claimed that important lessons had been learned from Allied failures. Not only was this assault to be a 'big push' in which successive waves would participate over time, but deep bunkers or *Stollen* had been constructed in which infantry could wait until needed. New rail lines were laid for the movement of prodigious quantities of stores. These included several hundred tons of barbed wire, a million sandbags and 2.5 million shells. The artillery fire plans pitted the heaviest artillery against the French forts, while the 21cm siege guns were to pulverize the front line. 'Boxes' of fire would cordon off sectors from reinforcement, and just before the attack French batteries would be treated to gas shoots. Importantly, it was reckoned that the 1,220 artillery pieces devoted to Verdun would so blast the enemy lines with 'an unbroken sheet' of shells that the infantry would be able to advance with only minor casualties. It was not the last time that such an assumption would prove fallacious.

Bad weather delayed the attack until it was feared that surprise was lost; but at 6am on 21 February 1916, the Germans unleashed a shattering bombardment which could be heard almost a hundred miles away. That afternoon the first infantry left the German trenches, wearing white brassards as a recognition sign; their mission was to seek out weak points which the main attack would exploit on the morrow. Yet so promising was the advance of these patrols that General von Zwehl's VII Reserve Corps was immediately pitched into the Bois d'Haumont, and fell upon an already decimated enemy. A battle that would last six months and cost a quarter of a million lives had begun. On 22 February, following further bombardment, full-scale attacks were led in by pioneers and flame-throwers, but again it was von Zwehl's corps that garnered the best success, clearing Haumont village. Over the next two days, despite bitter fighting and counter-attacks, the mauled French 72nd and 37th (African) divisions were expelled from the line, creating a dangerous gap.

On 25 February, the Germans achieved probably their greatest coup of the battle, almost by accident. That day Lochow's III Corps was programmed to advance to a point about half a mile short of Fort Douaumont. This was a self-contained moated rampart which, though planned 30 years previously, had been modernized as recently as 1913, and was currently assumed to be beyond the power of the attacking forces. The French High Command had decided that locking large garrisons in forts was counter-productive; consequently, Douaumont's garrison had been reduced to about 60

Diagram of mine warfare; in fact the mines were usually much deeper than this, often 60–80ft (20–25m) below ground. We are looking across No Man's Land from behind the French front line (A); at (B) is an old mine crater now incorporated into the defences. (C) is a German offensive mine being dug under the French trenches; the gallery is shown here unrealistically small. (D) is a vertical shaft dug down from a communication trench behind the French front line, from which a transverse gallery (E) has been developed, with a listening post (F). This has detected the German working; a *camouflet* (G) defensive mine has been dug forward under the suspected position of the German gallery, with an explosive charge which will be set off to destroy it. Opposing teams of tunnellers sometimes broke into each others' works underground, leading to nightmarish hand-to-hand battles with small arms and grenades. (Stephen Bull)

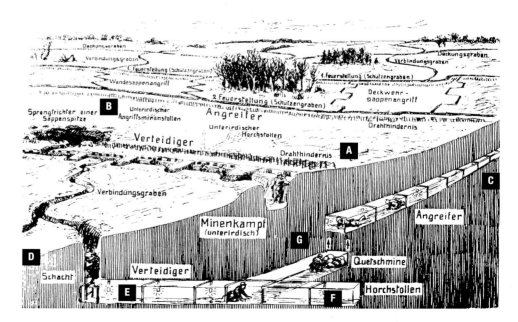

men, just enough to man her main armament. An order sent at the opening of the offensive for men to be poured back into her underground barracks and earth defences remained unfulfilled. So it was that when a section of Brandenburg pioneers fronting Infanterie-Regiment Nr.24 Grossherzog Friedrich Franz led the way unbidden down the ditch of the mound they called the 'coffin lid', others followed into what appeared to be simply a handy shelter from bombardment. Nearby French infantry assumed the enemy, now so far forward, to be friendly troops, and held their fire. A rather bemused pioneer sergeant named Kunze was first inside the fort. He captured some of the garrison,

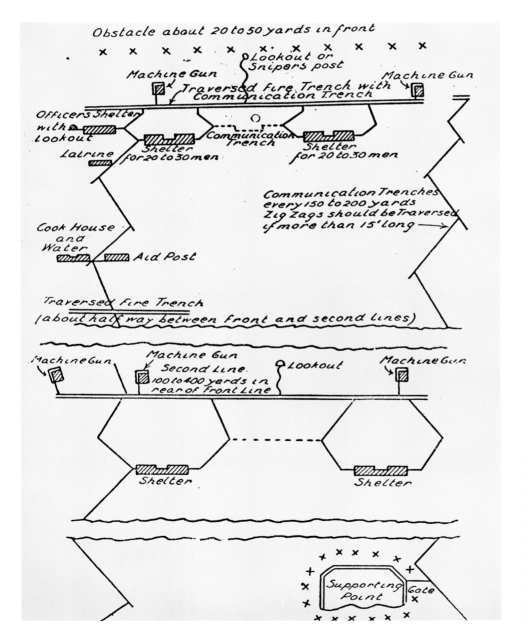

The ideal trench plan, from the British Army's *Notes From the Front (III)* of 1915. There are two main trench lines between 100 and 400 yards (91 and 365m) apart, and both lines are provided with machine gun posts and shelters. Latrines, cookhouse, and aid post are positioned on the communication trench joining the lines. (Stephen Bull)

then inadvertently let them go; but he was soon joined by two companies of the 24th, and the whole of Douaumont was secured. For this action two officers, Captain Haupt and First Lieutenant von Brandis, were decorated with the Pour le Mérite, Germany's highest decoration.

The collapse of their defences on the right bank of the Meuse during the first few days' fighting now stirred the French to well-nigh superhuman efforts. Von Falkenhayn had been optimistic in expecting that this reverse would break French resolve. The expansion of the British sector in the north had freed up the French Second Army, which was rapidly redeployed to fill the void. Second Army was led by the hitherto obscure 60-year-old General Philippe Pétain, who proved to be the ideal man for the task. Unimpressed by the 'Grandmaison' doctrine of attack at all costs, he was a respecter of firepower who would husband men and material when possible; he would nevertheless defend tenaciously, and would not shrink from huge sacrifices when these were demanded. German attacks had gained 5 miles in the first few days; from now on they would gain only a few hundred yards of what American ambulance driver Amos Wilder would call a 'calcinated and inhuman landscape'.

Where initial French stupefaction had helped to keep German casualties to sustainable proportions, repeated blows at the same places met with more stubborn resistance. One French artilleryman described the carnage he observed from the banks of the Meuse:

> At the top of the ravine, on the edge of the plateau, was a great heap of Germans. They looked like a great swarm of bees crawling over one another; not one was standing. The whole ravine was grey with corpses; one could not see the ground they were so numerous; and the snow was no longer white. We calculated there were fully 10,000 dead at that point alone, and the river ran past dappled with patches and streaks of blood.

Every push by the Crown Prince's Fifth Army would be met by fresh French battalions struggling along what became known as the 'Sacred Way' into the 'Meuse Mill'. Motor transport was deployed on a greater scale than ever before, with 3,500 lorries endlessly driving back and forth between Bar-le-Duc and Verdun, the much-shelled road being kept open only by the constant toil of Colonial troops posted at short intervals along its length.

By mid-March 1916, the Kaiser was admitting privately that he could see no end to Verdun; General von Gallwitz was heard to quip that the town would finally be reached, at the earliest, in 1920. Yet the battle went on, with bloody attacks up the feature known as the Morte Homme ('Dead Man's Hill'), and the capture of the Bois d'Avocourt on 20 March. The French responded doggedly to every reverse. On 9 April, the Germans launched a general assault on both banks of the Meuse; one unit struggled onto what they assumed to be the top of the Morte Homme only to find that they were on a false crest, short of the true summit; again French counter-attacks swept them down. As Lieutenant Raymond Jubert described it, the French infantry were assembled as stealthily as possible, and dumped their knapsacks in favour of extra ammunition and a day's rations before advancing under bombardment, and sometimes under machine gun fire capable of hurling men bodily into the air. They found the trench near the summit 'empty – but full of corpses', and regained possession.

The enemy were now reduced to tunnelling and blasting the hills ceaselessly with artillery. Eyewitnesses noted with macabre fascination how shells buried the dead, then disinterred them, then cut them into ever smaller portions. According to one estimate, the German artillery expended anything up to 17 trainloads of shells in a single day.

Perhaps strangely, Pétain now faced criticism for a perceived failure to counter-attack strongly enough. He was given a face-saving promotion away from Verdun to the command of Army Group Centre on 1 May, and was replaced by the more aggressive, even profligate General Robert Nivelle. An important French artillery position behind Hill 304 fell soon afterwards, and in the Crown Prince's memorable phrase the Morte Homme now flamed 'like a volcano'. It was finally taken at the end of May. Even so, the French continued to fight back, at one point almost regaining control of Douaumont. The moment of real crisis, which had 'threatened the very existence of France', was passing.

At the beginning of June 1916, Operation *May Cup* carried the Germans inch by inch over Fort Vaux, against a resistance which has gone down in the annals of French military history. The defenders under Major Raynal first fought off the enemy flame-throwers with bombing attacks, then called down artillery fire on their own position to kill German miners who attempted to tunnel in. Reduced to drinking their own urine, and fainting from explosive fumes and the concussion of shells, the last of the defenders were finally forced to show the white flag on 7 June.

The battle of 'annihilation' – a word said to have passed von Falkenhayn's lips in a private moment – eventually saw more than 50 German divisions pass through Verdun. An actual majority of the French Army was also rotated through the sector, under the so-called 'Noria' system designed to move battalions out before they became so wasted as to be useless. Yet even this most attritional battle, in what was fast becoming a total war, was not without tactical innovation.

The German experimental *Sturmabteilung*, or 'assault detachment', had been transferred to Fifth Army before the opening of the battle, and had been committed to the initial assaults in small groups wherever resistance was expected to be stiffest. By 1 April the unit had been increased to a battalion under Captain Willy Rohr. In its expanded form, the *Sturmbataillon* would field a complete machine gun company and a battery of mountain howitzers in place of the 3.7cm guns it had used previously. In May 1916, the High Command took the important decision that every army would send men to Rohr's battalion for training in the latest assault methods. These men would pass on their skills on returning to their formations, so that new regimental and divisional assault units could be established throughout the German Army.

For the time being, however, there would be fewer opportunities to put these new offensive lessons to the test. As Rupprecht of Bavaria, commander of Sixth Army, put it, von Falkenhayn seemed to have lost sight of the big picture while mesmerized by his *Ermattungsstrategie* or 'campaign of attrition'. On the other hand, as Winston Churchill noted at the time, the French had suffered more than they should 'by their valiant and obstinate retention of particular positions' which of themselves had no strategic value. While small unit tactics had undoubtedly advanced, coordination of the various arms and strategy had not kept pace. As Chief of Staff General von Knobelsdorf argued for the resources to finish the job, his leader now held back. The last triumph would be the capture of the ruins of Fleury on 23 June, by the Alpine Corps expertly supported by Rohr's assault battalion, the flame-throwers of the 3rd Guard Pioneers and phosgene gas. Another attack on 11 July was doomed to failure.

Towards the end of 1916 the French would succeed in regaining much of the ground lost around Verdun: but by now the war had entered a new chapter. The long-awaited all-out British offensive in the north had begun, von Falkenhayn had been sent off to the Eastern Front, and Joffre had been replaced. New players, and new ways of war, would now take centre stage.

THE SOMME AND BEYOND

Dr Stephen Bull

THE 'BIG PUSH'

At 7.30am on 1 July 1916, the first waves of 13 British divisions responded to the sound of officers' whistles, mounted ladders and sortie steps, and emerged from forward saps, to go 'over the top' into the teeth of machine guns and shrapnel. An officer of Württembergisches Infanterie-Regiment Nr.180 described the scene:

> A series of extended lines of infantry were seen moving forward from the British trenches. The first line appeared to continue without end to right and left. It was quickly followed by a second, then a third and fourth. They came on at a steady easy pace as though expecting to find nothing alive in our front trenches ... The front line, preceded by a thin line of skirmishers and bombers, was now halfway across No Man's Land ... when the British line was within a hundred yards, the rattle of machine gun and rifle fire broke out ... immediately afterwards a mass of shells from the German batteries in the rear tore through the air and burst among the advancing lines. Whole sections seemed to fall, and the rear formations, moving in close order, quickly scattered. The advance rapidly crumbled under this hail of shells and bullets. All along the line men could be seen throwing up their arms and collapsing ... Again and again the extended lines of British infantry broke against the German defence.

This resolute, profligate onslaught of manpower and material resources followed a week-long bombardment of 1,700,000 shells. It marked Britain's irreversible emotional and industrial commitment to the World War. No longer could England be accused of fighting 'to the last Frenchman', nor would French leadership be a foregone conclusion. Conscription would see to it that no British family or community was untouched by the war, and that all would have a stake in its outcome. It was no longer a war of diplomacy or commerce, but the Great War 'for Civilization', which would reshape society – and war itself. The first day of the 'Big Push' ended with 19,000 British dead and 57,000 wounded: Britain's bloodiest day in history.

Too often the tactics were what General Swinton would call 'fighting the rifle with the target', as Private Fred Ball of the King's Liverpools recorded of an attack later that July:

The fury of our barrage dropped like a wall of roaring sound before us. By some means the signal to advance was given and understood and we found ourselves advancing into the mist, feeling utterly naked. Who can express the sensations of men brought up in trench warfare suddenly divested of every scrap of shelter? ... So great was the noise that the order to keep in touch with one another was passed only by shouting our hardest, and our voices sounded like flutes in a vast orchestra of fiends. All at once I became conscious of another sound. A noise like the crisp crackle of twigs and branches, burning in a bonfire just beyond my vision in the mist, made me think I must be approaching some burning building. I realised, when my neighbour on the right dropped with a bullet in the abdomen, that the noise was rifle and machine gun fire, and I felt the tiniest bit happier when I touched my entrenching tool which, contrary to regulations, was attached to the front of my equipment instead of the side.

The 16th (Service) Battalion of the Northumberland Fusiliers were reported to have gone forward on 1 July 'like one man', and were found in several places to have fallen in lines, with 'ten or twelve dead or badly wounded, as if the platoons had just been dressed for parade'. The masses of shellholes were a mixed blessing: men kept stumbling into them, and they slowed the advance, but they provided welcome concealment on a bullet-swept field, as Second Lieutenant Alfred Bundy of the 2nd Middlesex recalled:

An appalling rifle and machine gun fire opened against us and my men commenced to fall. I shouted 'down' but most of those that were not hit had already taken what cover they could find. I dropped in a shellhole and occasionally attempted to move to my right or left but bullets were forming an impenetrable barrier and exposure of the head meant certain death. None of our men was visible but

Opposite:
A British officer. (Stephen Bull)

German infantry wearing variations on 'full marching order'. A mixture of long marching boots and ankle boots with puttees are seen, and one man appears to have improvised gaiters. Gasmask canisters are carried, and several men use bread bag straps round their necks to support their belt equipment. (Stephen Bull)

Trenches near Cambrai seen from the air; No Man's Land is at bottom right. This clear aerial photo shows the pocking of shellholes, the stark crenellated lines of two fire trenches, the lazy zig-zag of communication trenches, the shadows cast by belts of wire, and D-shaped advanced posts pushed out beyond them. (Stephen Bull)

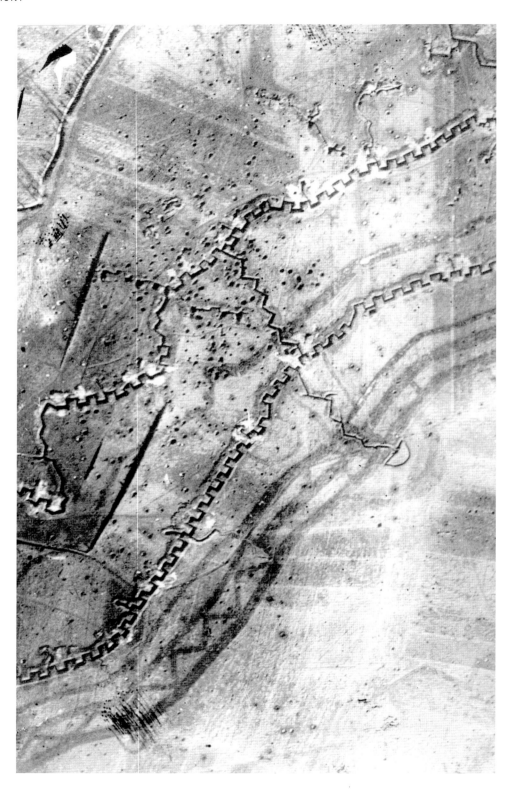

in all directions came pitiful groans and cries of pain. I began to suffer thirst as my water bottle had been pierced with a bullet ... I finally decided to wait till dusk and about 9.30 I started to crawl ... At last the firing ceased and after tearing my clothes and flesh on the wire I reached the parapet and fell over into our own trench now full of dead and wounded.

Though the German lines held along most of the front, the carnage was not one-sided. A single German regiment, the Baden Nr.169, took 591 casualties in the bombardment and assault. Even here, on the British 31st Division front where the Accrington and Barnsley Pals were decimated and left 'hanging like rags' on the wire, there were moments when things hung in the balance, and the British had to be driven out with grenades from front line trenches which they had managed to capture.

The Somme offensive would continue intermittently until November, bringing British casualties to over 400,000, in exchange for about 100 square miles (259km²) of churned mud. Though both the politicians and the High Command had sought a breakthrough, Sir Douglas Haig would redefine the objectives to fit the result. This had been, so it was now claimed, a 'wearing out' battle, a battle of attrition, which would ultimately lead to victory. Over the years the acknowledged 'sacrifice' of the Somme would become a watchword for futility.

Yet the Somme was not simply a blunder of mammoth proportions: it signified a stage in the evolution of organization, tactics and weaponry. Haig may have been a cavalryman at heart, but he also demanded ever more tanks, and ultimately encouraged new tactics. He also carried out the national will in bringing the war to a victorious conclusion, while politicians both took credit and distanced themselves from the 'butcher's bill'. Moreover, the main demand for the big offensive of 1916 came not from Britain, but from France, which was already reeling from Verdun. In short, the war was never simple to fight, nor static in its character – nor, given the numbers and skill of the enemy, would it ever be cheap. Lieutenant Charles Carrington of the Royal Warwickshire Regiment aptly summed it up:

A British Mk V 8in howitzer under a camouflage net near Carnoy, July 1916. For the Somme bombardment Fourth Army was assigned 64 of these weapons, which could send a 200lb (90kg) HE projectile out to a range of 10,500 yards (9.6km). (IWM, Q104)

Men from a battalion of the
West Yorkshire Regiment pose –
probably in late 1916 or early
1917 – in steel 'shrapnel
helmets', and the M1914 leather
equipment produced as a stop-
gap due to shortages of the Mills
M1908 webbing set. The leather
equipment was very widely
used by New Army formations
committed to battle for the first
time on 1 July 1916 – e.g. the
31st Division, including three
battalions of the West Yorks
serving in its 93rd Brigade.
The division suffered disastrous
casualties that day when
assaulting the German-fortified
village of Serre, on the northern
flank of Fourth Army operations.
(Stephen Bull)

The Great War on the Western Front began like most other wars ... when cavalry were employed on horseback and battles were short and sharp. It then passed into a period of stalemate, when infantry and guns burrowed underground and hammered at one another in prolonged trench to trench battles. In reality the period of fixed trench warfare was not so long as has been generally supposed, the lines were rigid only in 1915 and 1916 ... During 1917 bomb fighting in the trenches gave way to shellhole warfare, and in 1918 to open fighting ... in which tanks and cavalry played a large part.

Soldiers were changing, becoming an ever more accurate cross-section of the societies from which they were drawn. More importantly, they were less unthinking rifle-carriers, and ever more specialized. They may indeed have been less accurate shots and worse marchers than the regulars of 1914; but now they were bombers, snipers, tank crewmen, gas specialists, machine gunners, pioneers, signallers, drivers, and builders. A recent calculation regarding the French Army suggests that whereas 80 per cent of the troops had been infantry in 1914, the proportion was little over half by the end of the war. The situation was not so different for other nations. Soldiers were also being forced to be more self-reliant. As *Sturmtruppe* officer Ernst Jünger would notice, leaders now saw little of their men, who operated in increasingly scattered formation, and responsibility often devolved to a tank crew or a single machine gunner. Such men had to be capable of showing initiative rather than acting 'as puppets'.

THE TACTICS OF THE SOMME

By 1916 it had long been realized that lines of riflemen advancing on unprepared trenches stood little chance. The occupants of field fortifications could shoot them down more quickly than they could attack; machine guns and artillery locked the front solid, and local successes proved impossible to exploit due to poor communications and the difficulties of reinforcement. Even so, both sides were groping their way towards solutions.

Combat groups with grenade-throwers ('bombers') seemed to offer a way to enter enemy trenches and work through them; more open formations lessened the damage wrought by artillery; and greater autonomy at company level gave some tactical flexibility. Two lessons which had been painfully learned in 1914 and 1915 seemed to offer real answers. Firstly, enough heavy guns with enough shells appeared to open the inviting prospect of blasting the enemy from the face of the earth – with 'drum fire', as Beumelburg's memorable metaphor put it, turning men 'into apple sauce'. The French general Foch was already a disciple; as his memorandum of December 1915 stressed, offensives were made possible by their power of destruction. Artillery was the chief destructive force, which should be applied repeatedly, 'increasing all the time'. By the spring of 1916 he was stating that 'The completeness of the artillery preparation is the measure of the success which the infantry can obtain.' At long last Britain had the wherewithal for massive preparation. Total production of 18pdr shells in 1915 had been just over 5 million; in 1916 it would be nearly 35 million. Fewer than a thousand trench mortars were produced in the first two years of war, but 5,554 were made in 1916.

The second lesson was that organized mass attacks in successive, timetabled waves appeared to allow the possibility of advance right over the prostrate enemy, who would have no chance to react. In General Pétain's optimistic paraphrase, 'Artillery now conquers a position and the infantry occupies it.'

For the British in the summer of 1916 this doctrine was particularly seductive. Early failures had often been ascribed to the inability to marshal reserve formations into the gaps forced by the point of the attack. Scheduling reinforcement in advance, and maintaining constant pressure, were perceived as the antidote. Moreover, many British troops were inexperienced, whole New Armies of Kitchener's volunteers who had yet to see offensive action; and it seemed unreasonable to suppose that they would be capable of complex tactics which demanded independent action.

This digested wisdom became the 'Big Push' theory as expounded in the British official manual for the *Training of Divisions in Offensive Action* of May 1916. This stated that successive waves thrown into the attack would add 'fresh impetus' and 'driving power' to overwhelm the enemy. Fourth Army's *Tactical Notes* specified that each battalion be on a frontage of between two and four platoons, so that the advance was made in a depth of from four to eight successive waves, each no more than a hundred yards apart. The most difficult part was expected to be the point when it was necessary for waves to pass through one another after those ahead reached their objective. Ideally, entire fresh brigades would now pass over the holding points of those which preceded them, thus swallowing whole trench systems. On the micro scale it was imperative that individuals press on at all costs. Typical orders for 1 July, to 23rd Battalion, Northumberland Fusiliers, stressed that 'the advance must continue regardless of whether other units on our flanks are held up or delayed', and that on no account should anyone stop to help the wounded.

Though waves and timetables were the backbone of the system, officers and NCOs were encouraged to use their initiative to overcome specific local problems, and there was scope for the inclusion of bombers and skirmishers to precede the main attack. In places initiative took on greater significance. Some battalions of General Nugent's 36th (Ulster) Division, which had the good fortune of initial cover on the edge of Thiepval Wood, were advanced close to the German trenches before zero hour. As soon as the shelling ceased they immediately rushed the enemy, securing a portion of the line. Here close-quarter battle raged with a vengeance, as one Ulsterman recorded: 'The old sergeant kept going till we reached the German lines. With the first bomb he threw the door off a deep dug-out, and the next two he flung inside. He must have killed every German in it ... I had never killed a man with a bayonet before and it sent cold shivers up and down my spine many's a night afterwards just thinking about it.'

Private Devennie remembered grenades and trench mortar bombs being dropped down steps and through ventilation pipes. Private Irwin recalled an incident in which a man's torso was blown through the air. The result was the temporary capture of the Schwaben Redoubt; ironically, that evening the Ulstermen would meet the troops intended to relieve them as they were finally forced out and back to their own lines.

What was never clear in the British combat system of July 1916 was how artillery would coordinate its action with infantry as the battle unfolded. Many commanders, including General Rawlinson, had assumed that more and more shells fired prior to the infantry attack would pacify the enemy to the point of no resistance. It was the same mistake that the Germans had made at Verdun a few months previously.

One factor that has occasioned much comment was the amount of equipment that the British soldier had to carry. Yet not everyone carried the same weight. While many were overloaded, few went into the attack wearing 'full marching order', and precise equipment varied depending on unit and the function of the individual concerned. So it was that an order to the Royal Irish Rifles, 107th Brigade, specified that 'packs and greatcoats' would not be carried, but that haversacks (small packs) containing washing kit and iron rations would be worn on the back, with the ground sheet containing the cardigan 'rolled on the back of the belt'. Every man was supposed to have two bombs and two empty sandbags, and 170 rounds of ammunition; but forward platoons carried wire cutters, while those following up had pick or shovel. Wire cutter carriers were distinguished by a white cord on the shoulder strap. Though 23rd Battalion, Northumberland Fusiliers (Tyneside Scottish), also abandoned their main packs, they carried three bombs, four empty sandbags, and pick or shovel.

The diary of Lieutenant V. F. S. Hawkins shows that 2nd Battalion, Lancashire Fusiliers, carried neither packs nor greatcoats, tucking a pick or shovel under the braces of their equipment on their backs. Unit specialists carried no digging tools, the bombers having either a 'bomb bucket' or an improvised bomb carrier consisting of two sandbags tied around the neck. In this unit wire cutters were carried on a yellow lanyard. In a subsequent attack at Mametz the Royal Welsh Fusiliers were likewise committed 'in fighting kit' without warm clothing, and Captain Robert Graves recalled searching the carnage of the woods at night for German greatcoats. At the other end of the scale, men bringing up the rear carried trench mortar ammunition, barbed wire and other stores, which could raise their burdens to more than a hundredweight (112lbs/51kg) – proportionately more of these men survived to tell the tale.

Towards the end of the Somme battle Major Christopher Stone with 22nd Battalion, Royal Fusiliers, held the opinion that there was actually too much planning and thought put into what the men carried:

Zero day was postponed over and over again; the plans for the attack altered and enlarged; the attack itself practised whenever dry ground could be obtained, over dummy trenches. New ideas of 'battle order', bomb carriers, distinctive badges, etc., were dished out to the men till everyone was heartily sick of the battle long before it began. There was, at any rate, no excuse for not being prepared for it, or of not knowing the various objectives.

HELMETS AND ARMOUR

Very early in the war it had been realized that many fatal head wounds were caused by relatively small, low-velocity fragments. The French Intendant-General, August-Louis Adrian, was inspired by a 16th-century idea, and by soldiers' experiments, to design a steel skull cap to be worn under the képi. About 700,000 of these *calottes* were issued in early 1915, and the British followed with an order for 1,000 during June 1915. On the Vosges front the Germans made limited use of a steel skull defence with a nasal bar on a leather cap, developed by Colonel Hesse, Chief of Staff to Army Group Gaede.

From such crude beginnings sprang the drive to introduce universal defensive headgear; but armies differed over specifications. The French priority was to protect their men quickly, in a form

A famous photo of Irish Guardsmen examining a German MG08 machine gun at Pilckem Ridge, 1917, while wearing captured *Sappenpanzer* body armour. (Stephen Bull)

225

that was easily identified as French; the British requirement was for a 'shrapnel' helmet that would give the best possible protection against missiles from above; and the Germans' need was for a helmet that protected against low-velocity fragments of shell, mortar bomb, and grenade, while covering the forehead and neck. The three major types of helmet were therefore very different, but influenced many nations: the Russians, Belgians, Italians, Romanians and Allied Czech Legion adopted French-manufactured or French-style helmets; the Americans and Portuguese, the British type; and the Austrians and Turks, variations on the German theme.

The French Adrian helmet (see p.64) in some ways resembled a fireman's headgear; it was of light, multi-piece construction, built around a roughly hemispherical skull made in one of three sizes. A two-part brim was fixed to the crimped border of the skull front and rear, and a fore-and-aft crest covered a ventilation slot in the top. The lining comprised a corrugated aluminium spacer and a 'Cuban goat skin' sweat band with a segmented liner, the segments meeting above the cranium and adjusted with a cord. The helmet was finished with a chin strap and an applied metal badge denoting arm of service. Initially the helmet was painted *gris-bleu*, 'grey-blue'; this was altered to a darker, less reflective *bleu-terne*, 'dull blue', from September 1916. Khaki-painted helmets were worn by Colonial troops. The Adrian was not of good ballistic quality, being of relatively poor metal, weakened by the perforations in the bowl. British testers reckoned that it might stop three shrapnel balls out of four. Against this had to be set the fact that the first helmets were on their way to the troops by the summer of 1915, and that 3 million had been made by Christmas.

A Belgian grenadier – wearing the French Adrian helmet – demonstrates the use of the British Mills bomb. (Musée Royal de l'Armée, Brussels)

The British obtained a trial batch of Adrian helmets, and officers also made private purchases before the introduction of their own helmet. John L. Brodie's distinctive one-piece 'soup bowl' steel helmet was patented in August 1915 (see p.101). Though initially made of mild steel, by October the shell had been changed to non-magnetic, hardened manganese steel – virtually impervious to shrapnel balls, provided that they came from above. That same month the initial delivery was made to the front. The original paint scheme, suggested by Brodie himself, was a mottled light green, blue and orange, which produced a bronzed camouflage effect; but helmets were also painted in green or blue-grey.

The Brodie helmet undoubtedly reduced casualties, but was not without its critics. General Plumer complained that it was too shallow, too reflective, too sharp at the rim, with a lining that was too slippery. These criticisms led to the production of the 'Mark I' model helmet in early 1916. This had a separate folded rim, a two-part liner and khaki paint finished with a sprinkling of sand or sawdust to matt the surface texture. Initially there were nothing like enough helmets to go round, so they were designated as a 'trench store', to be kept in the front line and used by each unit that occupied the sector. It was only with the summer of 1916, when the first million had been produced, that the British helmet could be regarded as a general issue.

Designed by Dr Friedrich Schwerd, the German *Stahlhelm* was arguably the best of these first generation helmets (see p.18). It was the result of thoughtful initial specification, and rigorous practical testing, which included placing a selection of German and Allied headgear on the range at Kummersdorf and pounding them with artillery fire. The deep-pressed shell, in six different sizes, benefited from a light and simple three-pad liner system. Though trialled by Captain Willy Rohr's original *Sturmbataillon* in December 1915, it was not approved for general issue until the new year, and is thus often referred to as the 'Model 1916'. The prominent side lugs of the *Stahlhelm* were intended to take a heavy additional frontal plate or *Schutzschild* which would render it bulletproof, at least from the front. In the event this proved the least practical part of the system, and saw only limited use. About 300,000 helmets had been produced by July 1916.

In 1918 there were minor improvements to the German helmet which saw the chin strap fixings moved from the shell to the liner band, producing what is usually called the 'Model 1918'. In August of that year another variation with cut-outs to the shell skirt at each side was introduced experimentally, with the intention of improving the wearer's hearing; trials were still incomplete at the Armistice. Originally the German helmet was painted field grey, but the troops improved its camouflage qualities with mud, foliage, sacking covers and blotches of paint. Official issue white and grey cloth covers made their appearance in late 1916 and early 1917. The famous disruptive 'lozenge pattern' camouflage paint scheme, in which geometric areas of green, yellow ochre and rust brown were divided by 'finger wide' strips of black paint, was not formally announced by the General Staff until 7 July 1918; thereafter it was widespread.

Eye protection remained a vexed question: preserving sight was vital, but all the patterns of eye defence proposed were inconvenient in combat. No army therefore issued visors or 'splinter goggles' as a matter of course, but they were used experimentally, given to certain specialists or bought privately. 'Splinter goggles' usually took the form of a slotted sheet metal defence held to the head with bands. They were used on a very limited basis by the British and French, but were still being taken seriously enough for American forces to consider their use in 1917. One interesting experimental type was devised by American occultist Colonel W. H. Wilmer, who based his helmet-mounted, sponge rubber-cushioned design on the anti-snow blindness eye shields of the Native Americans of the North-West. The mask used by British tank crews was also essentially a 'splinter goggle' design, with a leather-covered face piece, slotted eye pieces, and a ringmail section hanging to cover the lower face.

Visors were the subject of much investigation, and the French Bureau of Inventions was hopeful of designing a practical helmet-visor combination. Majors Le Maistre and Polack devised models that were either a hinged front to the Adrian helmet, or formed part of a new helmet set. The Dunand brothers worked independently of the French government and invented a number of separate visors before producing a helmet with visor, which was offered to the Americans in 1917. Manufacturing problems and the difficulty of using a rifle with the visor down precluded widespread use. The British 'Cruise visor', which saw limited use in 1916 and 1917, consisted of a hanging curtain of mail, but again it was never a standard issue item.

Body armours were widely trialled, but for reasons of weight and cost were used only on a limited basis. Early in the war many companies, particularly on the Allied side, offered body armours and 'coat of plate' defences for private purchase. In 1915 and 1916 the idea of a 'Bomber's Shield' was investigated by the British Design Committee, Trench Warfare Section, which experimented with materials as diverse as steel, Shantung silk, vulcanized fibre, 'woodite', rubber and resinated kapok. A British silk 'necklet' for the neck and shoulders entered service in 1915, and was issued on a scale of 400 per division. It had surprisingly good ballistic qualities, but was expensive and degraded quickly. The 'Chemico' body armour worked on similar principles, being a sandwich of different materials including linen, cotton, and silk. Limited official use was also made of the Dayfield body shield from 1916, and in 1917 an 'EOB' breastplate was introduced.

French specialist troops, 1917–18, including an officer of the tank arm, the Artillerie Spéciale (left); a sergent of the 8e Régiment de Génie, the parent administrative unit for nearly 180 dispersed signal companies and detachments on the Western Front (centre); and a machine gunner of the 103e Régiment d'Infanterie (right). (Adam Hook © Osprey Publishing Ltd)

The French made some use of commercial body armour, but by 1916 General Adrian had introduced a light metal abdominal defence, 100,000 examples of which were manufactured. Groin and leg pieces were also produced but were not used on any scale. From February 1916 very large numbers of shoulder pieces – *épauliers Adrian* – were manufactured and issued; covered with old coat cloth, these were sewn to the shoulders of greatcoats. Issue was ordered discontinued in August 1916, however.

The Germans began to issue a set of silicon-nickel steel armour to a few men of each company in late 1916. This *Sappenpanzer* consisted of a breastplate hooked over the shoulders, to which three hanging abdominal and groin plates were articulated by means of webbing straps. The armour came in two sizes, weighing about 9kg and 11kg respectively (20lb and 24lb), and was capable of stopping small fragments, or even bullets from longer ranges. Though effective enough for static sentries or machine gun crews it was too cumbersome to be practical for offensive operations. An improved version of 1918 featured a stop for the rifle butt and stowage hooks for equipment. A total of about 500,000 sets were issued.

Armour shields and mantlets were also provided. Early in the war the Germans attempted to use small hand-held shields during advances. Later several nations introduced shields which were dual purpose, and could be either worn or used as a free-standing protective 'loophole' when rested on the ground. These included a heavy Austrian set with folding panels and a shuttered shooting hole; and the French Diagre, which was covered in blue cloth and featured a right-angled cut-out in the top corner for use as a rifle rest. The Italian Ansaldo system consisted of a steel body plate, available in slightly varying sizes and weights, which could be worn back or front, and was capable of resisting a rifle bullet at 100 metres. For use prone a pair of legs were rotated to support the shield, while a slot was opened for the rifle.

Loops were made for use on the ground, or set into the parapets of trenches; according to one estimate the Allies had deployed 200,000 on the Western Front by 1917. At Béthune, Royal Engineers workshops cut loops from standard plates using oxy-acetylene torches; and a type with canvas cover and rear prop was made by Rosenwasser Brothers of Brooklyn for the Belgians. On the German side, the M1916 loophole plate became commonplace; this was made of silicon-nickel steel about 6mm thick, and had a prop and an off-set rifle hole with swivelling shutter. It was proof against rifle and machine gun fire at 100 metres. An even more substantial plate, sometimes referred to as the '1916–17' model, was 11mm thick, with a 'mousehole' aperture, and could stop even armour-piercing rounds. This was held up by 3mm thick 'wings' at the rear which offered some side protection, but at 23kg (51lb) it was virtually immobile.

RAIDS

It is claimed that the very first trench raid occurred as early as 4 October 1914, when a platoon of 1st Battalion, Coldstream Guards, under Lieutenant Beckwith Smith rushed an enemy sap at Troyon Factory Road. In February 1915 General Sir John French called for 'constant activity' even though the army stood on the defensive. At about the same time the history of the 2nd Battalion, Royal Welsh Fusiliers, describes how the commanding officer 'kept alive the fighting spirit' of the battalion by means of 'patrols' intended to deny No Man's Land to the enemy: 'Patrolling was done by an officer who was rarely accompanied by more than four to six men, often by only one. Knowledge of the enemy's wire, reliefs, troops and so on, was sought. The capture of an enemy patrol, a dead man's identification marks, overhearing talk and recognizing dialect, aided intelligence.'

Many escapades aimed at snuffing out enemy listening posts ended in fights with rifles, pistols and bombs. In one of the larger skirmishes, on 12 March 1915, three officers and 21 men got close by bluff, using a German-speaking officer, and extricated themselves by whistle and lamp signals. In May 1915 the Canadians were reported as mounting many aggressive 'scouting patrols' led by NCOs. The 5th Battalion, Northumberland Fusiliers, executed a three-man night patrol in August 1915 to investigate a screen that the enemy had erected, but were sprayed with machine gun fire. Another group of seven went to their aid, and were lucky that there was only one fatality. Such exploits by aggressive units helped to develop small unit tactics. They added trench knives, coshes, knobkerries, knuckledusters, blackened faces, pullovers, cap comforters and muffled boots to the close combat repertoire; but these early raids aimed only at local goals. Trench raids as an official instrument of policy were slower to evolve.

The raid adopted as a model for future action was by 5th and 7th Canadian battalions on the Douvre River on the night of 16 November 1915; its keynote was minute preparation. A copy of the front line was laid out and attacks, the building of 'blocks', the use of bridging ladders and mats for crossing wire were practised. Artillery, trench mortars and infantry were all coordinated, while the raiders themselves were divided into two 70-man groups. Within each of these groups were sections devoted to different tasks: five 'wire cutters'; two bombing and blocking groups, each with seven men; two bridge cover parties with three men each; a trench rifle group of ten; a listening post support group of 13; and a reserve of 22. This organization ensured that once the enemy line had been penetrated, bombing groups could attack down the trench in both directions, blocks being established to prevent counter-attack.

British 9.45in 'flying pig' trench mortar at Pigeon Wood, Gommecourt, March 1917. (Stephen Bull)

On the day of the raid, artillery targeted a troublesome machine gun post and the wire, but this was incompletely cut and after dark the task had to be completed by hand. During the raid one group was discovered by the enemy, drawing fire. The raiders replied with bombs but, being compromised, were forced to withdraw. The other group was entirely successful, stabbing a sentry before bombing dug-outs, taking prisoners, and withdrawing according to plan. Artillery cooperation worked well; throughout the proceedings German rear lines were shelled, but when the attackers retired the guns turned on the sector that had just been raided, deterring counter-attack. The cost to the Canadians had been just one man wounded, and another killed by a 'negligent discharge'.

From this time on Allied raiding became more frequent and was sanctioned at the highest level. Haig had several good reasons for embracing what he called 'winter sports'. There was pressure from the French: they wanted him to attack, but he protested that as yet he had only a collection of 'divisions untrained for the field'. Raids would both help pacify the French and bring practical experience without committing the army to a premature offensive. This activity also seemed to offer the prospect of wearing down the enemy and forcing him to keep substantial garrisons constantly alert.

Raids, euphemistically called 'minor enterprises', were now also accepted as the prime antidote to staleness, as *Notes For Infantry Officers* pointed out:

> There is an insidious tendency to lapse into a passive and lethargic attitude, against which officers and all ranks have to be on their guard, and the fostering of the offensive spirit, under such unfavourable conditions, calls for incessant attention. Minor local enterprises and constant occupation during the tour of duty in the trenches furnish the best means of maintaining the efficiency of the troops ... Constant activity in harassing the enemy may lead to reprisals at first, and for this reason is sometimes neglected, but if persevered in, it always results in an ultimate mastery, it gives the troops a healthy interest and wholesome topics of conversation, and it achieves the double purpose of raising the morale of our own troops whilst lowering that of the enemy.

It should not be assumed that the advantage always lay on the side of the raiders. Most 'enterprises' had mixed results; many were bloody fiascos. At 'Y Sap' on the Somme on the night of 26 March 1916, the 1st Dorsets threw 86 men forward under cover of a mine explosion. Two parties entered the German lines, but the enemy fled, calling down artillery and machine gun fire on their abandoned posts. The Dorsets suffered four dead and 17 wounded, some of whom were initially left behind and had to be perilously extracted. They claimed one German hit. On 2 June 1916, also on the Somme, 22nd Battalion of the Manchesters launched a raid into uncut wire which resulted in 30 casualties, three of the four dead plainly visible the next morning 'tangled in a heap' among the wire.

That very night, not far away at Serre, 14th Battalion, York and Lancasters, made another raid optimistically claimed as a 'partial success'. This comprised three officers and 80 NCOs and men, and was intended to 'gain any information possible ... secure prisoners and to increase the morale of our troops'. Preparation was reported to have been good, but the intense 10-minute bombardment was insufficient; moreover, an officer and several men were wounded by a 'premature'. A Bangalore torpedo supposed to blow a hole in the wire was too short, and the break-through was made with wire cutters. Then 'the detailed order of procedure appears to have broken

American infantry, summer 1918. The private on the left is from the US 371st Infantry Regiment, one of the few African-American units to see combat. The other two figures, a Chauchat gunner and loader, are part of an automatic rifle team, 137th Infantry Regiment. (Adam Hook © Osprey Publishing Ltd)

down'. Just two officers and a dozen men got into the German trenches and promptly became involved in a bombing duel. After three minutes the raiders were recalled. Three men were killed and four wounded; the luckiest of these was Private McKelvey, who was spotted out in No Man's Land the next morning and rescued by a comrade.

A multiple raid launched by 55th Division on 28 June 1916 in the vicinity of Blaireville Wood, also on the Somme, was suddenly exposed when its covering cloud of gas and smoke was blown away. When they were just 50 yards (46m) from the enemy trench, the enemy started firing:

> He opened out with machine guns, rifles and trench mortars. It was Hell let loose, but someone shouted 'On the Kellys', and on we went, but we were cut down like corn. The Jerrys were two deep in their trench, and we realized we were done. Sixteen men answered the roll call out of 76. The worst part of a stunt is always after, when they have a roll call. To stand there and listen to the names being called and try to answer 'He's killed' – no one can picture it who hasn't seen one.

The total proceeds of this raid were one German cap and a Victoria Cross for a private who attempted to hold off the Germans during the retirement. As the Scottish trench proverb put it, 'Many a muddle means a medal.'

At Arrow Head Copse on 6 August 1916, two platoons of D Company, 1/4th Loyal North Lancashire Regiment, attempted to raid a ridge occupied by snipers, only to run into machine guns and shelling. Lieutenant Hague and two men were killed and 25 wounded to no effect. In October and November 1916, the 10th and 11th battalions, South Wales Borderers, gained 'undisputed possession of No Man's Land' in their sector, but not without cost. In one raid, Captain Charlton surprised an enemy sap and 'disposed' of its six-man garrison, only to beat a hasty retreat before

German reinforcements; Charlton and a private were killed, another officer wounded. On another raid, Lieutenant Moore was wounded and was lucky to be retrieved by Sergeant Edwards. On 28 September, 12th Battalion of the same regiment had attempted a 30-man raid on the Maroc sector, but were defeated by a combination of wire 45 feet (13.7m) wide and the explosion of a small mine which threw them into disorder.

According to recent calculation, there were a total of 310 trench raids made by the British alone during the battle of the Somme. Near Ypres, Captain Meysey-Thompson of the 21st Battalion, King's Royal Rifle Corps, may well have been correct when he observed that there were so many raids that they only served to keep the enemy ready and alert to intercept them. Captain Henry

British raiders, 1916–18. The figure on the left is dressed for winter daytime patrol in the Arleux area. In the centre is an officer after a night raid near Wailly, carrying an unusual self-cocking handgun. The private on the right is based on a photograph of a patrol ready to go out near Roclincourt on 12 January 1918. In addition to the SMLE rifle, he carries regulation wire cutters on a wrist loop and a No.36 Mills bomb. (Adam Hook © Osprey Publishing Ltd)

Dundas recorded a complex raid by 1st Battalion, Scots Guards, in early 1917 which involved crossing two canal lines, only to find that the Germans had already withdrawn, thus avoiding both bombardment and raiders.

Neither were the colonials immune to failure: at Celtic Wood in October 1917 only 14 of 80 Australian raiders would return unscathed. At Vimy, the Canadians got into a vicious cycle of tit-for-tat raiding during the winter of 1916/17. In the first three weeks of December 1916 alone, the Canadians received reports of 23 hostile patrols, and minor raids escalated into small battles. On 22 December, the whole of the 1st Canadian Mounted Rifles attacked with over 400 men; but on the night of 28 February 1917 similar mass tactics met with disaster. A gas cloud blew back over the assembling raiders; the Germans, unsuppressed and alert, proceeded to mow down large parts of the Canadian 54th and 75th battalions, and a total of 687 casualties was reported, including both battalion commanders.

With raids an established part of trench warfare, it is not surprising that the dress and equipment of raiders improved. Once troops had been content to discard equipment, fix bayonets, and turn their Service Dress caps backwards – being thus less likely to knock them off, and more likely to be taken for Germans. One A. S. Dolden of the London Scottish recorded that C and D companies of that unit even made a raid in kilts, with bayonets dulled, and both 'faces and knees blackened'. As experience mounted, however, raiders often adopted a complete new outfit. 'Boiler' or 'crawling' suits made their appearance during 1916; and the Royal Army Clothing Department produced a sealed pattern 'Suit Overall Light Scout' in 1917. Photos of 1918 also show the use of a snow camouflage white boiler suit. The history of 1/4th Battalion, Loyal North Lancashire Regiment, describes the night patrol attire as 'boiler suits and cap-comforters' with all identifying marks left behind.

Systematic raiding was addressed by the manual *Scouting and Patrolling* in December 1917. Under the heading of 'night patrols', it recommended that all night activities should be well planned, the objectives being to gain information; to kill or take prisoners; or to protect an area. All patrollers were to accustom their eyes to the dark before going out, and patrols were to move in parts, leaving at least one man listening at any time. They should freeze when any flare was let off, and should return to their own lines cautiously and by a different route. Depending on how many men were in the patrol, different formations were recommended; and though small numbers were thought best, the larger patrols might include up to 20, complete with Lewis guns. In such an instance scouts would be put out ahead and a box formation of patrollers formed around the gun teams. For small patrols pairs might advance one behind the other, threes in a rough arrowhead. Tip-and-run bombing groups could be formed with a pair of bombers to the fore and three men behind as a covering party. Equipment was an important consideration:

> Men on patrol should be lightly equipped. A cap-comforter is least visible, the face and hands should be darkened and gloves may be worn. Each man should carry two bombs, a bayonet or knobkerrie, and a revolver or rifle. A revolver is more convenient, but men so armed should be expert in its use. The rifle is best for purposes of protection. Scouts going out on patrol should have nothing on them which would assist the enemy if they were captured.

If all else failed the raider was encouraged to resort to 'hand-to-hand fighting and various jiu-jitsu methods of offence and self defence', as were taught in the Army Scouting Schools.

A message-carrying dog reaches German infantry sheltering in shallow scrapes or shellholes. Note the improvised 'assault packs' worn by the riflemen, with their tent sections rolled and strapped around mess tins carried on the back. (IWM, Q23697)

In 1916, German raiders are recorded as wearing 'attack order without greatcoat or cap, belts to be worn without pouches'. Perhaps more frightened of being shot by their own sentries, the Germans also experimented with triangles of white linen sewn to their jackets, and with 'white brassards'. Orders from 1917, however, suggest that white marks tended to be abandoned as impractical. Notes of Reserve-Infanterie Regiment Nr.261 refer to the carrying not only of pistols on lanyards, torches, flare pistols, daggers and trench clubs, but also of tent sections for removal of wounded and booty.

Like Allied efforts, German raids met with mixed results. In the flurry of raids at Vimy in mid-March 1917, there were at least two instances when alert Canadian sentries helped artillery and machine gun fire to decimate raiders before they reached their target. Yet in other actions Canadian 2nd Division lost 15 men, and two men went missing from an outpost. The Germans used similar techniques to the British and could raid on a large scale, as the Americans of Company F, 16th Infantry, famously discovered on the night of 2 November 1917. Corporal Frank Coffman recalled the following:

At three o'clock in the morning the Germans turned loose ... several thousand shells. The only thing that prevented our platoon from being entirely wiped out was the fact that our trenches were deep, and the ground soft and muddy with no loose stones. After the shelling had lasted three-quarters of an hour the range was suddenly lifted in a half circle box barrage in our rear to prevent our supports coming up, and 240 Bavarians, the widely advertised cut throats of the German army, hopped down on us. The first raid on American troops was in full swing. They had crawled up to the wire under cover of their barrage and the moment it lifted were right on top of us.

Two men were killed immediately; a third, Private Thomas Enright, was found on top of the parapet with his throat cut and a dozen bayonet wounds – it was assumed that he had been captured but had put up a struggle. Seven Americans were wounded, 11 captured: half the platoon was out of action.

SNIPING

Though a very different activity, the objectives of sniping were essentially the same as those of raiding: to gain mastery of No Man's Land, to wear down the enemy both numerically and morally, and to obtain information. Sniping was more than a century old in 1914, yet the skills were either poorly developed or forgotten in the major European armies. The first snipers were therefore French and German gamekeepers and foresters, Scottish stalkers, and big game hunters, who transferred civilian techniques to the battlefield. It was a game in which the Germans achieved an early dominance, which lasted through 1915.

The effect, both physical and mental, was considerable. The American Herbert McBride, serving with the Canadians, made close observation of the impact of the enemy sniper's bullet:

At short ranges, due to the high velocity, it does have an explosive effect and not only that effect but, when it strikes, it sounds like an explosion ... all of a sudden, you hear a 'whop' and the man alongside goes down. If it is daylight and you are looking that way, you may see a little tuft sticking out from his clothes. Wherever the bullet comes out it carries a little of the clothing ... the sound of a bullet hitting a man can never be mistaken for anything else ... the effect of the bullet, at short range, also suggests the idea of an explosion, especially if a large bone be struck. I remember one instance where one of our men was struck in the knee and the bullet almost amputated the leg. He died before he could be taken to the dressing station.

German sniper and observer team pose for a photograph in the trenches, 1916 – in actual combat they would obviously not expose themselves like this. (Stephen Bull)

Medics observed exit wounds up to 5 inches (12.7cm) across and the backs blown from craniums. As one account so graphically put it, the German pointed bullet 'was apt to keyhole so that the little hole in the forehead where it entered often became a huge tear, the size of a man's fist, on the other side'. Conversely, where the victim was caught unawares at long range, he might be unconscious of being 'sniped'. McBride recalled that unless a long-range bullet hit the head, it slipped in with little sound. One Canadian, leaving the latrines, was under the impression that he had scratched his leg on barbed wire. Many hours later the 'scratch' was still stinging, and the surgeon extracted a bullet from the wound.

Initially, equipment supply was problematic. In Germany the Duke of Ratibor is credited with initiating the collection of sporting weapons, and the Bavarians are believed to have received their first 'scoped rifles in December 1914. Bavarian regiments were soon supplied at the rate of one sniper rifle per company, rising to three per company by 1916. From Britain and the colonies came game rifles like the Rigby, Jeffreys high-velocity .333in and Ross Model 1905. Yet at first Britain was severely hamstrung by the dominance of the German optics industry. An appeal by Field Marshal Lord Roberts eventually netted 14,000 pairs of binoculars; but as far as sniper 'scopes were concerned, only 1,260 government orders had been placed by July 1915. By this time the Canadians were operating on a scale of four Ross rifles with telescopic sights per battalion, and Sir Max Aitken's *Canada in Flanders* claimed that a Native American, Private Ballendine, had already achieved a tally of 36 Germans.

In the British Army, the efforts of individual enthusiasts like Major F. Crum of the King's Royal Rifles, Major T. F. Fremantle, and Lieutenant L. Greener of the Warwickshires bulked large. Yet one officer more than any other has been identified with the systemization of sniping and the establishment of army schools. Hesketh Vernon Hesketh-Pritchard, a big game hunter and former Hampshire County cricketer, was at first turned down by the army on grounds of age, but succeeded in reaching the front, escorting war correspondents in 1915. In his luggage he brought 'scoped sporting rifles, and was soon preaching his creed 'to shoot but not be shot'. His mission was, as he saw it, to 'invent ways to irritate Germans'. In July 1915 he conducted experiments with 'elephant guns' against the metal loophole plates which the Germans were already using, and by August was lobbying generals Lynden Bell, Munro and others with a scheme to set up an official sniping establishment.

Appointed as sniping officer to 4th Division, Hesketh-Pritchard was soon in his element, as his painstaking account of a sniping duel on 6 October records. At 3.10pm a German was spotted: 20 minutes later hands were seen fixing a board to use as a rifle rest, which Hesketh-Pritchard observed with a telescope from 420 yards (384m) away:

At 4.15 we could see the brim of his cap, and he lighted a pipe – I could see the tobacco smoke ... Then he fired a shot resting his rifle on the board ... I think he was shooting at a dummy plate ... Then at 4.55 he looked over, his chin resting on the parapet. The rifle was well laid, and I had not to move it more than an inch; then the shot. Later a Bosche with a beard looked over, and this man was killed by the sergeant major ... .

Though there were some spectacular long-range shots, moving targets and weather made hits over 300 yards (274m) the exception, and some of the best tallies were achieved at relatively close ranges.

Men would fall, and their comrades would take cover, scanning the horizon, not realizing that the predator was low down and close at hand. The most skilled would crawl out at night to a good position, lay up possibly for many hours, take one or two shots as they presented themselves and crawl back again under cover of darkness.

Yet sniping soon developed into more than the chilling game of 'assassination'. Battalions acquired dedicated sniping or intelligence officers, and British Army schools of sniping were begun in 1916; eventually not only British, but American and Portuguese troops would pass through them. The work of the sniper officers increasingly focused on teaching and training, inventing, and supplying snipers' requisites. Hesketh-Pritchard developed a 'double loop' which made it difficult to be hit from any angle other than directly to the front, and a system of dummy heads which could be raised and lowered to attract enemy snipers. Major Crum specialized in masks; while Lieutenant Gray made a board to which sandbags were attached to be inserted into the parapet at night to conceal the placement of new loopholes. Head 'veils' in light and dark brown, which had already been used unofficially, were produced as standard 'sealed patterns' in 1916.

It was also about this time that the Royal Engineers first established a 'Special Works Park' for the provision of camouflage. Apart from huge quantities of netting, screens, canvas and scrim for regular tasks, this would also produce special equipment for snipers and observers. At one end of the scale were complete observation posts, dummy trees, and giant 'Ross' periscopes more than 10 feet (3m) in length; at the other, painted canvas robes and dummy heads. An unusual item made from May 1917 was the 'Chinese attack' figure; these were cut-outs which could be raised suddenly to simulate an attack, distracting the enemies' attention or encouraging them to open fire. The French, who had already established their own facilities, also had some extraordinary products. Amongst these were dummies representing dead or wounded men and horses. Some would be used as hides, others made to move so as to attract enemy snipers. Later the Americans would embrace the camouflage idea, setting up not only a central camouflage 'Shop & Replacement Battalion' but also one camouflage battalion per army.

On the other side of the line the enemy were moving in similar directions, adopting painted canvas and burlap robes, and head veils. The British *Summary of Recent Information Regarding the German Army and its Methods*, issued in January 1917, noted that 'snipers have been discovered wearing uniforms made of sandbags, merging themselves with the parapet'. Untidy parapets consisting of irregular lines, different coloured sandbags and odd piles of debris were turned to positive advantage to camouflage loopholes and break up outlines. Splodges of dark-coloured paint on sandbags, odd bits of pipe and reflective pieces of glass were used by both sides to keep the enemy guessing where real apertures and observers actually were. The most commonly encountered German sniper weapons were Scharfschützen Gewehr 98, specially selected examples of the ordinary service rifle modified by means of a turned-down bolt handle and the addition of Goerz, Zeiss or Hensoldt telescopic sights. By the latter part of the war, the Germans were operating on a norm of 24 snipers per battalion; yet there was every indication that the British were gaining ground.

British sniping methods were finally codified as part of the manual *Scouting and Patrolling* in December 1917. In defence, it was recommended that snipers be found in a number of 'battle positions' in long grass, shellholes, trees or piles of bricks, from which they could inflict casualties on attackers or overlook captured lines. In the attack, it was the sniper's duty to work himself into vantage points and ruined trenches. Though good camouflage would be difficult to obtain on the attack, targets were more likely to be numerous.

In trench warfare, a system of posts would be established from which the entire enemy front could be kept under observation. These posts were carefully camouflaged with multiple loopholes and curtains so positioned as to prevent light showing. Once the enemy had discovered such a position it would be abandoned, temporarily or permanently. Working with each observer would be a sniper, 'a picked shot capable of hitting any head that shows itself up to a distance of 300 yards'. Snipers were warned to look out for enemy observers and smash any periscopes that appeared, preventing the enemy from seeing them and gaining 'moral superiority'. Camouflage, and what we might now call 'field craft', were vital:

> The sniper should make use of veils, sniper suits, camouflage, etc. when available, and scout officers should keep themselves up to date with the latest ideas. The study of protective colouring is interesting and of value; but it must be impressed on the sniper that, however well his disguise may conform with his surroundings, if he does not at the same time learn to keep still, or, move only with stealth and cunning, he is likely to disclose his position. Great patience and constant practice in moving very slowly are required. Disguises may be improvised by using grass, leaves, etc., and by smearing the hands and face to harmonise with the surroundings. A regular outline of any shape attracts attention.

Sniping at night was thought to be particularly advantageous since most movement occurred after dark, and for such work the Aldis sight with its large object glass was most suitable. Night sights could also be improvised by winding a little white cotton around the ordinary front and rear sight lugs of the rifle. Similarly, 'rifle batteries' or rifles set on weighted ammunition boxes could be left trained on enemy sap heads, machine gun posts or gaps in the wire. They could then be used at any sign of danger, or as a distraction from friendly patrols.

Though textbook sniper establishments might be as low as eight men per battalion, by the latter part of the war many units were fielding a dozen or more. Major Crum recommended from 16 to 24, while the 2nd Worcestershires had an unlucky 13. What had started as 'sport' would end as an enduring feature of modern war.

New Defensive Tactics

Dispersal in Depth – the 'Empty Battlefield'

Part of the reason for the continued failure of offensives in 1916 and 1917 was the increasing power of defence: not only were positions ever deeper, but the methods of holding them were more subtle. From ground level this was the 'empty battlefield': single lines of trenches, manned by the whole of the available garrison, had now become multiple complexes, often several kilometres wide, with numerous belts of wire and deep *Stollen* or dug-outs for reinforcements. Linear obstacles became defended areas, which presented no easy target upon which overwhelming firepower could be concentrated. For the romantically minded this scientific approach to war was a particular kind of tragedy, as Friedrich Steinbrecher expressed in 1916:

The poetry of the trenches is a thing of the past. The spirit of adventure is dead ... We have become wise, serious and professional. Stern duty has taken the place of keenness ... a frigid mechanical doing of one's duty ... Formerly the dug-out walls were adorned with pictures – now they are covered with maps, orders and reports. Formerly the men christened their dug-outs ... now they are numbered.

Allied field works were similar, though intended to be less permanent. Considerable planning went into trench systems, but the worm's-eye view was often one of unremitting toil and confusion. A member of 1/4th Battalion, Loyal North Lancashire Regiment, described 'Beek Trench' near Ypres in 1916 in the following gruesome terms:

a mass of slime and rotten sandbags which it was part of our job to drain, duck board and rivet [sic] with corrugated iron. As nearly every trench in the salient was in like state, and repairs were soon spotted and strafed by the Hun ... it will be seen that 'Old Bill's' opinion, that the war would only end when the whole of Belgium had been put into sandbags, had much to justify it. Going up Beek trench on a dark night was no picnic. You started along a long narrow alley winding uphill, your hands feeling the slimy sandbag walls, your feet wary for broken duck boards; now and again a hot, stuffy smell, a void space in the wall, and the swish of pumped up water under foot proclaimed the entrance to a mine. Gradually the sandbag walls got higher and the alley narrower, and in places you stumbled where the trench had been blown in and got covered in blue slime ... round corners you dived under narrow tunnels two or three feet high, finally emerging into the comparative open of the front line trench.

The British intelligence *Summary of Recent Information Regarding the German Army and its Methods* of January 1917 observed that enemy defences now comprised two, or usually three, defended zones with at least a kilometre between them. Each position was itself made up of three trench lines, with gaps of from 50 to 200 metres (55 to 219yd), and communication trenches and linking 'diagonals'. When any part was broken into, the remainder would naturally form a 'pocket' able to converge heavy fire upon the intruders. Strongpoints and redoubts in woods, villages and depressions formed the core of defences.

The 1916 German 'Construction of Field Positions' manual *Stellungsbau* recommended that major strongpoints and 'holding on' points could be gradually linked and locked together to form new lines of defence. Dummy positions would be used to mislead enemy airmen. Lines were best laid out so that the forward positions overlooked the enemy, aiding artillery observation. Further back trenches housing the main garrisons were on reverse slopes unseen by the enemy. Individual fire trenches were ideally traversed, and not much more than a metre wide, sufficient to allow a deep passageway behind the fire step, but not so wide as to present a shell trap. A field of fire of as little as 100 metres (109yd) was perfectly acceptable if this protected the troops. Machine gun positions were to form the 'framework' of the line, a minority of them placed well forward, with surprise increasing their potency. Trench mortars were best placed in their own pits, not in the main trenches, so as to be out of the likely enemy bombardment zone. Some of the details were seen by John Masefield on the expensively won Somme battlefield:

Whenever the enemy has a bank of any kind, at all screened from fire, he has dug in it for shelter. In the Y Ravine ... he sank shafts into the banks, tunnelled long living rooms, both above and below the gully bottom, linked the rooms together with galleries, and cut hatchways and bolting holes to lead to the surface. All this work was securely done, with baulks of seasoned wood, iron girders, and concreting ... When our attacks came during the early months of the battle, they were able to pass rapidly and safely ... bringing their machine guns with them.

The German wire – which had '16 barbs to the foot' – was secured to crossed irons or corkscrew supports, making thick webs, 'about 4 feet [1.2m] high and from 30 to 40 feet [9 to 12m] across'; these were supplemented by trip wires, low entanglements and iron spikes or 'calthrops'. Though the British bombardment on the Somme had been massive, it had been lacking in important respects. Its duration had ruined any element of surprise, and its wire-cutting potential had been overestimated. Worse, although just over 2,029 guns had been deployed, only 452 were 'heavies' capable of dealing with deep bunkers. This was a smaller proportion of heavy artillery than the Germans had managed at Verdun.

Some of the latest defensive tactics appeared in the American manual *Notes on the Construction and Equipment of Trenches* of May 1917, just weeks after the US declaration of war. This readily accepted that commanders of sectors 'do not count on holding their firing trenches in case of violent attack, but always have arrangements made in every detail for a counter-attack'. It also recommended the provision of narrow 'slit trenches' and dispersed shelters for use during bombardment. The American Expeditionary Force's ideas were a mixture of Allied and German methods, and its troops would initially occupy trenches which had already been dug. Yet *Notes on the Construction* ... also contained evidence of zeal to the point of overconfidence, as when it recommended the occupation of forward slopes, which were 'certainly exposed to view and

British troops attempt to clear a road across a sea of devastation. This woodland is in a relatively lightly shelled area. In the most heavily bombarded forward areas autumn rains could turn the pulverized ground to a deeply saturated soup of mud, making the movement of infantry and heavy weapons almost impossibly difficult. The third battle of Ypres in autumn 1917 became notorious for the depth of the mud and the frustrating and exhausting difficulty of movement, even when not under direct fire. (Stephen Bull)

A quiet time for German machine gunners playing 'skat' in a solidly constructed trench near Ypres, 1916. It was in such peaceful moments that a careless man might briefly expose his head above the parapet, offering a target to a sniper. Details visible here include a mess tin and gasmask canister hanging from nails, and a periscope wrapped in sacking propped on the firing step. The machine gun on its 'sledge' mount is emplaced in the sandbag parapet; the large object in the right foreground is an armoured shield for the MG08. (Stephen Bull)

bombardment', on the grounds that 'high ground gives a feeling of superiority to the troops and acts favourably on their morale'. Elsewhere it also suggested that about half the trench garrison might be put in the foremost line.

By the time the third Battle of Ypres (or Passchendaele) opened 31 July 1917, German systems had advanced considerably. The front was divided into divisional sectors 5,000 metres (3.1 miles) wide, within which were regimental sectors each about 2,000 metres (1.2 miles) across. The battalions of the regiments were placed one behind the other, in forward, battle and rear zones, to a total depth of at least 4 kilometres (2.5 miles). Even the battalion within the forward zone or *Vorveldzone* was not in one line, but was divided up to form a defence a kilometre or more in depth. The sub-divisions within the *Vorveldzone* included the 'security line' within about 250 to 500 metres (270 to 550 yards) of the enemy, in which a mere 50 or so troops would man perhaps a dozen scattered outposts. Behind this would be a better defended *Widerstand* or 'resistance' line, where about 200 men, including some machine gun teams, would provide a checkerboard formation of squad-sized positions.

The last part of the forward zone was the 'main' line of resistance, in which the remainder of the battalion would man two or three trenches. In the event of all-out attack, the outlying

posts could retire on the main line, and the whole of the area between here and the opposition would be counted a 'barrage' zone for German artillery. Attacking troops would therefore have to struggle through a kilometre of churned ground, potentially under artillery fire, machine guns and snipers, from a variety of directions, before they reached anything approximating a solid 'front' which they could attack. The new emphasis was on individual, but mutually supporting, positions.

REINFORCED CONCRETE

The increasing use of reinforced concrete was a material aid to stand-alone defences and economy of manpower. The Germans were pioneers of MEBUs, *Mannschafts Eisenbeton Understande* or 'reinforced concrete personnel dug-outs', for which they barged huge quantities of materials down the Rhine, beginning in late 1915. Over time considerable technological progress was made, and early sandwich constructions and the use of heavy rails gave way to new methods such as thin reinforcing rods and pre-cast blocks. The Royal Engineers examined such structures with professional appreciation, noting one particular farm with concrete positions which had been bombarded 'by ourselves and by the enemy for over a month' without yielding, as 'the effect of shell fire on these structures has been practically nil, though the surrounding ground is a mass of interlocking shellholes'. In some spectacular instances super-heavy shells burst next to bunkers, which did not shatter, but settled at drunken angles into the craters.

Some bunkers had embrasures, but many were 'blinds' having no vulnerable apertures, allowing the occupants to sit out bombardments in relative safety; even so, direct hits could cause casualties

A German *Schützengraben* or 'fire trench' in wooded country, showing firing steps, grenade dumps, and helmets and bandoliers at the ready. (Stephen Bull)

through concussion or the flaking of dangerous lumps of concrete off the insides of the walls. When firing ceased, the garrisons rushed out to man shellholes or fired machine guns over the roof of the bunker. Only when the enemy took the position completely by surprise did this scheme become a liability, and then there were instances when dozens of trapped men were captured by one or two Allied soldiers.

By 1917, the concrete pillbox had become the cornerstone of the new system of defence, with many small machine gun posts boasting cover 1.5 metres thick. Bunkers nestled into folds in the ground or were camouflaged with turf, rubble or wood to suit the environment, as General Gough noted at Ypres:

> The Germans had built small but very powerful concrete shelters. These were covered with mud and scattered throughout the desert of wet shellholes ... They were impossible to locate from a distance, and in any case were safe against anything but the heaviest shells. The farms, most of which were surrounded by very broad, wet ditches, or moats, had also been heavily concreted.

Artilleryman George Wear had a similar perspective:

> The bombardments of the Somme ... were nothing to those round Ypres. Batteries jostled each other in the shell marked waste of mud, barking and crashing night and day. There were no trees, no houses, no countryside, no shelter, no sun. Wet, grey skies hung over the blasted land, and in the mind a gloomy depression spread. Trenches had disappeared. 'Pill boxes' and shellholes took their place ...

'Plugstreet' Wood, January 1917: men of the Lancashire Fusiliers emerge from a built-up section of 'box trench' onto a duckboard path. This is the rear entrance of a communication trench; in the coastal sector of Flanders, where the water table was very high, fire trenches also had to be constructed above ground in this way. (Stephen Bull)

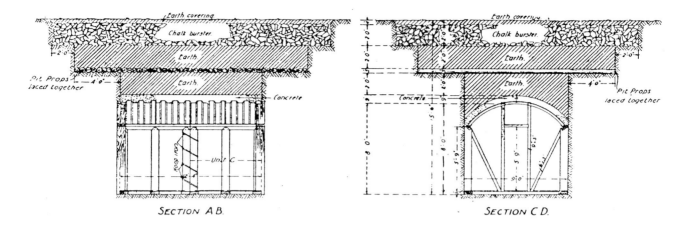

SECTION A B.

SECTION C D.

Diagrams showing how British corrugated iron 'elephant' shelters could be shellproofed using layers of concrete, earth, chalk rubble and pit props: AB side view, CD end view. The idea was to make sure the shell burst close to the surface, so that the underlying strata absorbed the shock and fragments. (Stephen Bull)

Fighting for such monoliths could be brutal indeed, with even the Australian official history admitting that having been savagely and repeatedly raked with machine gun fire on the way in, troops were apt to butcher the first enemy to emerge. Once captured, concrete posts were a mixed blessing, since the entrance and the thickest defence were now on the wrong sides. One possibility was to block up the old doorway and blow a new entrance; another was to throw up a new defence in front of the existing portal. Either way it was highly dangerous under fire.

One unit, 1st Battalion, Cambridgeshire Regiment, endured days of such fighting at St Julien in the summer of 1917. The battalion's C Company first seized a trench line and two concrete bunkers, holding them 'like a breakwater' against successive counter-attacks until they were crowded with delirious wounded. Private Muffet distinguished himself by repeatedly crossing open ground to fetch ammunition. The Cambridgeshires' battalion commander ensconced himself in another enemy position:

> Our gun pit, with roof and sides of concrete, was open at each end. To protect us from the German
> side we had piled up a mound of earth ... Over the concrete roof, and for five or six yards beyond the
> concrete sides, the Germans had heaped earth, which was now overgrown with grass. It was not a
> residence calculated to command a high rent in time of peace, but at that hour many a soldier would
> have given all he possessed to stay beneath its shelter.

Local defence of this impromptu headquarters was provided by a Lewis gun dismounted from a stranded tank. Despite bombardment and the killing or wounding of most in the vicinity, the gun pit held out against German infantry attack. Only when British guns erroneously targeted the pit was the order to withdraw given. Even then, Private Muffet refused to abandon the position called 'Border House' and leave the two wounded men who remained alive until given a written order. Muffet was recommended for the Victoria Cross, but it was refused.

Not far away, Guy Chapman saw a similar battle given a diabolical twist:

> Then the defenders suddenly saw advancing towards them a wave of fire. The enemy were attacking
> under cover of a *Flammenwerfer* ... When the nozzles were lighted, they threw out a roaring, hissing
> flame 20 to 30 feet [6 to 9m] long, swelling at the end to a whirling oily rose six feet [1.8m] in

'New model' 7.6cm German light *Minenwerfer*, pictured August 1917. Capable of rapid fire and a range of 1,300 metres (1,420 yards) with high explosive or gas bombs, the 7.6cm was mounted on a traversing plate and fired by means of a pull on a lanyard. The crew shown here includes an NCO and, behind him, a telephonist. (Stephen Bull)

diameter. Under cover of these hideous weapons, the enemy surrounded the advance pill box, stormed it and killed the garrison ... the enemy was consolidating the pill-box; but Whitehead and C. S. M. Edmonds, collecting a few men to carry for them, furiously assaulted the place and bombed their way into it. Most of the occupants were killed, and six surrendered.

As Colonel E. G. L. Thurlow observed, the British had a tendency to assume that elaborate concrete works were not worth the immense efforts required, and that they engendered a 'lack of offensive spirit'. They therefore made limited front line use of this material, although some British concrete machine gun positions had been built as early as 1915, and corrugated iron 'elephant shelters' were covered in layered concrete to create 'bomb proofs'. Some individual strongpoints were also well protected. Yet from summer 1917, with their capture of Messines Ridge overlooking Ypres, the Allies were forced to take concrete construction far more seriously. The British Army's first concrete factory, opened at Arques in the winter of 1916, was joined by a second at Aire a year later. The Aire facility was entirely given over to the manufacture of blocks and beams, and at the height of production was making 7,000 and 700 of each per day, respectively.

Early in 1918, Aire also formed a 'School of Concrete', and Royal Engineer Transport Works companies were formed specifically to deal with concrete. In addition to block-built pillboxes, 'mix in place' cement was used, as were Moir pre-cast pillboxes with steel domes which were imported to France from Richborough in Kent. Additionally, Major-General Hobbs of the Australian 5th Division conceived the Hobbs armoured machine gun emplacement, which was produced in Glasgow and transported to the front, mainly for use in Australian sectors. Unfortunately, work was not far advanced at the time of the German offensive in the spring of 1918, and both the concrete factories were in danger of being overrun, necessitating the establishment of new facilities further back.

With the turn of the tide in the summer of 1918, the Allies found themselves up against the Hindenburg Line, arguably the best set of works to date, having been constructed out of range of Allied artillery. Here networks of light railways connected the new defensive line with dumps of raw materials and 'mixing places'. Even as the Hindenburg Line was being breached, a British 'GHQ Defence Line' was begun with the idea of forming an ultimate back-stop against any future German advance. This used the latest techniques, including the innovative 'ferro-concrete pancake shelter' in which a hole was dug in the shape of a dug-out wall and filled with reinforced concrete, the edifice then being capped and the enclosed earth literally 'dug out'.

Though the Allies never managed the concentration of concrete achieved by the enemy, attempts were made to modernize. In late 1917, Haig established a committee under Major-General Jeudwine, commander of 55th (West Lancashire) Division, to examine defensive methods. Although in the event his recommendations were not accepted in total, General Headquarters did now issue a memorandum on defence which was little more than an abbreviated translation of German manuals circulated earlier in the year. Where the British were hampered was in unwillingness to give up ground – doubtless because of French sensibilities, and because home opinion would have taken a dim view of yielding territory bought with blood. The result was a relative lack of flexibility. Often front lines had to remain front lines, and the creation of proper 'outpost zones' was not always possible.

A German MG08 on an improvised 'trench mount'. This arrangement was less stable than the 'sledge' mount but much easier to move. (Stephen Bull)

Nevertheless, by the end of the war the similarities were greater than the differences. As the preamble to the British handbook *Diagrams of Field Defences* explained, defence systems should now 'take the form of a network of posts and localities sited for mutual support in considerable depth. These posts and localities are to be connected for purposes of command and covered communication on certain portions of the front.'

The handiest temporary strongpoint was the ubiquitous shellhole, as described by *The Organisation of Shell Hole Defences* of December 1917. This appreciated that no two holes were the same, nor should they be, as this was bound to draw enemy attention. Concealment, both direct and from the air, was of paramount importance, all work being 'assimilated as far as possible to the surrounding ground, and regularity of outline avoided'. Alterations were best disguised with mud-splashed waterproof sheets, painted corrugated iron or other camouflage. Dug earth was disposed of in empty holes, thus deceiving the enemy as to which were occupied. Duckboards or tracks were to be varied or concealed, and any connecting trenches narrow and camouflaged.

A pair of shellholes was usually enough for a section. Typical modifications included drainage, firing positions, overhead cover and wiring. In very wet ground, it was recommended that men cut a slot or scrape behind or in the front lip of the crater, and use the shellhole as a sump to drain water into. In other locations the two holes could be connected so that the ground in between had the effect of a large traverse. In vulnerable locations, firing positions would be cut into the shellholes, but permanent three- or four-man weapons pits would be dug nearby and preferably camouflaged to look like further shellholes. Another method was to pick two or more holes close together, but not in a straight line, and link them with short irregular trenches. Where the holes were deeper than the trenches they became natural drains. Reverse slope shellholes were thought particularly suitable, as they were difficult for the enemy to observe and water would run away naturally.

Wiring was best used inconspicuously and sparingly, on short screw pickets, 30 to 50 yards (27 to 46m) in front of holes. Even a single strand of wire had the useful side effect of preventing ration parties or reliefs wandering past in the dark and into the enemy. Shellholes which the enemy might use to approach could be denied by filling them with wire.

LIGHT MACHINE GUNS

Despite the existence of weapons that might be described as 'automatic rifles' or 'light machine guns', like the Danish Madsen and the Mexican-designed Mondragon, hardly any were in service prior to 1914. Neither was there any sophisticated tactical theory for their use. In Britain a committee had been formed to look at automatic rifles as early as 1909, and Major McMahon of the School of Musketry suggested the provision of one per company, but they were not part of the establishment on the outbreak of war.

In the face of acute shortages of automatic weapons during the first year of war, a number of nations took up whatever 'light' guns were available. Sometimes these were treated merely as additional machine guns; sometimes they were given a specific role. In the German instance a small number of Musketen battalions were formed during mid-1915 (see pp.24–5), in which four-man squads used Madsen-type weapons with 25-round magazines, primarily in defence. The French, interested in the possibility of automatic 'walking fire' supporting the advance, continued the

May 1918: 'doughboys' of the US 77th Division under instruction by a sergeant of the British Machine Gun Corps on the Vickers machine gun. American orders for the Vickers were placed, but it was soon superseded by the M1917 Browning. (Stephen Bull)

development of Captain Louis Chauchat's pre-war automatic rifles. The culmination of their endeavours was the Chauchat (CSRG) M1915, a relatively light, air-cooled, highly innovative sheet metal and tubing weapon with a 20-round magazine (see pp.71–2). Unfortunately, it suffered from overheating, poor ergonomics and frequent malfunctions.

It was the British who made best progress, adopting a .303in version of the American-designed Lewis gun (see p.107) and beginning a general issue of four per battalion in July 1915. By 1916 the establishment was increased to 16 per battalion, or one per platoon; and with the removal of the Vickers medium machine guns from infantry battalions to Machine Gun Corps companies, the Lewis carved out its own tactical niche. This was defined in *Notes on the Tactical Employment of Machine Guns and Lewis Guns* as both offensive and defensive: to provide covering fire during the attack; to consolidate positions won; to provide a mobile reserve of firepower; to economize on troops; to defend parts of lines which could not be covered by ordinary machine guns; and even to take part in 'small enterprises' or raids. Although initially viewed with suspicion as an inferior replacement for the Vickers in the infantry, and by no means mechanically infallible, the Lewis soon proved its value.

By early 1917, each platoon would have a Lewis serviced by its own nine-man section, many of whom would be detailed as carriers for the 30-odd drums of ammunition required to keep it firing. During 1918 a second gun was added to each platoon, which, counting the four for anti-aircraft defence, meant that each battalion deployed 36 Lewis guns. On the march, the guns were pulled in handcarts, while the horse-drawn limbers that were later introduced could carry four guns and 22 magazine boxes.

In the British cavalry, Hotchkiss light machine guns, known to the Americans as Benèt-Mercié 'machine rifles', replaced the Maxims. Fed from rigid 30-round cartridge strips, these were compact enough, though arguably less effective than the Lewis.

In the close cooperation of the Lewis with other weapons was identified a means by which attacking infantry could overcome enemy machine guns. The ideal method was described in the instruction *Notes On Dealing With Hostile Machine Guns*, issued in April 1917. First choice to remove the threat would be trench mortars and cross-fire from friendly machine guns, but if this was impossible the Lewis gun section would work their way forward to fire 'from the nearest cover available'. This would almost certainly attract the enemy fire, allowing rifle sections to move on the flanks. When close enough, these would either silence the enemy machine gun with a barrage of rifle grenades, or attack with rifle fire and the bayonet.

Though best used prone, in short bursts, it was just possible to fire the Lewis standing up. Edmund Blunden recorded firing from the shoulder in early 1917 when a Lewis gunner fired at enemy raiders, but was killed for his pains. A sling, originally intended for carrying the gun when hot, was introduced in late 1916, but before long this was being used not just for portability but for firing the gun on the move. One of the most dramatic instances was provided by the Australian Corps at Hamel in July 1918. As the official report put it, 'where a tank was not available to clear up a hostile nest, one of the guns of the L. G. section, carried on a sling, and fired from the hip, gave sufficient cover for the remaining gun to come into action deliberately'. The Lewis guns thereby performed 'invaluable work', often in conjunction with rifle grenade fire.

Such effective mobile firepower was soon noticed. As early as 5 July 1916, on the Somme, General von Stein was remarking on the 'large number of Lewis guns which were brought into action very quickly and skilfully in newly captured positions'. He further recommended that 'our infantry should be equipped with a large number of light machine guns of this description'. The Lewis gun soon became a prized piece of booty for German assault troops, yet the capture of relatively few British weapons by no means solved the problem. The Germans had already experimented with improvised 'trench mounts' for their MG08 weapons, and now struggled to introduce a light machine gun of their own.

Various weapons were tried, including a Bergmann-designed automatic rifle, but the gun ultimately adopted as standard was the MG08/15 (see p.25). This would certainly facilitate the development of German small unit tactics, but was an uneasy compromise; for while the MG08/15 retained the familiar Maxim mechanism and a reasonable sustained fire capability from its 100-round belt-carrying drum, it also kept much of the weight. Theoretically, a web and leather sling allowed fire on the move, but how practical this really was with 22kg (48¹/₂lb) of gun, water and ammunition was open to question.

The Americans, unwisely adopting the French Chauchat and slow to realize the importance of the Lewis, actually came up with one of the best light support weapons at the eleventh hour. The first Browning Automatic Rifles or 'BARs' (see pp.146–7) were shipped to France in the summer of 1918 and first saw action in September: firing from 20-round box magazines, and weighing just over 7kg (15¹/₂lb), they were particularly handy. As the official report stated, the guns were 'highly praised', and although they received 'hard usage, being on the front for days at a time in the rain and when the gunners had little opportunity to clean them, they invariably functioned well'.

NEW OFFENSIVE TACTICS – GERMAN

To break trench deadlock would require three things: new weapons, numerical or qualitative superiority, and new tactics. Of the weapons, arguably the light machine gun contributed most to the return of fluidity, providing a potent support around which a platoon or squad could operate. The tank was very useful, particularly as a 'breaking-in' weapon for Allied advances, but lacked the range of operations or the reliable communications required for a long range 'break-out'. Grenades, trench mortars, gas and improved artillery technology all played important supporting roles.

French unsteadiness and the collapse of Russia in late 1917 offered Germany a window of opportunity to fight on a single front with local superiority. Not to seize this chance in 1918 was unthinkable; while British strength on the Western Front was set to rise to 1.5 million effectives during 1918, the Americans were arriving and France fought on, Germany was running short of men. Moreover, the Royal and US Navy blockade ensured the dwindling of both food and military supplies to the Central Powers. There were many curious minor miracles with *Ersatz* or 'supplementary' materials: gasmasks made of Bulgarian sheep leather, uniforms made of shoddy, 'war soap' with sand or clay additives, black pudding 'sausages' and acorn coffee, but the downward spiral towards industrial and literal starvation was clear.

The result was the *Kaiserschlacht* of spring 1918. Yet, though a breakthrough was achieved, open warfare gobbled up even more men than trench warfare. Paradoxically, there was imminent danger that much more of this success would cost Germany the war. The attack faltered, and the Germans resumed positional warfare. Now it would be the Allies' turn to try to finish the job. The *Materialschlacht* of industrial production had turned in their favour, with tanks and guns sufficient to

The German trench mortar 'family' on wheeled carriages, 1918: (left to right) 'new pattern' 7.6cm light; 17cm medium; and 24cm heavy models. Four *Minenwerfer* shells are shown, because the heavy projectile came in two different lengths. (Stephen Bull)

break the Hindenburg Line and deal the Germans a blow from which they would not recover during the 'hundred days'. Yet Allied victory was not just a matter of numerical preponderance. British infantry tactics were little inferior to those of the enemy, and British tanks were without equal. After initial heavy casualties, the Americans learned fast. The Browning machine gun and Browning Automatic Rifle would more than prove their worth. From August 1918 General Pershing had his own sector to fight at St Mihiel, fielding half a million Americans supported by French tanks and aircraft. Later US pressure would be switched to the Argonne.

Much recent debate has revolved around the idea of stormtroops, and whether British or German methods were superior. Yet such discussion tends to obscure rather than enlighten. Most nations had begun experimenting with new assault tactics as soon as their old tactics failed, whether this was the German *Stosstruppen*, the British 'grenadier parties', or the Italian 'death companies'. The combatants copied each others' weapons and techniques, and captured and translated their manuals. The 'assault trooper' did not spring from the ether in 1918; and the idea of the German *Sturmbataillone* was not to form a permanent elite, but to make practical experiments before spreading the knowledge acquired through the army as a whole. They were, as Ludendorff put it, 'examples to be imitated'. So it was that following Kaslow's and Rohr's initial efforts in 1915, one *Sturmbataillon* was formed per army during late 1916 and early 1917, sometimes by using the existing divisional *Sturmabteilung* as their raw material. On the British side, 'army schools' of sniping and scouting, bombing, gas and other specialisms may have been less integrated and arguably less dynamic; but they were ultimately more successful in achieving a uniform standard of training.

German offensive technique was summed up in *The Attack in Positional Warfare*, a slim volume issued down to battalion level by the Chief of the General Staff in January 1918, with additional amendments later that year. Troops were to be massed for the attack in secret, to penetrate the enemy position 'rapidly', to the 'furthest possible objective' on the *Schwerpunkt* or 'centre of gravity' of the attack, usually on a frontage of 2,000–3,000 metres (1.2–2 miles) per division. Overcrowding was to be avoided, though careful preparation might allow initial deployment forward of the enemy barrage zone. Reserves were to be committed on successful sectors, not where resistance was most stubborn.

German Landwehr, armed with obsolete Gewehr 71 rifles, guard Russian prisoners of war. The collapse of the Russian Army following the costly failure of its summer 1917 offensive, and the Bolshevik revolution in October, allowed the best German troops to be transferred to fight in the West. (Stephen Bull)

Artillery preparation would no longer consist of an all-out bombardment lasting days, but was 'concentrated in relation to time and space in order to increase surprise and moral effect'. Trench mortars, infantry guns and batteries firing over open sights would not be used prior to the day of the attack, so as to maintain surprise. The preface to the assault would last from minutes to hours depending upon circumstances. Pauses, sudden bursts of shells and the 'fire waltz' back and forth across the target were all useful ruses. During the infantry attack, a 'creeping barrage' would move ahead of the troops, who would advance 'immediately behind ... in spite of any loss from stray "shorts" and injury to our own men from shell splinters'. The objective was not pure destruction, nor mere weight of metal projected, but *Sturmreifschiessen* – to shoot the enemy into a condition where they were literally 'ripe for attack'. Artillery was to be coordinated at army level to neutralize key points, as had been pioneered by Colonel Brüchmuller in 1916 and was now common practice.

Though detailed instructions were to be prepared in advance, and command and control were seen as critical, the manual intended that 'scope for independent action and initiative is left even to the private soldier'. This took one stage further the idea of 'directive' command, in which it was the job of senior officers to state the objective and provide the resources. It was not believed wise to give too many orders, as these would place constraints and limit the ability of subordinates to take opportunities. Numbers were not the main predictor of success, but quality or 'combat power' achieved by training, equipment, preparation, rest, speed of execution and intelligence of command and troops.

Seizing the enemy's gun line on the first day, and rapidly bringing up the mass of artillery and fresh infantry, was important. Attacks were generally guided by scouts, followed by assault

German assault troops take cover in a shellhole. Grenade bags and entrenching tools in improvised carriers are slung round the body; helmets are smeared with mud for camouflage. (Stephen Bull)

detachments and skirmishers, but whether 'to employ waves formed of lines of skirmishers or waves of assault detachments, or a combination of both, must be decided according to each particular case'. Where assault detachments were deployed these were often organized in eight-man squads led by an NCO. With the enemy positions thoroughly penetrated, the main body of the infantry could follow, feeding the advanced detachments, widening the breakthroughs and destroying the isolated and demoralized pockets of opposition. Each battalion was instructed to take two light *Minenwerfer* forward with it, and in the last year of war *Wurfgrenaten*, or 'jam pot' grenades fired from rifle cup dischargers, filled the gap left by the discontinuation of rodded rifle grenades.

Machine guns were not to be regarded as auxiliary weapons; they were as important to the infantry as the rifle. Close cooperation was vital, with numerous machine guns attached to the lead troops so that 'they may be able to cover the advance of the riflemen and bombers by keeping down the fire from hostile nests, or to repulse hostile counter-attacks'. Light MG08/15 machine gun 'troops' consisting of as few as four men could even be mixed in to form all-arms *Gruppen*. It was readily acknowledged that the élan of the attack might take troops beyond their first objective; but with the understanding that 'the boldest decision is always the best', it was suggested that attacking formations should not be held back unless the advance had become an unconsidered rush.

The individual infantryman's battle was carried out with the *Nahkampfsmittel* or 'weapons of close combat', as described in the German General Staff instruction of 1917. Firearms were supplemented by grenades: blast effect stick grenades and small iron 'egg' grenades, as the instructions explained:

> The equipment of bombers varies with their task. The following is often suitable – steel helmet; slung rifle or carbine or pistol; two sandbags containing hand grenades slung round the neck or over both shoulders, or two special hand grenade carriers; entrenching implement; gasmask; haversack with four 'iron rations'; two water bottles; no valise or pouches (cartridges being carried in the pockets or the haversack).

The men were trained to throw accurately, to long range, and in brief but heavy volleys. When opposed from a trench beyond hand grenade range, bombers were taught to 'close on the trench at all possible speed, throwing their grenades; lie down while the grenades burst, and then rush the trench without hesitation'. Fighting for shellholes or bunkers would normally entail trench mortar, artillery or machine gun preparation and supporting fire during the attack. If resistance continued, a machine gun or snipers would fire on enemy loopholes while bombers worked around the flanks.

The limitations of a long-barrelled bolt-action rifle with a five-round magazine like the standard issue Gewehr 98 in trench fighting and the assault were widely appreciated. Luger P08 and other pistols, trench knives, clubs and entrenching tools were all used in close combat, but none was ideal in all circumstances. Carbines such as the 98A had been on issue to specialists since before the war, and their use was extended; but this did nothing to speed operation or increase the number of rounds in the magazine. Another idea was the development of a 20-round 'trench magazine' for the Gewehr 98; this certainly helped the infantryman to keep firing and was quite widely used, but was no handier than the ordinary rifle. In 1917 the Prussian War Ministry began a programme to produce a new rifle, while Mauser experimented with a 'trench and close combat' rifle with various sizes of magazine. Neither of these would see general issue, and it was only in the last months of the war that a major breakthrough was achieved with the deployment of the Maschinenpistole 18.

This was arguably the world's first effective sub-machine gun, a *Kugelspritz* or 'bullet squirter' firing 32 rounds of 9mm pistol ammunition from a 'snail' magazine – first developed for the P08 pistol – on full automatic. Its most effective range was under 50m (55yd), and it was capable of causing havoc in the confines of a trench. It was planned to give sub-machine guns to 10 per cent of the infantry, but fortunately for the Allies the MP18 would see only very limited distribution before the end of the war.

NEW OFFENSIVE TACTICS – BRITISH

The various editions of *The Training and Employment of Divisions*, published in the last 18 months of the Great War, presented a synthesis of British offensive tactics that were far removed from 1914. While 'general principles' might remain unchanged, methods, application and timing were all drastically revised. Though British tactical plans were arguably less radical than their German counterparts, in that they spoke of 'a methodical and progressive battle, beginning with limited objectives and leading up by gradual stages to an attack on deep objectives' and finally to 'open warfare', the similarities were far greater than the differences. The history of 1/4th Battalion, Loyal North Lancashires, published as early as 1921, actually claimed that its performance at Third Ypres, for which 16 medals were awarded, 'raised us to the status of Storm Troops'.

Shorter, more responsive artillery bombardments were a key factor. Where bombardments had to be long, aerial photographs now checked progress so that corps commanders could single out undamaged positions for further attention. Guns now used high explosive shells with 'instantaneous' fuses that were capable of bursting on, rather than under, ground level. With better munitions, wire-cutting with shells improved, and efforts were made to keep cleared lanes open during the night by means of rifle and machine gun fire. The objectives of the artillery were similarly more subtle: smoke and gas shoots were mixed with 'box' and 'creeping' barrages, intended to surprise, neutralize or isolate, rather than simply to blast the enemy.

In the ideal barrage plan, the majority of the 18pdr field guns would form the creeping barrage, with the attacking infantry advancing about 50 yards (46m) behind it, as the manual described:

The barrage does not lift direct from one trench to another, but creeps slowly forward, sweeping all the intervening ground in order to deal with any machine guns or riflemen pushed out into shellholes in front of or behind the trenches. This creeping barrage will dwell for a certain time on each definite trench line to be assaulted. The infantry must be trained to follow close behind the barrage from the instant it commences and then, taking advantage of this 'dwell', to work up as close as possible to the objective ready to rush it the moment that the barrage lifts.

Where enemy trench lines were close, the infantry would be placed as near as possible, and rush them as artillery fire ceased. With the bulk of the field guns employed on really close work, the 4.5in howitzers and the remainder of the 18pdrs would form a barrage 'in depth', concentrating on strongpoints and working up communication trenches, perhaps with a 'machine gun barrage' superimposed over it. The 60pdrs and other medium and heavy pieces would provide a third barrage, searching the line of advance. Finally, the long range and super-heavy pieces would fire over the objectives, picking out areas where reserves might be gathered for counter-attack or transport routes. Despite the emphasis on intelligent shooting, the British artillery on the Western Front was now firing more shells than ever – anything from 1 to 3 million rounds per week from April 1918 to the end of the war.

By 1918, infantry attack was no longer a matter of rigid lines, going in strictly by company and battalion, but a series of more or less flexible 'waves'. The first skirmishing wave followed the barrage into the enemy front line and homed in on 'points of resistance'; the second, or 'main weight of the attack', came on in platoons of section columns or single file lines. The third wave was 'small handy columns' of reinforcements; and the fourth, troops who were intended to defend the captured territory. The 'files' and 'small columns' were in no way intended as parade ground formations, but loose gaggles – colloquially referred to as 'worms' – taking advantage of the ground. Moreover, as was explained in *The Training and Employment of Platoons*, each platoon now contained within it 'all the weapons with which the infantry soldier is armed – namely rifle and bayonet, Lewis gun, rifle bomb, and bomb'. Each platoon was supposed to have a minimum of 24 and a maximum of 40 men, divided into four sections and a headquarters comprising an officer and three other ranks.

Each section was led by an NCO, and numbered from five to nine other ranks – five being regarded as the minimum number required to work together 'efficiently as a section', and nine the maximum number that could be controlled 'in the conditions of modern battle' by a junior NCO. One section of the platoon was the Lewis gun section, the others, rifle sections. Though pretty well everyone was regarded as first and foremost a 'rifleman', all were trained in the use of the bomb, and at least half with the rifle bomb; it was recommended that one of the rifle sections be trained to act as a specialist 'bombing team'. Each section was to be able to provide two men capable of acting as scouts.

Wherever possible, men of a section were to be kept together, with drill, fatigues and team games fostering 'spirit'. Section commanders were encouraged to know the names and characters of every man under their direction. This became more than theory, as an officer of the 8th Battalion, the Norfolk Regiment, recorded:

> Men lived, ate, slept and worked in their sections and platoons in which they were to fight in France. Some sections never actually changed between the day of their first formation and the day on which they first suffered casualties in France. The officers not only knew their men by sight and by name, and by their military proficiency, but knew many details of their private lives ... Thus was the morale and ésprit de corps of the battalion fostered.

Though they were expected to cooperate and provide mutual supporting fire, platoons were now used as tactical units in their own right. In the attack, they could advance without halting, but 'leap-frogging' movement was accepted as the norm, with lead troops taking up one objective while others then passed through them and on to the next. Rather than have waves committed specifically to the clearing of linear trenches, dug-outs and 'mopping up', it was now usual to have to clear areas of the battlefield where the enemy were ensconced in shellholes or strongpoints. Lewis

A Royal Engineer demonstrates the use of the No.36 Mills grenade with the cup discharger, 1917. With a range of 240 yards (220m), the discharger was eventually issued on a scale of 96 per battalion. The rifle is held butt to the ground and trigger guard upward, and the grenade inserted into the cup so that the firing lever is confined after the safety pin is removed. It is discharged by firing a bulletless ballistite cartridge. (Stephen Bull)

guns aided platoon advances in various ways: directly by firing ahead or to either flank while the riflemen 'leap-frogged', or more covertly by advancing first under cover of night or fog to occupy shellholes or other cover close to the enemy. During major attacks, bombing along trenches was now frowned upon, but grenades were used generally for clearing and rifle bombs as 'section howitzers'. Light trench mortars were expected to be manhandled forward, one or two immediately behind each attacking battalion for support.

Given the apparent modernity of platoon action it is perhaps surprising that the bayonet continued to receive so much attention. Yet it continued to bulk large, at least in preparation for battle, as *Assault Training* spelt out in September 1917:

> The bullet and the bayonet belong to the same parent, the rifle, which is still the deciding factor on the battlefield ... It is the spirit of the bayonet that captures the position, and the bullet that holds it. The bullet also shatters the counter attack and kills outside bayonet distance. Bayonet training and musketry training are therefore complementary to one another and must be taught as one subject ... The principles of the assault and counter charge should also be made clear. Throughout the training the instructors should foster the fighting spirit and encourage the desire to kill.

American 'bombers' advance through wire with sandbags of grenades. The US Army wore British-made steel helmets until contracts could be placed for their own M1917A1 copy with home firms such as Crosby of Buffalo, the American Can Company, Budd, and Worcester Pressed Steel. (Stephen Bull)

At the same time, it was acknowledged that bayonet fighting was rare: 'Two lines advancing against each other with the bayonet will seldom meet. The one stimulated with the greater fury and confidence, by the force of its determination to conquer, will cause the other line to waver and turn.' This was confirmed by statistics: according to the British official history, just one-third of one per cent of casualties were caused by bayonets. The soldier's contempt for his bayonet was summed up by an entry in *Routine Orders* which noted that many returned to base were found to have lost their temper. Instructions were therefore given that 'on no account are bayonets to be used as pokers or toasting forks, or for any other purpose which will result in their being heated and thus rendered useless as a weapon'.

Gas technology was reaching peak efficiency. From late 1916, British troops were protected with a new 'SBR' or 'small box respirator', which combined an effective face mask with a breathing tube and a box of neutralizing granules. By the end of the war, Britain had produced in excess of 13 million of these masks, and so effective were they that the US also adopted them. America would make another five million of an 'improved' model, known as the 'CE'. Though they were now better protected, from the summer of 1917 the British were plagued by a highly toxic, persistent and insidious gas which attacked not only the respiratory system and eyes, but burned the skin wherever it touched. Originally this was known as 'HS', standing, it was said, for 'Hun Stuff'. Later the compound was discovered to be dichlorethylsulphide, and became better known as 'mustard gas'. After a struggle of some months British chemists replicated it, and the troops replied in kind.

From April 1917 and the action at Vimy Ridge onwards, gas shells and cylinders were joined by the more effective 'projector' designed by Captain W. H. Livens. This was a simple steel tube, standing in a sombrero-shaped base plate, set at a predetermined angle towards the enemy. By means of electric firing, batteries of Livens Projectors could hurl dozens of large, thin-walled gas bombs into the enemy line to create an instantaneous cloud. The method was more reliable than cylinder release, able to deliver more gas more quickly than artillery shells, and justly feared, as one German instruction observed:

> The British use this 'Gasmine' very cleverly. When the weather conditions are suitable, especially at night, the Projectors are thrown, in a sudden burst of fire, in salvos of six or more, on to our front line trenches. This is usually preceded by an apparently normal bombardment ... On account of the effectiveness of this new British Gasmine, the mask will always be carried in the alert position when within 3km of the enemy's trenches, and under no circumstances whatever will it be removed ... In addition, working parties, men sleeping in dug-outs, etc., must be protected by gas sentries.

TANK TACTICS

Tank tactics made major advances over the last two years of the war. As early as December 1915, Winston Churchill, then First Lord of the Admiralty, had suggested to the War Committee that the new 'caterpillars' should be, above all, a surprise weapon, for breaking enemy wire 'and the general domination of his firing line'. A more detailed appraisal, submitted by Lieutenant-Colonel Swinton to the Committee in February 1916, exhorted that tanks should not be used 'in driblets' but in one great 'combined operation' with the infantry, gas and smoke. They should be at least a hundred yards apart, with 90 machines advancing on a frontage of about 5 miles.

Yet Swinton's early aspiration for the tank as a majestic 'breakthrough' weapon was premature, for unarguable practical reasons. While it had been hoped that the first battle machines might have sufficient mileage to cross the entirety of the German defensive zones in one operation, the actual range of the Mk I tank without refuelling was 23 miles. Moreover, even on good ground, the maximum speed was little more than 3 miles an hour, while start lines, in order to remain even moderately safe and secret, had to be 2 miles behind the British front. Neither were tanks inviolate: they were very prone to mechanical failure, and as General Headquarters noted in August 1916, they were vulnerable to shellfire, so were instructed to return to cover as soon as their immediate task was completed. Though the machine gun armament of the Mk I was reasonable, only part of the production, designated 'Male' tanks, carried 6pdr guns. Tank communications were at best haphazard: they depended on waving signal flags or flashing lamps, or – for longer range messaging – on releasing carrier pigeons.

So it was that when C and D companies of the Machine Gun Corps Heavy Branch were at last committed to the renewed Somme offensive at Flers on 15 September 1916, their impact was local and their tactics relatively simple. The 32 vehicles that finally made it to the start line were directed to attack specific points in groups or pairs, advancing just ahead of the infantry. They came under the command of the infantry divisions, many of which allotted small parties of troops to act as escort against close assault. Attempts were made to leave clear 'lanes' in the artillery barrage for the tanks.

Given the limited numbers and primitive nature of the equipment, it was perhaps surprising that the fledgling tank arm achieved as much as it did in its first battle. Nine machines forged ahead of the infantry and managed to straddle trench lines, interfere with enemy machine guns or hose down concentrations of enemy troops with their Lewis guns. One machine got all the way to Flers; yet 14 broke down or were ditched, and a total of ten suffered damage from enemy fire. One of these was Lieutenant Henriques' machine in C Company:

> As we approached the Germans they let fire at us with might and main. At first no damage was done and we retaliated, killing about 20. Then a smash against my flap at the front caused splinters to come in and the blood to pour down my face. Another minute and my driver got the same. Then our prism glass broke to pieces, then another smash, I think it must have been a bomb ... The next one wounded my driver so badly we had to stop. By this time I could see nothing at all ... How we got back I shall never understand.

Expansion of the role of the tanks would take time. Only 60 machines were ready for battle at Arras in April 1917, and bad weather and even snow severely hampered operations in which almost every vehicle suffered ditching, breakdown or damage from enemy shells. In 8 Company of C Battalion all ten tanks were disabled, but not before they had succeeded in knocking out several machine guns and snipers' lairs. In 9 Company only five machines would make it into action: of these, Lieutenant Williams' tank had the most hair-raising time, getting 'a whizz-bang [77mm shell] through the conning tower' and ditching twice, prior to being hit by a heavy shell which killed three of the crew and wounded three. In 10 Company on Easter Monday the tanks contributed to the attack on Telegraph Hill, but took heavy casualties. Even so, one machine remained in action for the better part of three days, helping the infantry.

In the appalling quagmire of Third Ypres in summer and autumn 1917, tanks were out of their natural element, often sinking into liquid mud until their relevance to modern war was brought into question. Despite acts of heroism, the majority were ditched or hit. Just one scene of many was recorded by Colonel J. F. C. Fuller:

> I waded up the road, which was swimming a foot or two in slush ... The road was a complete shambles and strewn with debris, broken vehicles, dead and dying horses and men; I must have passed hundreds of them as well as bits of men and animals littered everywhere. As I neared Poelcapelle our guns started to fire ... the nearest approach to a picture I can give is that it was like standing in the centre of a gigantic Primus stove. As I neared the derelict tanks the scene became truly appalling; wounded men lay drowned in the mud ... The nearest tank was a female. Her left sponson doors were open. Out of these protruded four pairs of legs; exhausted and wounded men had sought refuge in this machine, and the dead and dying lay in a jumbled heap inside.

By the time of Cambrai in November 1917, a new tactical formation known as the 'unicorn' had come into use. A section of three machines advanced in an equilateral triangle, the two rear tanks taking over with them a platoon of infantry in a 'snake' behind them. Cambrai would also see overwhelming numbers of machines used, on reasonable ground, and surprise was achieved with a dawn attack. In all, nine battalions of the enlarged Tank Corps were committed, with a total

1917: French 'assault artillery' crew inside a St Chamond tank, armed with a 75mm gun and four machine guns. This photo gives a hint of the gruelling conditions in all World War I tanks: the crews were crammed into a lurching steel box in the narrow gaps between exposed guns and engine, deafened, sickened by fumes and only partially protected from enemy fire and internal splinters. (Stephen Bull)

of 378 fighting tanks. Many of these carried brushwood fascines which were dropped into trenches to provide crossing points. A 6-mile hole was punched into German Second Army; but neither exploitation nor proper coordination with the infantry were achieved, with the result that German counter-attacks were able to plug the gap and reclaim much of the ground.

The theory of tank and infantry cooperation was consolidated in *The Training and Employment of Divisions*, where the main characteristics of the fighting tank were defined as mobility, security and offensive power – what we would still recognize as the armour 'triangle' of speed, armour and firepower. Yet the Mk IV tank was far from invincible, with a maximum speed of 3.7mph, and armour 12mm thick. According to the manual, this meant that in practical terms the tank was limited to 120 yards per minute on good flat ground, reducing to as little as 15 yards per minute at night. Against a direct hit from a shell the tank was defenceless, but it could expect to be 'proof against all bullets, shrapnel and most splinters'. It could expect to traverse dry shellholes at slow speed but was in danger of ditching in the wet, and could effectively regard 'swamp, thick woods, streams with marshy banks, or deep sunken roads' as impassable. Artillery were instructed to cooperate more with smoke and counter-battery fire than with heavy bombardments that would lead to cratering.

Infantry cooperation was assumed to depend on mutual understanding of limitations and tactics; comradeship through close acquaintance; combined reconnaissance; and rapid communication. At the beginning of 1918, the last of these was the least practicable, since signalling between tanks and infantry depended on a system of simple semaphore on the part of the troops and a system of coloured discs on the part of the tanks. A green or red disc signified respectively 'wire cut' or 'wire uncut'; and red and green shown together indicated that the objective had been reached. Infantrymen requiring the help of tanks held their rifle or helmet above their heads. Wireless signal tanks were still regarded as experimental; vehicles still carried two pigeons for sending messages over longer ranges.

Tank attacks now saw one vehicle allotted to each 100 or 200 yards of front, with a company of 12 to 16 per objective. Sections of four machines were not usually divided. Normally one section of a company acted as an advanced guard while the remainder followed, with each of the following vehicles lending cover to a platoon of infantry going forward in single file sections in its wake. These sections were directed to hold back at least 25 yards as the tanks crossed wire, because it was likely to spring back. On meeting a strongpoint, the role of the tanks was to engage, forcing the enemy to seek shelter, distracting and holding them until the infantry came up. The infantry files were instructed to 'move at considerable extension – 50 to 70 yards interval', making 'every use of the ground for cover', the whole attack moving forward 'under the protection of machine gun covering fire'.

German instructions issued in January 1918, shortly before the first use of their A7V tank, were brief but essentially similar. As their *Regulations For the Employment of Assault Tank*

Detachments put it, the task of the tank was to support the infantry and demolish obstacles, focusing on strongpoints and machine gun posts. Close contact with the troops was 'of the highest importance', and where necessary sections of engineers were to be attached to help overcome difficult ground. Smoke, night and other forms of concealment were to be used to hide the German vehicles, and when a mission had been accomplished tanks were instructed to disappear back into cover. German techniques were never thoroughly developed, no doubt because only about 20 of the lumbering, fortress-like A7Vs ever reached the Armoured Assault Detachments; the remainder of the German force comprised captured machines. The majority of these were British Mk IV tanks, and apart from modification to the armament, as for example mounting MG08 machine guns and some T-Gewehr anti-tank rifles, these *Beute Panzerwagen* ('Booty Tanks') were used much as they had been taken.

Though the British attack never became fully mechanized, the developments in the last few months of the war offered a clue to what armour might one day achieve. 'Whippet' tanks, capable of 8mph and with a radius of action of 80 miles, first saw action in March 1918 and played an important part in the advances of August. Supply tanks, wireless tanks, and tracked gun carriers all saw limited use. Moreover, there was exponential growth in the use of mechanical transport behind the lines.

Merely rotating divisions every two months required the movement of more than a division per day by rail. From late 1916, troop transport trains were typically made up of 50 coaches and trucks, with 1,760 passengers per train. Yet this was just a tiny fraction of the picture, since it was calculated that every mile of the front required 675 tons of stores per day. In October 1916 alone, 195,000 tons of stores crossed the Channel from England each week. Much of this was then delivered as trainload 'packs' to the front, with each trainload made up of a regulation number of wagons of each commodity – e.g. bread, groceries, oats and petrol. Trains were directed to the right divisional railhead by means of colour- or number-coded stickers. In total, 76,000 British troops were used to build, repair and run the railways. At the same time, there were also light railways, and the War Office was operating 548 craft for inland water transport. Fourth Army alone deployed a motor fleet of 4,671 lorries, 1,145 cars and 1,636 motorcycles.

Opposite:

German A7V tank 'Adalbert' in transit on a rail flat car, 1918. The A7V had a crew of no fewer than 18, and mounted one 57mm gun and seven machine guns; five tanks equipped each *Sturmpanzer Abteilung*, of which only three were fully equipped with A7Vs by July 1918. This particular vehicle saw plenty of action. Committed at Villers-Bretonneux in late April 1918 as 'Hagen', it broke down, but was repaired and rechristened 'König Wilhelm'. Under this name it was commanded by Lieutenant Heiland during the attack on the River Matz in June 1918, successfully pushing through heavy fighting at Orvillers. When it was decided that the names of royal personages were unsuitable for tanks it was renamed 'Adalbert', going on to serve in the final Marneschutz offensive in July, and at St Etienne. It was finally captured by the French after the Armistice. (Stephen Bull)

CONCLUSION

The Great War led to the deaths of about 12 million combatants, a majority of these on the Western Front. Germany lost 1.6 million; France, 1.3 million; Britain and her empire, 900,000. Russia's dead were 1.7 million; Austria-Hungary's, 800,000. The German, Russian, and Austrian empires passed into history. Britain spent £8,742,000,000, loaning another £1,465,000,000 to her Allies: the 'interim' reparations demanded of Germany were five billion dollars. The horrors of 'the trenches' led to calls for the abolition of war and a League of Nations. Yet, however catastrophic, 1914–18 was also a war of invention and change.

The Marne in 1914 may have had much in common with the Franco-Prussian War and the American Civil War; but by 1918 the war of material, mass conscription of populations, tanks, aircraft, concrete, and innovative minor tactics would bear more similarity to 1939 than many would care to admit.

FURTHER READING

Bach, André, *Fusillés pour l'exemple* (Paris, 2003)

Barbusse, Henri, *Le Feu* (Paris, 1916; English translation 1917)

Barrie, Alexander, *War Underground – The Tunnellers of the Great War* (Staplehurst, 2000)

Berry, Henry, *Make the Kaiser Dance: Living Memories of the Doughboy* (New York, 1978)

Brown, Malcolm, *Verdun 1916* (Stroud, 2000)

Campion Vaughan, Edwin, *Some Desperate Glory: The Diary of a Young Officer* (London, 1982)

Clayton, Anthony, *Paths of Glory: the French Army 1914–18* (London, 2003)

Coppard, George, *With a Machine-gun to Cambrai* (London, 1999)

Cru, Jean Norton, *Témoins* (originally published in 1929; reprinted in 1993)

Doughty, Robert A., *Pyrrhic Victory: French Strategy and Operations in the Great War* (Cambridge, Massachusetts, 2005)

Douie, Charles, *The Weary Road – Recollections of an Infantry Subaltern* (London, 1929)

Ducasse, André, Jacques Meyer and Gabriel Perreux, *Vie et mort des français 1914–18* (Paris, 1962)

Duffy, Christopher, *Through German Eyes: The British and the Somme 1916* (London, 2006)

Dunn, J. C., *The War the Infantry Knew* (London, 2004)

Ebelhauser, Gustav (Richard Baugartner, Ed), *The Passage – A Tragedy of the First World War*, (Huntington, West Virginia, 1984)

Edmonds, J. E. (Ed and Comp), *Military Operations France and Belgium* (14v London, published variously by HMSO and Macmillan, 1922–47)

Eisenhower, John S. D., *Yanks: The Epic Story of the American Army in World War One* (New York, 2001)

Farwell, Byron, *Over There: The United States in the Great War 1917–1918* (New York, 1999)

Ford, Nancy Gentile, *Americans All! Foreign-born Soldiers in World War One* (College Station, Texas, 2001)

Griffith, Paddy, *Battle Tactics of the Western Front* (New Haven, Connecticut, 1996)

Gudmundsson, Bruce I., *Stormtroop Tactics* (New York, 1989)

Horne, Alistair, *The Price of Glory* (London, 1963)

Infantry in Battle (Washington, D. C., 1939)

Jünger, Ernst, *Storm of Steel* (London, 1929)

Liddle, Peter H. (Ed), *Passchendaele in Perspective: The Third Battle of Ypres* (London, 1997)

Lucy, John F., *There's a Devil in the Drum* (London, 1938)

Mead, Gary, *The Doughboys: America and the First World War* (Woodstock, New York, 2000)

Meyer, Jacques, *La vie quotidienne des soldats pendant la Grande Guerre* (Paris, 1966)

Middlebrook, Martin, *The Kaiser's Battle* (London, 1978)

Middlebrook, Martin, *The First Day on the Somme* (London, 2006)

The Official History of Operations in France and Belgium 1917, Vol II (IWM London)

Passingham, Ian, *All The Kaiser's Men: The Life and Death of the German Army on the Western Front 1914–1918* (Stroud, 2003)

Prior, Robin and Trevor Wilson, *Command on the Western Front: The Military Career of Sir Henry Rawlinson* (Oxford, 1992)

Rawling, Bill, *Surviving Trench Warfare: Technology and the Canadian Corps 1914–1918* (Toronto, 1992)

Renn, Ludwig, *War*, English edition (London, 1929)

Richards, Frank, *Old Soldiers Never Die* (Uckfield, UK, 2001)

Robertshaw, Andrew, *Somme 1 July 1916: Tragedy and Triumph* (Oxford, 2006)

Rommel, Erwin, *Attacks* (Vienna, Virginia, 1989)

Samuels, Martin, *Doctrine and Dogma* (Westport, Connecticut, 1992)

Sassoon, Siegfried, *Memoirs of an Infantry Officer* (London, 1974)

Sheffield, Gary, *Forgotten Victory: The First World War – Myths and Realities* (London, 2001)

Sheffield, Gary and Dan Todman (Eds), *Command and Control on the Western Front 1914–1918: The British Experience* (Staplehurst, 2004)

Simkins, Peter, *Kitchener's Army* (Manchester, 1988)

Simpson, Andy (Ed), *Hot Blood and Cold Steel: Life and Death in the Trenches of the First World War* (London, 1995)

Simpson, Andy, *The Evolution of Victory: British Battle on the Western Front* (London, 1995)

Smith, Leonard V., *Between Mutiny and Obedience* (Princeton, 1994)

Spears, General Sir Edward, *Liaison 1914* (London, 1968)

Strachan, Hew, *The First World War: To Arms* (Oxford, 2001)

Terraine, John, *The Western Front 1914–1918* (London, 1964)

Terraine, John, *The Smoke and the Fire: Myths and Anti-Myths of War 1861–1945* (London, 1980)

Travers, Tim, *How The War Was Won* (London, 1982)

Travers, Tim, *The Killing Ground* (London, 1987)

INDEX

References to illustrations are shown in bold.